Constitutional History of India

Constitutional History of India

M.K. Singh

CENTRUM PRESS
NEW DELHI-110002 (INDIA)

CENTRUM PRESS
H.O.: 4360/4, Ansari Road, Daryaganj,
New Delhi-110002 (India)
Tel: 23278000, 23261597, 23255577, 23286875
B.O.: No. 1015, Ist Main Road, BSK IIIrd Stage,
IIIrd Phase, IIIrd Block, Bengaluru-560085 (INDIA)
Tel: 080-41723429
Email: centrumpress@gmail.com
Visit us at: www.centrumpress.com

Constitutional History of India

First Edition, 2013

ISBN 978-93-81938-84-3

PRINTED IN INDIA

Printed at Suman Printers, Delhi

Contents

Preface

The constitution of India is remarkable for many outstanding features which will distinguish it from other constitutions, even though there were members in the constituent Assembly who criticized the constitution which was going to be adopted as a slavish imitation of the west or not suited to the genius of the people.

Parliament's authority to amend the Constitution, particularly the chapter on the fundamental rights of citizens, was challenged as early as in 1951. After independence, several laws were enacted in the states with the aim of reforming land ownership and tenancy structures. This was in keeping with the ruling Congress party's electoral promise of implementing the socialistic goals of the Constitution contained in Article 39 (b) and (c) of the Directive Principles of State Policy that required equitable distribution of resources of production among all citizens and prevention of concentration of wealth in the hands of a few. Property owners adversely affected by these laws petitioned the courts. The courts struck down the land reforms laws saying that they transgressed the fundamental right to property guaranteed by the Constitution. Piqued by the unfavourable judgements, Parliament placed these laws in the Ninth Schedule of 2 the Constitution through the First and Fourth amendments (1951 and 1952 respectively), thereby effectively removing them from the scope of judicial review. Parliament added the Ninth Schedule to the Constitution through the very first amendment in 1951 as a means of immunising certain laws against judicial review. On 26 November 1949, after almost three years of deliberation, the Constituent Assembly of India adopted a constitution for what remains the world's largest liberal democracy. From our vantage point 50 years later, it is instructive to reflect on how the 'founding fathers' (along with a handful of 'mothers') sought to address issues of diversity. After all, in a world in which more than a third of all states possess constitutions acquired only in the first half of the 1990s, our constitution has survived the test of time far better than most of its post-colonial counterparts.

The constitution of India was adopted on November 26, 1949. Some provision of the constitution came into force on same day but the remaining provisions of the constitution came into force on January 26, 1950. This day is referred to the constitution as the "date of its commencement", and celebrated as the Republic Day. The Indian Constitution is unique in its contents and spirit. Through borrowed from almost every constitution of the world, the constitution of India has several salient features that distinguish it from the constitutions of other countries.

This concise and legible book will provide key text to all students, teachers and researchers.

—*Editor*

1

The Basic Structure of the Indian Constitution

According to the Constitution, Parliament and the state legislatures in India have the power to make laws within their respective jurisdictions. This power is not absolute in nature. The Constitution vests in the judiciary, the power to adjudicate upon the constitutional validity of all laws. If a law made by Parliament or the state legislatures violates any provision of the Constitution, the Supreme Court has the power to declare such a law invalid or *ultra vires*. This check notwithstanding, the founding fathers wanted the Constitution to be an adaptable document rather than a rigid framework for governance. Hence Parliament was invested with the power to amend the Constitution.

The argument on the 'basic structure' of the Constitution, lying somnolent in the archives of India's constitutional history during the last decade of the 20th century, has reappeared in the public realm. While setting up the National Commission to Review the Working of the Constitution (the Commission), the National Democratic Alliance government (formed by a coalition of 24 national and regional level parties) stated that the basic structure of the Constitution would not be tampered with. Justice M.N. Venkata chalaiah, Chairman of the Commission, has emphasized on several occasions that an inquiry into the basic structure of the Constitution lay beyond the scope of the Commission's work.

Respective political parties — notably the Congress (I) and the two Communist parties which are in the opposition — have made it clear that the review exercise was the government's ploy to seek legitimacy for its design to adopt radical constitutional reforms thus destroying the basic structure of the document. Much of the public debate has been a victim of partial amnesia as even literate circles of urban India are unsure of the ramifications of this concept, which was hotly debated during the 1970s and 1980s. The following discussion is an attempt to chart the waters of that period rendered turbulent by the power struggle between the legislative and the judicial arms of the State.

Article 368 of the Constitution gives the impression that Parliament's amending powers are absolute and encompass all parts of the document. But the Supreme Court has acted as a brake to the legislative enthusiasm of Parliament ever since independence. With the intention of preserving the original ideals envisioned by the constitution-makers, the apex court pronounced that Parliament could not distort, damage or alter the basic features of the Constitution under the pretext of amending it. The phrase 'basic structure' itself cannot be found in the Constitution. The Supreme Court recognised this concept for the first time in the historic *Kesavananda Bharati* case in 1973.[1] Ever since the Supreme Court has been the interpreter of the Constitution and the arbiter of all amendments made by Parliament.

Parliament's authority to amend the Constitution

Parliament's authority to amend the Constitution, particularly the chapter on the fundamental rights of citizens, was challenged as early as in 1951. After independence, several laws were enacted in the states with the aim of reforming land ownership and tenancy structures. This was in keeping with the ruling Congress party's electoral promise of implementing the socialistic goals of the Constitution contained in Article 39 (b) and (c) of the Directive Principles of State Policy that required equitable distribution of resources of production among all citizens and prevention of concentration of wealth in the hands of a few. Property owners adversely affected by these laws petitioned the courts. The courts struck down the land reforms laws saying that they transgressed the fundamental right to property guaranteed by the Constitution. Piqued by the unfavourable judgements, Parliament placed these laws in the Ninth Schedule of 2 the Constitution through the First and Fourth amendments (1951 and 1952 respectively), thereby effectively removing them from the scope of judicial review. Parliament added the Ninth Schedule to the Constitution through the very first amendment in 1951 as a means of immunising certain laws against judicial review.

Under the provisions of Article 31, which themselves were amended several times later, laws placed in the Ninth Schedule pertaining to acquisition of private property and compensation payable for such acquisition cannot be challenged in a court of law on the ground that they violated the fundamental rights of citizens. This protective umbrella covers more than 250 laws passed by state legislatures with the aim of regulating the size of land holdings and abolishing various tenancy systems. The Ninth Schedule was created with the primary objective of preventing the judiciary - which upheld the citizens' right to property on several occasions - from derailing the Congress party led government's agenda for a social revolution.

Property owners again challenged the constitutional amendments which placed land reforms laws in the Ninth Schedule before the Supreme Court, saying that they violated Article 13 (2) of the Constitution. Article 13 (2) provides for the protection of the fundamental rights of the citizen. 4 Parliament and the state legislatures are clearly prohibited from making laws that may take away or abridge the fundamental rights guaranteed to the citizen. They argued that any amendment to the Constitution had the status of a law as understood by Article 13 (2). In 1952 (*Sankari Prasad Singh Deo v. Union of India*) and 1955 (*Sajjan Singh v. Rajasthan*), the Supreme Court rejected both arguments and upheld the power of Parliament to amend any part of the Constitution including that which affects the fundamental rights of citizens. Significantly though, two dissenting judges in *Sajjan Singh v. Rajasthan* case raised doubts whether the fundamental rights of citizens could become a plaything of the majority party in Parliament.

The Golaknath Verdict

In 1967 an eleven-judge bench of the Supreme Court reversed its position. Delivering its 6:5 majority judgement in the *Golaknath v. State of Punjab* case, Chief Justice Subba Rao put forth the curious position that Article 368, that contained provisions related to the amendment of the Constitution, merely laid down the amending procedure. Article 368 did not confer upon Parliament the power to amend the Constitution. The amending power (constituent power) of Parliament arose from other provisions contained in the Constitution (Articles 245, 246, 248) which gave it the power to make laws (plenary legislative power). Thus, the apex court held that the amending power and legislative powers of Parliament were essentially the same. Therefore, any amendment of the Constitution must be deemed law as understood in Article 13 (2).

The majority judgement invoked the concept of implied limitations on Parliament's power to amend the Constitution. This view held that the Constitution gives a place of permanence to the fundamental freedoms of the citizen. In giving the Constitution to themselves, the people had reserved the fundamental rights for themselves. Article 13, according to the majority view, expressed this limitation on the powers of Parliament.

Parliament could not modify, restrict or impair fundamental freedoms due to this very scheme of the Constitution and the nature of the freedoms granted under it. The judges stated that the fundamental rights were so sacrosanct and transcendental in importance that they could not be restricted even if such a move were to receive unanimous approval of both houses of Parliament.

They observed that a Constituent Assembly might be summoned by Parliament for the purpose of amending the fundamental rights if necessary. In other words, the apex court held that some features of the Constitution lay at its core and required much more than the usual procedures to change them.

The phrase 'basic structure' was introduced for the first time by M.K. Nambiar and other counsels while arguing for the petitioners in the *Golaknath* case, but it was only in 1973 that the concept surfaced in the text of the apex court's verdict.

Abolition of Privy Purses

Within a few weeks of the *Golaknath* verdict the Congress party suffered heavy losses in the parliamentary elections and lost power in several states. Though a private member's bill - tabled by Barrister Nath Pai seeking to restore the supremacy of Parliament's power to amend the Constitution was introduced and debated both on the floor of the house and in the Select Committee, it could not be passed due to political compulsions of the time. But the opportunity to test parliamentary supremacy presented itself once again when Parliament introduced laws to provide greater access to bank credit for the agricultural sector and ensure equitable distribution of wealth and resources of production and by:

a) nationalising banks and
b) derecognising erstwhile princes in a bid to take away their Privy purses, which were promised in perpetuity - as a sop to accede to the Union - at the time of India's independence.

Parliament concluded that it was implementing the Directive Principles of State Policy but the Supreme Court struck down both moves. By now, it was clear that the Supreme Court and Parliament were at loggerheads over the relative position of the fundamental rights vis-à-vis the Directive Principles of State Policy. At one level, the battle was about the supremacy of Parliament vis-à-vis the power of the courts to interpret and uphold the Constitution.

At another level the contention was over the sanctity of property as a fundamental right jealously guarded by an affluent class much smaller than that of the large impoverished masses for whose benefit the Congress government claimed to implement its socialist development programme. Less than two weeks after the Supreme Court struck down the President's order derecognising the princes, in a quick move to secure the mandate of the people and to bolster her own stature Prime Minister Indira Gandhi dissolved the Lok Sabha and called a snap poll. For the first time, the Constitution itself became the electoral issue in India. Eight of the ten manifestos in the 1971 elections called for changes in the Constitution in order to restore the supremacy of Parliament. A.K. Gopalan of the Communist Party of India (Marxist) went to the extent of saying that the Constitution be done away with lock stock and barrel and be replaced with one that enshrined the real sovereignty of the people. The Congress party returned to power with a two-thirds majority. The electorate had endorsed the Congress party's socialist agenda, which among other things spoke of making basic changes to the Constitution in order to restore Parliament's supremacy.

Through a spate of amendments made between July 1971 and June 1972 Parliament sought to regain lost ground. It restored for itself the absolute power to amend any part of the Constitution including Part III, dealing with fundamental rights. Even the President was made duty bound to give his assent to any amendment bill passed by both houses of Parliament. Several curbs on the right property were passed into law. The right to equality before the law and equal protection of the laws (Article 14) and the fundamental freedoms guaranteed under Article 19 were made subordinate to Article 39 (b) & (c) in the Directive Principles of State Policy. Privy purses of erstwhile princes were abolished and an entire category of legislation dealing with land reforms was placed in the Ninth Schedule beyond the scope of judicial review.

CONCEPT OF SOCIAL JUSTICE UNDER INDIAN CONSTITUTION

The constitution of India was adopted on November 26, 1949. Some provision of the constitution came into force on same day but the remaining provisions of the constitution came into force on January 26, 1950. This day is referred to the constitution as the "date of its commencement", and celebrated as the Republic Day. The Indian Constitution is unique in its contents and spirit. Through borrowed from almost every constitution of the world, the constitution of India has several salient features that distinguish it from the constitutions of other countries.

Dr. Bhimrao Ambedkar, was chairman of the drafting committee. He was the first Law Minister of the India. He continued the crusade for social revaluation until the end of his life on the 6th December 1956. He was honoured with the highest national honour,' Bharat Ratna' in April 1990. B.R. Ambedkar was affectionately called Baba Saheb Ambedkar. Dr. Ambedkar is the man of millennium for social justice, since he was the first man in history to successfully lead a tirade of securing social to the vast sections of Indian humanity, with the help of a law. Dr. Ambedkar was the man who tried to turn the Wheel of the Law toward social justice for all. He has strong fervor to attain social justice among the Indian Communities for this purpose he began his vocation. At the time of independence, the constitution makers were highly influenced by the feeling of social equality and social justice. For the same reason, they incorporated such provisions in the constitution of India. These are as follows –

The words, "Socialist", "secular", "democratic" and "republic" have been inserted in the preamble. Which reflects it's from as a "social welfare state." The expression "socialist" was intentionally introduced in the Preamble.

In *D. S. Nakara v. Union of India*, the Supreme Court has held that the principal aim of a socialist state is to eliminate inequality in income, status and standards of life. The basic frame work of socialism is to provide a proper standard of life to the people, especially, security from cradle to grave. Amongst there, it envisaged economic equality and equitable distribution of income. This is a blend of Marxism & Gandhism, leaning heavily on Gandhian socialism. From a wholly feudal exploited slave society to a vibrant, throbbing socialist welfare society reveals a long march, but, during this journey, every state action, whenever taken, must be so directed and interpreted so as to take the society one step towards the goal.

In *Excel Wear v Union of India*, the Supreme Court held that the addition of the word 'socialist' might enable the courts to learn more in favour of nationalisation and state ownership of an industry. But, so long as private ownership of industries is recognised which governs an overwhelming large principles of socialism and social justice can not be pushed to such an extent so as to ignore completely, or to a very large extant, the interest of another section of the public, namely the private owners of the undertaking.

The term 'justice' in the Preamble embraces three distinct forms- social, economic and political, secured through various provisions of Fundamental Rights and Directive Principles. Social justice denotes the equal treatment of all citizens without any social distinction based on caste, colour, race, religion, sex and so on. It means absence of privileges being extended to any particular section of the society, and improvement in the conditions of backward classes (SCs, STs, and OBCs) and women. Economic justice denotes on the non- discrimination between people on the basis of economic factors. It involves the elimination of glaring in equalities in wealth, income and property. A combination of social justice and economic justice denotes what is known as 'distributive justice'. Political justice implies that all citizens should have equal political rights, equal voice in the government. The ideal of justice- social, economic and political- has been taken from the Russian Revaluation (1917).

The term 'equality' means the absence of special privileges to any section of the society, and provision of adequate opportunities for all individuals without any discrimination. The Preamble secures at all citizens of India equality of status an opportunity. This provision embraces three dimensions of equality- civic, political and economic.

The following provisions of the chapter on Fundamental Rights ensure civic equality:

a) Equality before the Law (Article 14).

b) Prohibition of discrimination on grounds of religion, race, caste, sex of place of birth (Article 15).

c) Equality of opportunity in matters of public employment (Article 16).

d) Abolition of untouchability (Article 17).

e) Abolition of titles (Article 18).

There are two provisions in the Constitution that seek to achieve political equality. One, no person is to be declared ineligible for inclusion in electoral rolls on grounds of religion, race, caste or sex (Article 325). Two, elections to the Lock Sabha and the state assemblies to be on the basis of adult suffrage (Article 326). Article 36 to 51 incorporate certain directive principles of State policy which the State must keep in view while governing the nation, but by Article 37 these principle have been expressly made non-justiciable in a court of law. Although these principles are not judicially enforceable, yet they are not without purpose. The report of the Sub-Committee said: "The principles of Policy set forth in this part are intended for the guidance of the State. While these principles shall not be cognizable by any Court they are nevertheless fundamental in the governance of the country and their application in the making of laws shall be the duty of the State."

According to Dr. B.R. Ambedkar, the Directive Principles of State Policy is a 'novel feature' of the Indian Constitution. They are enumerated in Part IV of the Constitution. They can be classified into three broad categories- socialistic, Gandhian and liberal- intellectual. The directive principles are meant for promoting the ideal of social and economic democracy. They seek to establish a 'welfare state' in India. However, unlike the Fundamental Right, the directives are non-justiciable in nature, that is, they are not enforceable by the courts for their violation. Yet, the Constitution itself declares that 'these principles are fundamental in the governance of the country and it shall be the duty of the state to apply these principles in making laws'. Hence, they impose a moral obligation on the state authorities for their application. But, the real force (sanction) behind them is political, that is, public opinion. In Minerva Mills case (1980), the Supreme Court held that 'the Indian Constitution is founded on the bedrock of the balance between the Fundamental Rights and the Directive Principles'.

Social Justice is the foundation stone of Indian Constitution. Indian Constitution makers were well known to the use and minimality of various principles of justice. They wanted to search such form of justice which could fulfill the expectations of whole revolution. Pt. Jawahar Lal Nehru put an idea before the Constituent Assembly

"First work of this assembly is to make India independent by a new constitution through which starving people will get complete meal and cloths, and each Indian will get best option that he can progress himself."

Social justice found useful for everyone in its kind and flexible form. Although social justice is not defined anywhere in the constitution but it is an ideal element of feeling which is a goal of constitution. Feeling of social justice is a form of relative concept which is changeable by the time, circumstances, culture and ambitions of the people.

Social inequalities of India expect solution equally. Under Indian Constitution the use of social justice is accepted in wider sense which includes social and economical justice both. According to Chief Justice Gajendragadkar.

"In this sense social justice holds the aims of equal opportunity to every citizen in the matter of social & economical activities and to prevent inequalities".

The constitution of India does not completely dedicated to any traditional ideology as – equalitarian, Utilitarian, Contractarian or Entitlement theory. Dedication of constitution is embedded in progressive concept of social justice and various rules of justice such as- Quality, Transaction, Necessity, Options etc. are its helping organs. Infact dedication of the constitution is in such type of social justice which can fulfill the expectations of welfare state according to Indian conditions.

So that in one way it has been told about the value of Equality which is known as the declaration of equal behaviour of equals to Aristotil, directs the state "The state shall not deny to any person equality before the law or the equal protection of the laws within the territory of India" that is distributive justice. In the other way it has been told the protective discrimination by special provision for other backwards of the society such as – SC, ST & Socially and educationally back ward classes, which is the attribute (symbol) of corrective and compensatory justice.

Original Principle of Equalitarian justice is propounded/ derived by Aristotle that is equal behaviour in equal matter. If there is unequal behaviour between equal, there will be injustice.

In State of U.P. Vs. Pradeep Tandon, the Supreme Court accepted reasonable classification justiciable on the basis of unequal behaviour between unequal people. In Chiranjeet Las Vs. Union Of India. and State of J.K. vs. Bhakshi Gulam Mohammad it is held by the Supreme Court that due to some special circumstances one person or one body can be treated as one class. But the question is how to determine inequality? In India it is not easy to determine inequality. In Air India vs. Nergis Mirza the Supreme Court declared the rule of Air India unreasonable and discriminatory. But accepting justiciable element in equality, it is try to make equality more effective and progressive. In E.P. Royappa vs. State of Tamilnadu Justice Bhagwati has held that equality is movable concept which has many forms and aspects. It can not be tightened in traditional and principlized circle. Equality with equal behaviour prohibits arbitrariness in action, inequality is surely be there.

To accept right to equality as an essential element of Justice, India Constitution prohibits unequal behaviour on the grounds of religion, race, caste, sex. But constitution accepts that strict compliance of formal equality will make up equality. But the system of special provision for backward classes of society, it is to try to make the principle of equality more effective. Under Article 15(4) the state shall make any special provision for the advancement of any socially and educationally backward classes of citizen or for the scheduled castes, and the Scheduled tribes and in the same manner by accepting the opportunity of equality to employment under state in Article 16 (1), it has excepted the principle of equalization under Article 16(4). If it is in the opinion of the state that any class of the citizens has not adequately representation under state employment, state shall make any provision for the reservation of appointments. According to Art 46 the State shall promote with special care the educational and economic interests of weaker sections of the people, and in particular, of the scheduled castes and the scheduled tribes, and shall protect them from social injustice and all forms of exploitation.

In a very important case of Indra Shahani vs. Union of India the Supreme Court declared 27% reservation legal for socially and economically backward classes of the society under central services.

Basically protective discrimination is used to fulfill those lacks which arise due to a long time deprivation. It is a part of corrective and compensatory justice. It has been told that peoples of backward class of society have been bearing injustice for generation to generation. Some peoples of the society made supremacy on the benefits of the society and made deprived to others. So this provision of protective discrimination has been made for those deprived people who are living in unbeneficial circumstances.

Through equal opportunity on the basis of quality the Supreme Court has tried to make a reasonable balance between distribution of benefits and distributive justice. In M.R. Balaji vs State of Mysure, the Supreme Court has held that for the object of compensatory justice, limit of reservation should not be more than 50%. In India Shahni vs. Union of India full bench of nine judges approved this balance between distributive justice through quality and compensatory justice.

There is a very wide planning of justice according to necessity in the constitution. It expects distribution of social benefits according to necessity by which more needy person can get benefits. It is expected to the state that the state shall in particular, direct its policy towards securing that children are given opportunities and facilities to develop in a healthy manner and in conditions of freedom and dignity and that childhood and youth are protected against exploitation and against moral and material abandonment. Under Article 41, it is expected to the state that the State shall, within the limits of its economic capacity and development, make effective provision for securing the right to work, to education and to public assistance in case of unemployment, old age, sickness and disablement, and in other cases of underserved want. It is provided under Article 42 that the state shall make provision for securing just and humane conditions of work and for maternity relief. In Article 43 it is expected that the State shall endeavour to secure, by suitable legislation or economic organization or in any other way, to all workers agricultural, industrial or otherwise, work, a living wage, conditions of work ensuring a decent standard of life and full enjoyment of leisure and social and cultural opportunities and, in particular, the state shall endeavour to promote cottage industries on an individual or co-operative basis in rural areas. In PUDR vs. Union of India, the Supreme Court has held that minimum wages must be given and not to pay minimum wages is the violation of human dignity and it is also known as exploitation.

In India, courts have performed a great role to make the Social justice successful. In the field of distributive Justice, Legislature and Judiciary both are playing great role but courts are playing more powerful role to deliver compensatory or corrective justice but these principles are known as mutually relatives not mutually opposites. Ideals and goals are to deliver social justice. Medium may be distributive or compensatory justice. The adopted type may be of quality, Necessity, Equality, Freedom, Common interest or other. Although the Supreme Court has not found any possible definition of Social Justice but has accepted it as an essential and an organ of legal system.

The supreme court of India has given a principal and dynamic shape to the concept of social justice. Social justice has been guiding force of the judicial pronouncements. In Sadhuram v. Pulin, the Supreme Court ruled that as between two parties, if a deal is made with one party without serious detriment to the other Court would lean in favour of weaker section of the society. The judiciary has given practical shape to social justice through allowing affirmative governmental actions are held to include compensatory justice as well as distributive justice which ensure that community resources are more equitably and justly shared among all classes of citizens. The concept of social justice has brought revolutionary change in industrial society by charging the old contractual obligations. It is no more a narrow or one sided or pedantic concept. It is founded on the basic ideal of socio-economic equality and its aim is to assist the removal of socio- economic disparities and inequalities. In J.K. Cotton Spinning. And Wiving. Co. Ltd. V. Labour Appellate Tribunal, the Supreme Court of India pointed out that in industrial matters doctrinaire and abstract notions of social justice are avoided and realistic and pragmatic notions are applied so as to find a solution between the employer and the employees which is just and fair.

Despite the well intentioned commitment of ensuring social justice through equalization or protective discrimination policy, the governmental efforts have caused some tension in the society. In the name of social justice even such activities are performed which have nothing to do with social justice. The need of hour is to ensure the proper and balanced implementation of policies so as to make social justice an effective vehicle of social progress.

English quotation if you want to succeed as a Judge/ lawyer in our profession and that quotation is:

"Work like a horse and live like a hermit." If you apply these standards in your daily lives you will be fulfilling the constitutional dharma and if each one of you live by the constitutional dharma our society shall be free of discrimination and each one of you will be the role model for others and all these religious and caste conflicts will end.

REFERENCES

- Austin, Granville: *The Indian Constitution: Cornerstone of a Nation*, Oxford, Clarendon Press, 1966.
- Best M.: *The New Competition. Institutions of Industrial Restructuring*, Cambridge, Polity Press, 1990.
- Chandra, R.: *Judicial System in India*, Lucknow, Print House (India), 1992.
- Friedrich, J.: *Constitutional Government and Democracy*, Boston, Ginn, 1950.

2

Criticism of Indian Constitution

THE CONSTITUTION OF INDIA

The constitution of India is remarkable for many outstanding features which will distinguish it from other constitutions, even though there were members in the constituent Assembly who criticized the constitution which was going to be adopted as a slavish imitation of the west or not suited to the genius of the people. The most criticism is following:

Firstly: The constitution of India is being criticized on the ground that it is the most lengthy and detailed constitutional document the world has so far produced.

Secondly: The constitution of India is called as the carbon copy of the Act of 1935. The fathers of the constitution have borrowed a large number of provisions from the Act of 1935 and made them part of the new constitution.

Thirdly: One of the frequent criticism of the constitution was that was a lawyer's paradise. It is true that the constitution is a complex document. The language in which it was drafted is that which is familiar only in courts of law.

Fourthly: The constitution has been criticized by a small but vocal section on the ground that it is un-Gandhian. The constitution did not embody the principles for which Mahatma Gandhi stood or the ideology of the Indian National Congress.

Fifthly: It is said that the Indian constitution is a bag of borrowings or is a more paper and scissors work. Parliamentary form of government is borrowed from the British constitution while federalism and judicial review is borrowed from the U.S. constitution.

Sixthly: According to some critics, the centre has been made to strong. There is too much centralisation and that eh states have been reduced to municipalities.

Seventhly: The new constitution is called as un Indian anti-Indian that no part of the constitution represents the ancient polity of India, its genius and the sprit of its hallowed and glorious traditions.

In spite of the above weakness the Indian Constitution occupied an important place in India.

DIRECTIVE PRINCIPLES IN INDIA

The Directive Principles of State Policy are guidelines to the central and state governments of India, to be kept in mind while framing laws and policies. These provisions, contained in Part IV of the Constitution of India, are not enforceable by any court, but the principles laid down therein are considered fundamental in the governance of the country, making it the duty of the State to apply these principles in making laws to establish a just society in the country. The principles have been inspired by the Directive Principles given in the Constitution of Ireland and also by the principles of Gandhism; and relate to social justice, economic welfare, foreign policy, and legal and administrative matters. Directive Principles are classified under the following categories: Gandhian, economic and socialistic, political and administrative, justice and legal, environmental, protection of monuments and peace and security.

History

The concept of Directive Principles of State Policy was borrowed from the Irish Constitution. The makers of the Constitution of India were influenced by the Irish nationalist movement. Hence, the Directive Principles of the Indian constitution have been greatly influenced by the Directive

Principles of State Policy. The idea of such policies "can be traced to the Declaration of the Rights of Man proclaimed Revolutionary France and the Declaration of Independence by the American Colonies." The Indian constitution was also influenced by the United Nations Universal Declaration of Human Rights. In 1919, the Rowlatt Acts gave extensive powers to the British government and police, and allowed indefinite arrest and detention of individuals, warrant-less searches and seizures, restrictions on public gatherings, and intensive censorship of media and publications. The public opposition to this act eventually led to mass campaigns of nonviolent civil disobedience throughout the country demanding guaranteed civil freedoms, and limitations on government power. Indians, who were seeking independence and their own government, were particularly influenced by the independence of Ireland and the development of the Irish constitution. Also, the directive principles of state policy in Irish constitution were looked upon by the people of India as an inspiration for the independent India's government to comprehensively tackle complex social and economic challenges across a vast, diverse nation and population.

In 1928, the Nehru Commission composing of representatives of Indian political parties proposed constitutional reforms for India that apart from calling for dominion status for India and elections under universal suffrage, would guarantee rights deemed fundamental, representation for religious and ethnic minorities, and limit the powers of the government. In 1931, the Indian National Congress (the largest Indian political party of the time) adopted resolutions committing itself to the defence of fundamental civil rights, as well as socioeconomic rights such as the minimum wage and the abolition of untouchability and serfdom. Committing themselves to socialism in 1936, the Congress leaders took examples from the constitution of the erstwhile USSR, which inspired the fundamental duties of citizens as a means of collective patriotic responsibility for national interests and challenges. When India obtained independence on 15 August 1947, the task of developing a constitution for the nation was undertaken by the Constituent Assembly of India, composing of elected representatives under the presidency of Dr. Rajendra Prasad. While members of Congress composed of a large majority, Congress leaders appointed persons from diverse political backgrounds to responsibilities of developing the constitution and national laws. Notably, Bhimrao Ramji Ambedkar became the chairperson of the drafting committee, while Jawaharlal Nehru and Sardar Vallabhbhai Patel became chairpersons of committees and sub-committees responsible for different subjects. A notable development during that period having significant effect on the Indian constitution took place on 10 December 1948 when the United Nations General Assembly adopted the Universal Declaration of Human Rights and called upon all member states to adopt these rights in their respective constitutions.

Both the Fundamental Rights and the Directive Principles of State Policy were included in the I Draft Constitution (February 1948), the II Draft Constitution (17 October 1948) and the III and final Draft Constitution (26 November 1949), being prepared by the Drafting Committee.

Characteristics

DPSPs aim to create social and economic conditions under which the citizens can lead a good life. They also aim to establish social and economic democracy through a welfare state. They act as a check on the government, theorised as a yardstick in the hands of the people to measure the performance of the government and vote it out of power if it does not fulfill the promises made during the elections. The Directive Principles are non-justiciable rights of the people. Article 31-C, inserted by the 25th Amendment Act of 1971 seeks to upgrade the Directive Principles. If laws are made to give effect to the Directive Principles over Fundamental Rights, they shall not be invalid on the grounds that they take away the Fundamental Rights. In case of a conflict between Fundamental Rights and DPSP's, if the DPSP aims at promoting larger interest of the society, the courts shall have to uphold the case in favour of the DPSP. The Directive Principles, though not justiciable, are fundamental in the governance of the country. It shall be the duty of the State to apply these principles in making laws. Besides, all executive agencies should also be guided by these principles. Even the judiciary has to keep them in mind in deciding cases.

Directives

The directive principles ensure that the State shall strive to promote the welfare of the people by promoting a social order in which social, economic and political justice is informed in all institutions of life. Also, the State shall work towards reducing economic inequality as well as inequalities in status and opportunities, not only among individuals, but also among groups of people residing in different areas or engaged in different vocations. The State shall aim for securing right to an adequate means of livelihood for all citizens, both men and women as well as equal pay for equal work for both men and women. The State should work to prevent concentration of wealth and means of production in a few hands, and try to ensure that ownership and control of the material resources is distributed to best serve the common good. Child abuse and exploitation of workers should be prevented. Children should be allowed to develop in a healthy manner and should be protected against exploitation and against moral and material abandonment.

The State shall provide free legal aid to ensure that equal opportunities for securing justice is ensured to all, and is not denied by reason of economic or other disabilities. The State shall also work for organisation of village panchayats and help enable them to function as units of self-government. The State shall endeavour to provide the right to work, to education and to public assistance in cases of unemployment, old age, sickness and disablement, within the limits of economic capacity, as well as provide for just and humane conditions of work and maternity relief. The State should also ensure living wage and proper working conditions for workers, with full enjoyment of leisure and social and cultural activities. Also, the promotion of cottage industries in rural areas is one of the obligations of the State. The State shall take steps to promote their participation in management of industrial undertakings.

Also, the State shall endeavour to secure a uniform civil code for all citizens, and provide free and compulsory education to all children till they attain the age of 14 years. This directive regarding education of children was added by the 86th Amendment Act, 2002. It should and work for the economic and educational upliftment of scheduled castes, scheduled tribes and other weaker sections of the society. The directive principles commit the State to raise the level of nutrition and the standard of living and to improve public health, particularly by prohibiting intoxicating drinks and drugs injurious to health except for medicinal purposes. It should also organise agriculture and animal husbandry on modern and scientific lines by improving breeds and prohibiting slaughter of cows, calves, other milch and draught cattle It should protect and improve the environment and safeguard the forests and wild life of the country. This directive, regarding protection of forests and wildlife was added by the 42nd Amendment Act, 1976.

Protection of monuments, places and objects of historic and artistic interest and national importance against destruction and damage, and separation of judiciary from executive in public services are also the obligations of the State as laid down in the directive principles. Finally, the directive principles, in Article 51 ensure that the State shall strive for the promotion and maintenance of international peace and security, just and honourable relations between nations, respect for international law and treaty obligations, as well as settlement of international disputes by arbitration.

Implementation

The State has attained many efforts to implement the Directive Principles. The Programme of Universalisation of Elementary Education and the five year plans has been accorded the highest priority in order to provide free education to all children up to the age of 14 years. The 86th constitutional amendment of 2002 inserted a new article, Article 21-A, into the Constitution, that seeks to provide free and compulsory education to all children aged 6 to 14 years. Welfare schemes for the weaker sections are being implemented both by the Central and state governments. These include programmes such as boys' and girls' hostels for scheduled castes' or scheduled tribes' students. The year 1990-1991 was declared as the "Year of Social Justice" in the memory of B.R. Ambedkar. The government provides free textbooks to students belonging to scheduled castes or scheduled tribes pursuing medicine and engineering courses. During 2002-2003, a sum of Rs. 4.77 crore was released for this purpose. In order that scheduled castes and scheduled tribes are protected from atrocities, the Government enacted the *Prevention of Atrocities Act* in 1995, which provided severe punishments for such atrocities.

Several Land Reform Acts were enacted to provide ownership rights to poor farmers. Up to September 2001, more than 20,000,000 acres (80,000 km^2) of land had been distributed to scheduled castes, scheduled tribes and the landless poor. The thrust of banking policy in India has been to improve banking facilities in the rural areas. The *Minimum Wages Act* of 1948 empowers government to fix minimum wages for employees engaged in various employments. The *Consumer Protection Act* of 1986 provides for the better protection of consumers. The act is intended to provide simple, speedy and inexpensive redressal to the consumers' grievances, award relief and compensation wherever appropriate to the consumer. The *Equal Remuneration Act* of 1976, provides for equal pay for equal work for both men and women. The *Sampoorna Grameen Rozgar Yojana* was launched in 2001 to attain the objective of gainful employment for the rural poor. The programme was implemented through the Panchayati Raj institutions.

Panchayati Raj now covers almost all states and Union territories. One-third of the total number of seats have been reserved for women in Panchayats at every level; in the case of Bihar, half the seats have been reserved for women. Legal aid at the expense of the State has been made compulsory in all cases pertaining to criminal law, if the accused is too poor to engage a lawyer. Judiciary has been separated from the executive in all the states and Union territories except Jammu and Kashmir and Nagaland.

India's Foreign Policy has also to some degree been influenced by the DPSPs. India has in the past condemned all acts of aggression and has also supported the United Nations' peacekeeping activities. By 2004, the Indian Army had participated in 37 UN peacekeeping operations. India played a key role in the passing of a UN resolution in 2003, which envisaged better cooperation between the Security Council and the troop-contributing countries. India has also been in favour of nuclear disarmament.

Amendments

Alterations in Directive Principles require a Constitutional amendment which has to be passed by a special majority of both houses of the Parliament. This means that an amendment requires the approval of two-thirds of the members present and voting. However, the number of members voting should not be less than the simple majority of the house — whether the Lok Sabha or Rajya Sabha.

- Article 31-C, inserted into the Directive Principles of State Policy by the 25th Amendment Act of 1971 seeks to upgrade the DPSPs. If laws are made to give effect to the Directive Principles over Fundamental Rights, they shall not be invalid on the grounds that they take away the Fundamental Rights.
- Article 45, which ensures *Provision for free and compulsory education for children*, was added by the 86th Amendment Act, 2002.
- Article 48-A, which ensures *Protection and improvement of environment and safeguarding of forests and wild life*, was added by the 42nd Amendment Act, 1976.

FUNDAMENTAL RIGHTS, DIRECTIVE PRINCIPLES AND FUNDAMENTAL DUTIES OF INDIA

The Fundamental Rights, Directive Principles of State Policy and Fundamental Duties are sections of the Constitution of India that prescribe the fundamental obligations of the State to its citizens and the duties of the citizens to the State. These sections comprise a constitutional bill of rights for government policy-making and the behaviour and conduct of citizens. These sections are considered vital elements of the constitution, which was developed between 1947 and 1949 by the Constituent

Assembly of India. The *Fundamental Rights* are defined as the basic human rights of all citizens. These rights, defined in Part III of the Constitution, apply irrespective of race, place of birth, religion, caste, creed or gender. They are enforceable by the courts, subject to specific restrictions.

The *Directive Principles of State Policy* are guidelines for the framing of laws by the government. These provisions, set out in Part IV of the Constitution, are not enforceable by the courts, but the principles on which they are based are fundamental guidelines for governance that the State is expected to apply in framing and passing laws. The *Fundamental Duties* are defined as the moral obligations of all citizens to help promote a spirit of patriotism and to uphold the unity of India. These duties, set out in Part IV–A of the Constitution, concern individuals and the nation. Like the Directive Principles, they are not legally enforceable.

The Fundamental Rights and Directive Principles had their origins in the Indian independence movement, which strove to achieve the values of liberty and social welfare as the goals of an independent Indian state. The development of constitutional rights in India was inspired by historical documents such as England's Bill of Rights, the United States Bill of Rights and France's Declaration of the Rights of Man. The demand for civil liberties formed an important part of the Indian independence movement, with one of the objectives of the Indian National Congress (INC) being to end discrimination between the British rulers and their Indian subjects. This demand was explicitly mentioned in resolutions adopted by the INC between 1917 and 1919. The demands articulated in these resolutions included granting to Indians the rights to equality before law, free speech, trial by juries composed at least half of Indian members, political power, and equal terms for bearing arms as British citizens.

The experiences of the First World War, the unsatisfactory Montague-Chelmsford reforms of 1919, and the rise to prominence of M. K. Gandhi in the Indian independence movement marked a change in the attitude of its leaders towards articulating demands for civil rights. The focus shifted from demanding equality of status between Indians and the British to assuring liberty for all Indians. The Commonwealth of India Bill, drafted by Annie Beasant in 1925, specifically included demands for seven fundamental rights – individual liberty, freedom of conscience, free expression of opinion, freedom of assembly, nondiscrimination on the ground of sex, free elementary education and free use of public spaces. In 1927, the INC resolved to set up a committee to draft a "Swaraj Constitution" for India based on a declaration of rights that would provide safeguards against oppression. The 11 member committee, led by Motilal Nehru, was constituted in 1928. Its report made a number of recommendations, including proposing guaranteed fundamental rights to all Indians. These rights resembled those of the American Constitution and those adopted by postwar European countries, and several of them were adopted from the 1925 Bill. Several of these provisions were later replicated in various parts of the Indian Constitution, including the Fundamental Rights and Directive Principles.

In 1931, the Indian National Congress, at its Karachi session, adopted a resolution committing itself to the defence of civil rights and economic freedom, with the stated objectives of putting an end to exploitation, providing social security and implementing land reforms. Other new rights proposed by the resolution were the prohibition of State titles, universal adult franchise, abolition of capital punishment and freedom of movement.

Drafted by Jawaharlal Nehru, the resolution, which later formed the basis for some of the Directive Principles, placed the primary responsibility of carrying out social reform on the State, and marked the increasing influence of socialism and Gandhian philosophy on the independence movement. The final phase of the Independence movement saw a reiteration of the socialist principles of the 1930s, along with an increased focus on minority rights – which had become an issue of major political concern by then – which were published in the Sapru Report in 1945. The report, apart from stressing on protecting the rights of minorities, also sought to prescribe a "standard of conduct for the legislatures, government and the courts".

During the final stages of the British Raj, the 1946 Cabinet Mission to India proposed a Constituent Assembly to draft a Constitution for India as part of the process of transfer of power. The Constituent Assembly of India, composed of indirectly elected representatives from the British provinces and Princely states, commenced its proceedings in December 1946, and completed drafting the Constitution of India by November 1949. According to the Cabinet Mission plan, the Assembly was to have an Advisory Committee to advise it on the nature and extent of fundamental rights, protection of minorities and administration of tribal areas. Accordingly, the Advisory Committee was constituted in January 1947 with 64 members, and from among these a twelve-member sub-committee on Fundamental Rights was appointed under the chairmanship of J.B. Kripalani in February 1947.

The sub-committee drafted the Fundamental Rights and submitted its report to the Committee by April 1947, and later that month the Committee placed it before the Assembly, which debated and discussed the rights over the course of the following year, adopting the drafts of most of them by December 1948. The drafting of the Fundamental Rights was influenced by the adoption of the Universal Declaration of Human Rights by the U.N. General Assembly and the activities of the United Nations Human Rights Commission, as well as decisions of the U.S. Supreme Court in interpreting the Bill of Rights in the American Constitution. The Directive Principles, which were also drafted by the sub-committee on Fundamental Rights, expounded the socialist precepts of the Indian independence movement, and were inspired by similar principles contained in the Irish Constitution. The Fundamental Duties were later added to the Constitution by the 42nd Amendment in 1976.

The Fundamental Rights

The Fundamental Rights, embodied in Part III of the Constitution, guarantee civil rights to all Indians, and prevent the State from encroaching on individual liberty while simultaneously placing upon it an obligation to protect the citizens' rights from encroachment by society. Seven fundamental rights were originally provided by the Constitution

– right to equality, right to freedom, right against exploitation, right to freedom of religion, cultural and educational rights, right to property and right to constitutional remedies. However, the right to property was removed from Part III of the Constitution by the 44th Amendment in 1978. The purpose of the Fundamental Rights is to preserve individual liberty and democratic principles based on equality of all members of society. They act as limitations on the powers of the legislature and executive, under Article 13, and in case of any violation of these rights the Supreme Court of India and the High Courts of the states have the power to declare such legislative or executive action as unconstitutional and void.

These rights are largely enforceable against the State, which as per the wide definition provided in Article 12, includes not only the legislative and executive wings of the federal and state governments, but also local administrative authorities and other agencies and institutions which discharge public functions or are of a governmental character. However, there are certain rights – such as those in Articles 15, 17, 18, 23, 24 – that are also available against private individuals. Further, certain Fundamental Rights – including those under Articles 14, 20, 21, 25 – apply to persons of any nationality upon Indian soil, while others – such as those under Articles 15, 16, 19, 30 – are applicable only to citizens of India.

The Fundamental Rights are not absolute and are subject to reasonable restrictions as necessary for the protection of public interest. In the *Kesavananda Bharati v. State of Kerala* case in 1973, the Supreme Court, overruling a previous decision of 1967, held that the Fundamental Rights could be amended, subject to judicial review in case such an amendment violated the basic structure of the Constitution. The Fundamental Rights can be enhanced, removed or otherwise altered through a constitutional amendment, passed by a two-thirds majority of each House of Parliament. The imposition of a state of emergency may lead to a temporary suspension any of the Fundamental Rights, excluding Articles 20 and 21, by order of the President.

The President may, by order, suspend the right to constitutional remedies as well, thereby barring citizens from approaching the Supreme Court for the enforcement of any of the Fundamental Rights, except Articles 20 and 21, during the period of the emergency. Parliament may also restrict the application of the Fundamental Rights to members of the Indian Armed Forces and the police, in order to ensure proper discharge of their duties and the maintenance of discipline, by a law made under Article 33.

The Right to Equality

The Right to Equality is one of the chief guarantees of the Constitution. It is embodied in Articles 14–16, which collectively encompass the general principles of equality before law and nondiscrimination, and Articles 17–18 which collectively further the philosophy of social equality. Article 14 guarantees equality before law as well as equal protection of the law to all persons within the territory of India. This includes the equal subjection of all persons to the authority of law, as well as equal treatment of persons in similar circumstances. The latter permits the State to classify persons for legitimate purposes, provided there is a reasonable basis for the same, meaning that the classification is required to be non-arbitrary, based on a method of intelligible differentiation among those sought to be classified, as well as have a rational relation to the object sought to be achieved by the classification.

Article 15 prohibits discrimination on the grounds only of religion, race, caste, sex, place of birth, or any of them. This right can be enforced against the State as well as private individuals, with regard to free access to places of public entertainment or places of public resort maintained partly or wholly out of State funds. However, the State is not precluded from making special provisions for women and children or any socially and educationally backward classes of citizens, including the Scheduled Castes and Scheduled Tribes. This exception has been provided since the classes of people mentioned therein are considered deprived and in need of special protection.

Article 16 guarantees equality of opportunity in matters of public employment and prevents the State from discriminating against anyone in matters of employment on the grounds only of religion, race, caste, sex, descent, place of birth, place of residence or any of them. It creates exceptions for the implementation of measures of affirmative action for the benefit of any backward class of citizens in order to ensure adequate representation in public service, as well as reservation of an office of any religious institution for a person professing that particular religion.

The practice of untouchability has been declared an offence punishable by law under Article 17, and the Protection of Civil Rights Act, 1955 has been enacted by the Parliament to further this objective. Article 18 prohibits the State from conferring any titles other than military or academic distinctions, and the citizens of India cannot accept titles from a foreign state. Thus, Indian aristocratic titles and titles of nobility conferred by the British have been abolished. However, awards such as the *Bharat Ratna* have been held to be valid by the Supreme Court on the ground that they are merely decorations and cannot be used by the recipient as a title.

The Right to Freedom

The Right to Freedom is covered in Articles 19–22, with the view of guaranteeing individual rights that were considered vital by the framers of the Constitution, and these Articles also include certain restrictions that may be imposed by the State on individual liberty under specified conditions. Article 19 guarantees six freedoms in the nature of civil rights, which are available only to citizens of India. These include the freedom of speech and expression, freedom of assembly, freedom of association without arms, freedom of movement throughout the territory of India, freedom to reside and settle in any part of the country of India and the freedom to practice any profession.

All these freedoms are subject to reasonable restrictions that may imposed on them by the State, listed under Article 19 itself. The grounds for imposing these restrictions vary according to the freedom sought to be restricted, and include national security, public order, decency and morality, contempt of court, incitement to offences, and defamation. The State is also empowered, in the interests of the general public to nationalise any trade, industry or service to the exclusion of the citizens.

The freedoms guaranteed by Article 19 are further sought to be protected by Articles 20–22. The scope of these articles, particularly with respect to the doctrine of due process, was heavily debated by the Constituent Assembly. It was argued, especially by Benegal Narsing Rau, that the incorporation of such a clause would hamper social legislation and cause procedural difficulties in maintaining order, and therefore it ought to be excluded from the Constitution altogether. The Constituent Assembly in 1948 eventually omitted the phrase "due process" in favour of "procedure established by law". As a result, Article 21, which prevents the encroachment of life or personal liberty by the State except in accordance with the procedure established by law, was, until 1978, construed narrowly as being restricted to executive action. However, in 1978, the Supreme Court in the case of *Maneka Gandhi v. Union of India* extended the protection of Article 21 to legislative action, holding that any law laying down a procedure must be just, fair and reasonable, and effectively reading due process into Article 21. In the same case, the Supreme Court also ruled that "life" under Article 21 meant more than a mere "animal existence"; it would include the right to live with human dignity and all other aspects which made life "meaningful, complete and worth living". Subsequent judicial interpretation has broadened the scope of Article 21 to include within it a number of rights including those to livelihood, clean environment, good health, speedy trial and humanitarian treatment while imprisoned. The right to education at elementary level has been made one of the Fundamental Rights under Article 21A by the 86th Constitutional amendment of 2002.

Article 20 provides protection from conviction for offences in certain respects, including the rights against ex post facto laws, double jeopardy and freedom from self-incrimination. Article 22 provides specific rights to arrested and detained persons, in particular the rights to be informed of the grounds of arrest, consult a lawyer of one's own choice, be produced before a magistrate within 24 hours of the arrest, and the freedom not to be detained beyond that period without an order of the magistrate. The Constitution also authorises the State to make laws providing for preventive detention, subject to certain other safeguards present in Article 22. The provisions pertaining to preventive detention were discussed with skepticism and misgivings by the Constituent Assembly, and were reluctantly approved after a few amendments in 1949. Article 22 provides that when a person is detained under any law of preventive detention, the State can detain such person without trial for only three months, and any detention for a longer period must be authorised by an Advisory Board. The person being detained also has the right to be informed about the grounds of detention, and be permitted to make a representation against it, at the earliest opportunity.

The Right against Exploitation

The Right against Exploitation, contained in Articles 23–24, lays down certain provisions to prevent exploitation of the weaker sections of the society by individuals or the State. Article 23 provides prohibits human trafficking, making it an offence punishable by law, and also prohibits forced labour or any act of compelling a person to work without wages where he was legally entitled not to work or to receive remuneration for it. However, it permits the State to impose compulsory service for public purposes, including conscription and community service. The Bonded Labour system (Abolition) Act, 1976, has been enacted by Parliament to give effect to this Article. Article 24 prohibits the employment of children below the age of 14 years in factories, mines and other hazardous jobs. Parliament has enacted the Child Labour (Prohibition and Regulation) Act, 1986, providing regulations for the abolition of, and penalties for employing, child labour, as well as provisions for rehabilitation of former child labourers.

The Right to Freedom of Religion

The Right to Freedom of Religion, covered in Articles 25–28, provides religious freedom to all citizens and ensures a secular State in India. According to the Constitution, there is no official State religion, and the State is required to treat all religions impartially and neutrally. Article 25 guarantees all persons the freedom of conscience and the right to preach, practice and propagate any religion of their choice. This right is, however, subject to public order, morality and health, and the power of the State to take measures for social welfare and reform. The right to propagate, however, does not include the right to convert another individual, since it would amount to an infringement of the other's right to freedom of conscience.

Article 26 guarantees all religious denominations and sects, subject to public order, morality and health, to manage their own affairs in matters of religion, set up institutions of their own for charitable or religious purposes, and own, acquire and manage property in accordance with law. These provisions do not derogate from the State's power to acquire property belonging to a religious denomination. The State is also empowered to regulate any economic, political or other secular activity associated with religious practice. Article 27 guarantees that no person can be compelled to pay taxes for the promotion of any particular religion or religious institution. Article 28 prohibits religious instruction in a wholly State-funded educational institution, and educational institutions receiving aid from the State cannot compel any of their members to receive religious instruction or attend religious worship without their (or their guardian's) consent.

The Cultural and Educational Rights

The Cultural and Educational rights, given in Articles 29 and 30, are measures to protect the rights of cultural, linguistic and religious minorities, by enabling them to conserve their heritage and protecting them against discrimination. Article 29 grants any section of citizens having a distinct language, script culture of its own, the right to conserve and develop the same, and thus safeguards the rights of minorities by preventing the State from imposing any external culture on them. It also prohibits discrimination against any citizen for admission into any educational institutions maintained or aided by the State, on the grounds only of religion, race, caste, language or any of them. However, this is subject to reservation of a reasonable number of seats by the State for socially and educationally backward classes, as well as reservation of up to 50 percent of seats in any educational institution run by a minority community for citizens belonging to that community.

Article 30 confers upon all religious and linguistic minorities the right to set up and administer educational institutions of their choice in order to preserve and develop their own culture, and prohibits the State, while granting aid, from discriminating against any institution on the basis of the fact that it is administered by a religious or cultural minority. The term "minority", while not defined in the Constitution, has been interpreted by the Supreme Court to mean any community which numerically forms less than 50% of the population of the state in which it seeks to avail the right under Article 30. In order to claim the right, it is essential that the educational institution must have been established as well as administered by a religious or linguistic minority. Further, the right under Article 30 can be availed of even if the educational institution established does not confine itself to the teaching of the religion or language of the minority concerned, or a majority of students in that institution do not belong to such minority. This right is subject to the power of the State to impose reasonable regulations regarding educational standards, conditions of service of employees, fee structure, and the utilisation of any aid granted by it.

The Right to Constitutional Remedies

The Right to Constitutional Remedies empowers citizens to approach the Supreme Court of India to seek enforcement, or protection against infringement, of their Fundamental Rights. Article 32 provides a guaranteed remedy, in the form of a Fundamental Right itself, for enforcement of all the other Fundamental Rights, and the Supreme Court is designated as the protector of these rights by the Constitution. The Supreme Court has been empowered to issue writs, namely *habeas corpus*, *mandamus*, *prohibition*, *certiorari* and *quo warranto*, for the enforcement of the Fundamental Rights, while the High Courts have been empowered under Article 226 – which is not a Fundamental Right in itself – to issue these prerogative writs even in cases not involving the violation of Fundamental Rights. The Supreme Court has the jurisdiction to enforce the Fundamental Rights even against private bodies, and in case of any violation, award compensation as well to the affected individual. Exercise of jurisdiction by the Supreme Court can also be *suo motu* or on the basis of a public interest litigation. This right cannot be suspended, except under the provisions of Article 359 when a state of emergency is declared.

The Directive Principles of State Policy

The Directive Principles of State Policy, embodied in Part IV of the Constitution, are directions given to the State to guide the establishment of an economic and social democracy, as proposed by the Preamble. They set forth the humanitarian and socialist instructions that were the aim of social revolution envisaged in India by the Constituent Assembly. The State is expected to keep these principles in mind while framing laws and policies, even though they are non-justiciable in nature. The Directive Principles may be classified under the following categories: ideals that the State ought to strive towards achieving; directions for the exercise of legislative and executive power; and rights of the citizens which the State must aim towards securing. Despite being non-justiciable, the Directive Principles act as a check on the State; theorised as a yardstick in the hands of the electorate and the opposition to measure the performance of a government at the time of an election. Article 37, while stating that the Directive Principles are not enforceable in any court of law, declares them to be "fundamental to the governance of the country" and imposes an obligation on the State to apply them in matters of legislation. Thus, they serve to emphasise the welfare state model of the Constitution and emphasise the positive duty of the State to promote the welfare of the people by affirming social, economic and political justice, as well as to fight income inequality and ensure individual dignity, as mandated by Article 38.

Article 39 lays down certain principles of policy to be followed by the State, including providing an adequate means of livelihood for all citizens, equal pay for equal work for men and women, proper working conditions, reduction of the concentration of wealth and means of production from the hands of a few, and distribution of community resources to "subserve the common good". These clauses highlight the Constutuional objectives of building an egalitarian social order and establishing a welfare state, by bringing about a social revolution assisted by the State, and have been used to support the nationalisation of mineral resources as well as public utilities. Further, several legislations pertaining to agrarian reform and land tenure have been enacted by the federal and state governments, in order to ensure equitable distribution of land resources. Articles 41–43 mandate the State to endeavour to secure to all citizens the right to work, a living wage, social security, maternity relief, and a decent standard of living. These provisions aim at establishing a socialist state as envisaged in the Preamble. Article 43 also places upon the State the responsibility of promoting cottage industries, and the federal government has, in furtherance of this, established several Boards for the promotion of khadi, handlooms etc., in coordination with the state governments. Article 39A requires the State to provide free legal aid to ensure that opportunities for securing justice are available to all citizens irrespective of economic or other disabilities. Article 43A mandates the State to work towards securing the participation of workers in the management of industries. The State, under Article 46, is also mandated to promote the interests of and work for the economic uplift of the scheduled castes and scheduled tribes and protect them from discrimination and exploitation. Several enactments, including two Constitutional amendments, have been passed to give effect to this provision.

Article 44 encourages the State to secure a uniform civil code for all citizens, by eliminating discrepancies between various personal laws currently in force in the country. However, this has remained a "dead letter" despite numerous reminders from the Supreme Court to implement the provision. Article 45 originally mandated the State to provide free and compulsory education to children between the ages of six and fourteen years, but after the 86th Amendment in 2002, this has been converted into a Fundamental Right and replaced by an obligation upon the State to secure childhood care to all children below the age of six. Article 47 commits the State to raise the standard of living and improve public health, and prohibit the consumption of intoxicating drinks and drugs injurious to health. As a consequence, partial or total prohibition has been introduced in several states, but financial constraints have prevented its full-fledged application. The State is also mandated by Article 48 to organise agriculture and animal husbandry on modern and scientific lines by improving breeds and prohibiting slaughter of cattle. Article 48A mandates the State to protect the environment and safeguard the forests and wildlife of the country, while Article 49 places an obligation upon the State to ensure the preservation of monuments and objects of national importance. Article 50 requires the State to ensure the separation of judiciary from executive in public services, in order to ensure judicial independence, and federal legislation has been enacted to achieve this objective. The State, according to Article 51, must also strive for the promotion of international peace and security, and Parliament has been empowered under Article 253 to make laws giving effect to international treaties.

The Fundamental Duties

The Fundamental Duties of citizens were added to the Constitution by the 42nd Amendment in 1976, upon the recommendations of the Swaran Singh Committee that was constituted by the government earlier that year. Originally ten in number, the Fundamental Duties were increased to eleven by the 86th Amendment in 2002, which added a duty on every parent or guardian to ensure that their child or ward was provided opportunities for education between the ages of six and fourteen years. The other Fundamental Duties obligate all citizens to respect the national symbols of India, including the Constitution, to cherish its heritage, preserve its composite culture and assist in its defence. They also obligate all Indians to promote the spirit of common brotherhood, protect the environment and public property, develop scientific temper, abjure violence, and strive towards excellence in all spheres of life. Citizens are morally obligated by the Constitution to perform these duties. However, like the Directive Principles, these are non-justifiable, without any legal sanction in case of their violation or noncompliance. There is reference to such duties in international instruments such as the Universal Declaration of Human Rights and International Covenant on Civil and Political Rights, and Article 51A brings the Indian Constitution into conformity with these treaties.

Fewer children are now employed in hazardous environments, but their employment in nonhazardous jobs, prevalently as domestic help, violates the spirit of the constitution in the eyes of many critics and human rights advocates. More than 16.5 million children are in employment. India was ranked 88 out of 159 countries in 2005, according to the degree to which corruption is perceived to exist among public officials and politicians. The year 1990–1991 was declared as the "Year of Social Justice" in the memory of B.R. Ambedkar. The government provides free textbooks to students belonging to scheduled castes and tribes pursuing medicine and engineering courses. During 2002–2003, a sum of Rs. 4.77 crore (47.7 million) was released for this purpose. In order to protect scheduled castes and tribes from discrimination, the government enacted the *Prevention of Atrocities Act* in 1995, prescribing severe punishments for such actions.

The *Minimum Wages Act* of 1948 empowers government to fix minimum wages for people working across the economic spectrum. The *Consumer Protection Act* of 1986 provides for the better protection of consumers. The act is intended to provide simple, speedy and inexpensive redressal to the consumers' grievances, award relief and compensation wherever appropriate to the consumer. The *Equal Remuneration Act* of 1976 provides for equal pay for equal work for both men and women. The *Sampoorna Grameen Rozgar Yojana* (Universal Rural Employment Programme) was launched in 2001 to attain the objective of providing gainful employment for the rural poor. The programme was implemented through the Panchayati Raj institutions.

A system of elected village councils, known as Panchayati Raj covers almost all states and territories of India. One-third of the total number of seats have been reserved for women in Panchayats at every level; and in the case of Bihar, half the seats have been reserved for women. The judiciary has been separated from the executive "in all the states and territories except Jammu and Kashmir and Nagaland." India's foreign policy has been influenced by the Directive Principles. India supported the United Nations in peacekeeping activities, with the Indian Army having participated in 37 UN peacekeeping operations.

The implementation of a uniform civil code for all citizens has not been achieved owing to widespread opposition from various religious groups and political parties. The Shah Bano case (1985–86) provoked a political firestorm in India when the Supreme Court ruled that Shah Bano, a Muslim woman who had been divorced by her husband in 1978 was entitled to receive alimony from her former husband under Indian law applicable for all Indian women. This decision evoked outrage in the Muslim community, which sought the application of the Muslim personal law and in response the Parliament passed the Muslim Women (Protection of Rights on Divorce) Act, 1986 overturning the Supreme Court's verdict. This act provoked further outrage, as jurists, critics and politicians alleged that the fundamental right of equality for all citizens irrespective of religion or gender was being jettisoned to preserve the interests of distinct religious communities. The verdict and the legislation remain a source of heated debate, with many citing the issue as a prime example of the poor implementation of Fundamental Rights.

Relationship between the Fundamental Rights, Directive Principles and Fundamental Duties

The Directive Principles have been used to uphold the Constitutional validity of legislations in case of a conflict with the Fundamental Rights. Article 31C, added by the 25th Amendment in 1971, provided that any law made to give effect to the Directive Principles in Article 39(b)–(c) would not be invalid on the grounds that they derogated from the Fundamental Rights conferred by Articles 14, 19 and 31. The application of this article was sought to be extended to all the Directive Principles by the 42nd Amendment in 1976, but the Supreme Court struck down the extension as void on the ground that it violated the basic structure of the Constitution. The Fundamental Rights and Directive Principles have also been used together in forming the basis of legislation for social welfare. The Supreme Court, after the judgment in the *Kesavananda Bharati* case, has adopted the view of the Fundamental Rights and Directive Principles being complementary to each other, each supplementing the other's role in aiming at the same goal of establishing a welfare state by means of social revolution. Similarly, the Supreme Court has used the Fundamental Duties to uphold the Constitutional validity of statutes which seeks to promote the objects laid out in the Fundamental Duties. These Duties have also been held to be obligatory for all citizens, subject to the State enforcing the same by means of a valid law. The Supreme Court has also issued directions to the State in this regard, with a view towards making the provisions effective and enabling a citizens to properly perform their duties.

DIRECTIVE PRINCIPLES OF STATE POLICY IN INDIA

An authoritative feature of the constitution is the Directive Principles of State Policy. Although the Directive Principles are asserted to be "fundamental in the governance of the country," they are not legally enforceable. Instead, they are guidelines for creating a social order characterised by social, economic, and political justice, liberty, equality, and fraternity as enunciated in the constitution's preamble. The Forty-second Amendment, which came into force in January 1977, attempted to raise the status of the Directive Principles by stating that no law implementing any of the Directive Principles could be declared unconstitutional on the grounds that it violated any of the Fundamental Rights.

The amendment simultaneously stated that laws prohibiting "antinational activities" or the formation of "antinational associations" could not be invalidated because they infringed on any of the Fundamental Rights. It added a new section to the constitution on "Fundamental Duties" that enjoined citizens "to promote harmony and the spirit of common brotherhood among all the people of India, transcending religious, linguistic and regional or sectional diversities."

However, the amendment reflected a new emphasis in governing circles on order and discipline to counteract what some leaders had come to perceive as the excessively freewheeling style of Indian democracy. After the March 1977 general election ended the control of the Congress (Congress (R) from 1969) over the executive and legislature for the first time since independence in 1947, the new Janata-dominated Parliament passed the Forty-third Amendment (1977) and Forty-fourth Amendment (1978). These amendments revoked the Forty-second Amendment's provision that Directive Principles take precedence over Fundamental Rights and also curbed Parliament's power to legislate against "antinational activities."

The Directive Principles of State DPSP are Policy (contained in part IV, articles 36 to 50,) of the Indian Constitution. Many of the provisions correspond to the provisions of the ICESCR. For instance, article 43 provides that the state shall endeavour to secure, by suitable legislation or economic organisation or in any other way, to all workers, agricultural, industrial or otherwise, work, a living wage, conditions of work ensuring a decent standard of life and full enjoyment of leisure and social and cultural opportunities, and in particular the state shall endeavour to promote cottage industries on an individual or cooperative basis in rural areas. This corresponds more or less to articles 11 and 15 of the ICESCR. However, some of the ICESCR rights, for instance, the right to health (art. 12), have been interpreted by the Indian Supreme Court to form part of the right to life under article 21 of the Constitution, thus making it directly enforceable and justiciable. As a party to the ICESCR, the Indian legislature has enacted laws giving effect to some of its treaty obligations and these laws are in turn enforceable in and by the courts.

Article 37 of the Constitution declares that the DPSP "shall not be enforceable by any court, but the principles therein laid down are nevertheless fundamental in the governance of the country and it shall be the duty of the state to apply these principles in making laws." It is not a mere coincidence that the apparent distinction that is drawn by scholars between the

ICCPR rights and ESC rights holds good for the distinction that is drawn in the Indian context between fundamental rights and DPSP. Thus the bar to justiciability of the DPSP is spelled out in some sense in the Constitution itself.

It was said by several members in the Constituent Assembly that the directive principles are superfluous or mere guidelines or pious principles or instructions. They have no binding force on the State. In his speech Dr. Ambedkar answered.

" The directive principles are like instruments of instructions which were issued to the Governor in General and Governors of colonies and to those of India by the British Government under the 1935 Act under the Draft Constitution. It is proposed to issue such instructions to the president and governors. The text of these instruments of the instructions shall be found in scheduled IV to the Constitution of India. What are called directive principles is that they are instructions to the Legislature and the Executive. Such a thing is, to my mind, to be welcomed.

Wherever there is grant or power in general terms for peace, order and good government that it is necessary that it should be accompanied by the instructions regulating its exercise." It was never intended by Dr. Ambedkar that the Directive Principles had no legal force but had moral effect while educating members of the Government and the legislature, nor can it be said that the answer referred to necessarily implied with the Directive Principles had no legal force.

THE FOLLOWING OBSERVATIONS OF PROF. FOOD BHAT

Firstly, about of the directive principles of State policy, which are related to distributive justice, moulded the property relations by influencing the interrelationship doctrine, both directly and indirectly.

Secondly, the interrelationship doctrine is very much influenced by Article 39A of the Constitution which provides for equal justice and free legal aid in the justice delivery system.

Thirdly, the directive principles of State shall strive to secure its citizens right to an adequate means of livelihood and make the effective provision for securing right to work.

Fourthly, the directive principle that ';tender age of children are not abused';, and that ';children are given opportunities and facilities to develop in a healthy manner and in a conditions of freedom and dignity that childhood and youth are protected against exploitation against moral and material abandonment'; Article 39(f) have provided the spirit of law to the Apex Court.

Fifthly, the directive principle of ';Equal pay for equal work'; and ';participation of workers in management'; were received through right to equality under Article 14 in Part III, in various cases, such as Randhir Singh (AIR 1982 SC 469) and National Textile Workers Union case (AIR 1983 SC 75).

Sixthly, the directive principles relating to uniform civil code has the potentiality of using the interrelationship doctrine for its implementation.

Seventhly, the promotion of educational and economic interest of Scheduled Caste and Scheduled Tribe and other weaker section of the society, contemplated under Article 46 provides a guidance for affirmative actions under Article 15(4) and 16(4) and a pointer for resolving tension between formal and substantive equality by laying emphasis on infusing of strength and ability to compete, through eduction and training to weaker sectors (M.R. Balaji vs. State of Mysore – AIR 1963 SC 649).

Finally, the directive principle that the State shall endeavour to foster respect for international law and treaty obligations has a great potentiality of absorbing the international principles relating to guarantee as under of human rights, and thus influence the interrelationship doctrine.

The convictions are reflected:

(i) The impact of directive principles upon the interrelationship doctrine or vice-versa is not only theoretical but also practical and rewarding. Interrelationship doctrine has given impetus to, and got animated by the process of reading the directive principles into Part III of the Constitution.

(ii) It is true to say that the interrelationship doctrine has its roots in the very text of the constitution. This can be seen when the objects set in the Preamble, followed by Juxtaposing of right to equality with classification, the flexibility imbibed in fundamental rights, the spirit of law (operation of whole Part-III of the Constitution visa-vis the impugned law) rejection of compartmentalised treatment of fundamental rights and finally, the distinction between citizens and non-citizens with regard to availability of fundamental rights and the possibility of invoking a fundamental right to avail a suspended fundamental right during emergency are taken into account with a conscious approach of unity in diversity.

Former Chief Justice of India Shri M.N. Venkatachelaiah, said that professor Bhat examines the relationship of fundamental rights inter se and the jurisprudential and constitutional foundations of that interrelationship. The interrelationship is also a necessary implication of constitutionalism and Rule of Law. It was viewed that professor Bhat, in his elegant analysis, indicates the ';parallel streams'; and 'cross-currents' of fundamental rights and how these rights inform and enrich each other. This discourse has its familiar ring in the International Human Rights Regime, and the principles of their universality, indivibility and interdependence Fundamental Rights and DPSP.

When the tussle for primacy between fundamental rights and DPSP came up before the Supreme Court in the case of State of Madras v. Champakam Dorairajan (1951) SCR 525 first, the court said, "The directive principles have to conform to and run subsidiary to the chapter on fundamental rights." Later, in the Fundamental Rights Case (referred to above), the majority opinions reflected the view that what is fundamental in the governance of the country cannot be less significant than what is significant in the life of the individual. Another judge constituting the majority in that case said: "In building up a just social order it is sometimes imperative that the fundamental rights should be subordinated to directive principles." This view, that the fundamental rights and DPSP are complementary, "neither part being superior to the other," has held the field since (V.R.Krishna Iyer, J. in State of Kerala v. N. M. Thomas (1976) 2 SCC 310 at para).

The DPSP have, through important constitutional amendments, become the benchmark to insulate legislation enacted to achieve social objectives, as enumerated in some of the DPSP, from attacks of invalidation by courts. This way, legislation for achieving agrarian reforms, and specifically for achieving the objectives of articles 39(b) and (c) of the Constitution, has been immunised from challenge as to its violation of the right to equality (art. 14) and freedoms of speech, expression, etc. (art. 19). However, even here the court has retained its power of judicial review to examine if, in fact, the legislation is intended to achieve the objective of articles 39(b) and (c), and where the legislation is an amendment to the Constitution, whether it violates the basic structure of the constitution. Likewise, courts have used DPSP to uphold the constitutional validity of statutes that apparently impose restrictions on the fundamental rights under article 19 (freedoms of speech, expression, association, residence, travel and to carry on a business, trade or profession), as long as they are stated to achieve the objective of the DPSP.

The DPSP are seen as aids to interpret the Constitution, and more specifically to provide the basis, scope and extent of the content of a fundamental right.

To quote again from the Fundamental Rights case: Fundamental rights have themselves no fixed content; most of them are empty vessels into which each generation must pour its content in the light of its experience. Restrictions, abridgement, curtailment and even abrogation of these rights in circumstances not visualised by the constitution makers might become necessary; their claim to supremacy or priority is liable to be overborne at particular stages in the history of the nation by the moral claims embodied in Part IV (Chandra Bhavan v. State of Mysore (1970) 2 SCR, note 1, SCC para. 1714).

The Maneka Gandhi Case and Thereafter Simultaneously, the judiciary took upon itself the task of infusing into the constitutional provisions the spirit of social justice. This it did in a series of cases of which Maneka Gandhi v. Union of India (1978) 1 SCC 248 was a landmark. The case involved the refusal by the government to grant a passport to the petitioner, which thus restrained her liberty to travel. In answering the question whether this denial could be sustained without a predecisional hearing, the court proceeded to explain the scope and content of the right to life and liberty. In a departure from the earlier view, A.K.Gopalan v. State of Madras 1950 SCR 88 the court asserted the doctrine of substantive due process as integral to the chapter on fundamental rights and emanating from a collective understanding of the scheme underlying articles 14 (the right to equality), 19 (the freedoms) and 21. The power the court has to strike down legislation was thus broadened to include critical examination of the substantive due process element in statutes. Once the court took a broader view of the scope and content of the fundamental right to life and liberty, there was no looking back. Article 21 was interpreted to include a bundle of other incidental and integral rights, many of them in the nature of ESC rights. In Francis Coralie v. union territory of India (AIR 1978 SC 597) the court declared: "The right to life includes the right to live with human dignity and all that goes with it, namely, the bare necessaries of life such as adequate nutrition, clothing and shelter and facilities for reading, writing and expressing oneself in diverse forms, freely moving about and mixing and commingling with fellow human beings. The magnitude and components of this right would depend upon the extent of economic development of the country, but it must, in any view of the matter, include the bare necessities of life and also the right to carry on such functions and activities as constitute the bare minimum expression of the human self."

The combined effect of the expanded interpretation of the right to life and the use of PIL as a tool led the court into areas where there was a crying need for social justice. These were areas where there was a direct interaction between law and poverty, as in the case of bonded labour and child labour, and crime and poverty, as in the case of under trials in jails. In reading several of these concomitant rights of dignity, living conditions, health into the ambit of the right to life, the court overcame the difficulty of justiciability of these as economic and social rights, which were hitherto, in their manifestation as DPSP, considered nonenforceable. A brief look at how some of these ESC rights were dealt with by the court in four specific contexts will help understand the development of the law in this area.

RIGHT TO WORK

Article 41 of the Constitution provides that "the State shall within the limits of its economic capacity and development, make effective provision for securing the right to work, to education and to public assistance in cases of unemployment, old age, sickness and disablement, and in other cases of undeserved want."(article 6 of the ICESCR) Article 38 states that the state shall strive to promote the welfare of the people and article 43 states it shall endeavour to secure a living wage and a decent standard of life to all workers. One of the contexts in which the problem of enforceability of such a right was posed before the Supreme Court was of large-scale abolition of posts of village officers in the State of Tamil Nadu in India. In negating the contention that such an abolition of posts would fall foul of the DPSP, the court said: It is no doubt true that Article 38 and Article 43 of the Constitution insist that the State should endeavour to find sufficient work for the people so that they may put their capacity to work into economic use and earn a fairly good living. But these articles do not mean that everybody should be provided with a job in the civil service of the State and if a person is provided with one he should not be asked to leave it even for a just cause. If it were not so, there would be justification for a small percentage of the population being in Government service and in receipt of regular income and a large majority of them remaining outside with no guaranteed means of living. It would certainly be an ideal state of affairs if work could be found for all the able-bodied men and women and everybody is guaranteed the right to participate in the production of national wealth and to enjoy the fruits thereof. But we are today far away from that goal.

The question whether a person who ceases to be a government servant according to law should be rehabilitated by being given an alternative employment is, as the law stands today, a matter of policy on which the court has no voice.(K.Rajendran v. State of Tamil Nadu (1982) 2 SCC 273, para. 34). But the court has since then felt freer to interfere even in areas which would have been considered to be in the domain of the policy of the executive. Where the issue was of regularising the services of a large number of casual (nonpermanent) workers in the posts and telegraphs department of the government, the court has not hesitated to invoke the DPSP to direct such regularisation. The explanation was: Even though the above directive principle may not be enforceable as such by virtue of Article 37 of the Constitution of India, it may be relied upon by the petitioners to show that in the instant case they have been subjected to hostile discrimination. It is urged that the State cannot deny at least the minimum pay in the pay scales of regularly employed workmen even though the Government may not be compelled to extend all the benefits enjoyed by regularly recruited employees. We are of the view that such denial amounts to exploitation of labour. The Government cannot take advantage of its dominant position, and compel any worker to work even as a casual labourer on starvation wages. It may be that the casual labourer has agreed to work on such low wages. That he has done because he has no other choice. It is poverty that has driven him to that state. The Government should be a model employer. We are of the view that on the facts and in the circumstances of this case the classification of employees into regularly recruited employees and casual employees for the purpose of paying less than the minimum pay payable to employees in the corresponding regular cadres particularly in the lowest rungs of the department where the pay scales are the lowest is not tenable... It is true that all these rights cannot be extended simultaneously. But they do indicate the socialist goal. The degree of achievement in this direction depends upon the economic resources, willingness of the people to produce and more than all the existence of industrial peace throughout the country. Of those rights the question of security of work is of utmost importance.

In Bandhua Mukti Morcha v. Union of India, (1984) 3 SCC 161 a PIL by an NGO highlighted the deplorable condition of bonded labourers in a quarry in Haryana, not very far from the

Supreme Court. A host of protective and welfare-oriented labour legislation, including the Bonded Labour (Abolition) Act and the Minimum Wages Act, were being observed in the breach. In giving extensive directions to the state government to enable it to discharge its constitutional obligation towards the bonded labourers, the court said: The right to live with human dignity enshrined in Article 21 derives its life breath from the Directive Principles of State Policy and particularly clauses (e) and (f) of Article 39 and Article 41 and 42 and at the least, therefore, it must include protection of the health and strength of workers, men and women, and of the tender age of children against abuse, opportunities and facilities for children to develop in a healthy manner and in conditions of freedom and dignity, educational facilities, just and humane conditions of work and maternity relief. These are the minimum requirements which must exist in order to enable a person to live with human dignity and no State has the right to take any action which will deprive a person of the enjoyment of these basic essentials. Since the Directive Principles of State Policy contained in clauses (e) and (f) of Article 39, Articles 41 and 42 are not enforceable in a court of law, it may not be possible to compel the State through the judicial process to make provision by statutory enactment or executive fiat for ensuring these basic essentials which go to make up a life of human dignity, but where legislation is already enacted by the State providing these basic requirements to the workmen and thus investing their right to live with basic human dignity, with concrete reality and content, the State can certainly be obligated to ensure observance of such legislation, for inaction on the part of the State in securing implementation of such legislation would amount to denial of the right to live with human dignity enshrined in Article 21, more so in the context of Article 256 which provides that the executive power of every State shall be so exercised as to ensure compliance with the laws made by Parliament and any existing laws which apply in that State.

Thus the court converted what seemed a non-justiciable issue into a justiciable one by invoking the wide sweep of the enforceable article 21. More recently, the court performed a similar exercise when, in the context of articles 21 and 42, it evolved legally binding guidelines to deal with the problems of sexual harassment of women at the work place (Vishaka v. State of Rajasthan (1997) 6 SCC 241.). The right of workmen to be heard at the stage of winding up of a company was a contentious issue. In a bench of five judges that heard the case the judges that constituted the majority that upheld the right were three. The justification for the right was traced to the newly inserted article 43-A, which asked the state to take suitable steps to secure participation of workers in management.

The court observed: It is therefore idle to contend 32 years after coming into force of the Constitution and particularly after the introduction of article 43-A in the Constitution that the workers should have no voice in the determination of the question whether the enterprises should continue to run or be shut down under an order of the court.

It would indeed be strange that the workers who have contributed to the building of the enterprise as a centre of economic power should have no right to be heard when it is sought to demolish that centre of economic power National Textile Workers Union v. P. R. Ramakrishnan (1983) 1 SCC 249.

RIGHT TO SHELTER

Unlike certain other ESC rights, the right to shelter, which forms part of the right to an adequate standard of living under article 11 of the ICESCR, finds no corresponding expression in the DPSP. This right has been seen as forming part of article 21 itself. The court has gone as far as to say, "The right to life would take within its sweep the right to food and a reasonable accommodation to live in." However, given that these observations were not made in a petition by a homeless person seeking shelter, it is doubtful that this declaration would be in the nature of a positive right that could be said to be enforceable. On the other hand, in certain other contexts with regard to housing for the poor, the court has actually refused to recognise any such absolute right. In Olga Tellis v. Bombay Municipal Corporation (1985) 3 SCC 545 the court held that the right to life included the right to livelihood. The petitioners contended that since they would be deprived of their livelihood if they were evicted from their slum and pavement dwellings, their eviction would be tantamount to deprivation of their life and hence be unconstitutional. The court, however, was not prepared to go that far. It denied that contention, saying:

No one has the right to make use of a public property for a private purpose without requisite authorisation and, therefore, it is erroneous to contend that pavement dwellers have the right to encroach upon pavements by constructing dwellings thereon... If a person puts up a dwelling on the pavement, whatever may be the economic compulsions behind such an act, his use of the pavement would become unauthorised. Later benches of the Supreme Court have followed the Olga Tellis dictum with approval. In Municipal Corporation of Delhi v. Gurnam Kaur, (1989) 1 SCC 101. the court held that the Municipal Corporation of Delhi had no legal obligation to provide pavement squatters alternative shops for rehabilitation as the squatters had no legal enforceable right. In Sodan Singh case (1989) 4 SCC 155 a constitution bench of the Supreme Court reiterated that the question whether there can at all be a fundamental right of a citizen to occupy a particular place on the pavement where he can squat and engage in trade must be answered in the negative.

These cases fail to account for socioeconomic compulsions that give rise to pavement dwelling and restrict their examination of the problem from a purely statutory point of view rather than the human rights perspective. Fortunately, a different note has been struck in a recent decision of the court. In Ahmedabad Municipal Corporation v. Nawab Khan Gulab Khan, (1997) 11 SCC 123 in the context of eviction of encroachers in a busy locality of Ahmadabad city, the court said: Due to want of facilities and opportunities, the right to residence and settlement is an illusion to the rural and urban poor. Articles 38, 39 and 46 mandate the State, as its economic policy, to provide socioeconomic justice to minimise inequalities in income and in opportunities and status.

It positively charges the State to distribute its largesse to the weaker sections of the society envisaged in Article 46 to make socioeconomic justice a reality, meaningful and fruitful so as to make life worth living with dignity of person and equality of status and to constantly improve excellence. Though no person has a right to encroach and erect structures or otherwise on footpaths, pavements or public streets or any other place reserved or earmarked for a public purpose, the State has the constitutional duty to provide adequate facilities and opportunities by distributing its wealth and resources for settlement of life and erection of shelter over their heads to make the right to life meaningful.

RIGHT TO EDUCATION

Article 45 of the DPSP, which corresponds to article 13(1) of the ICESCR, states, "The State shall endeavour to provide, within a period of ten years from the commencement of this Constitution, for free and compulsory education for all children until they complete the age of fourteen years." Thus, while the right of a child not to be employed in hazardous industries was, by virtue of article 24, recognised to be a fundamental right, the child's right to education was put into the DPSP in part IV and deferred for a period of ten years.

The question whether the right to education was a fundamental right and enforceable as such was answered by the Supreme Court in the affirmative in Mohini Jain v. State of Karnataka (1992) 3 SCC 666. The correctness of this decision was examined by a larger bench of five judges in Unnikrishnan J.P. State of Andhra Pradesh (1993) 1 SCC 645. The occasion was the challenge, by private medical and engineering colleges, to state legislation regulating the charging of "capitation" fees from students seeking admission. The college management was seeking enforcement of their right to business. The court expressly denied this claim and proceeded to examine the nature of the right to education. The court refused to accept the nonenforceablity of the DPSP. It asked: It is noteworthy that among the several articles in Part IV, only Article 45 speaks of a time-limit; no other article does. Has it no significance? Is it a mere pious wish, even after 44 years of the Constitution? Can the State flout the said direction even after 44 years on the ground that the article merely calls upon it to endeavour to provide the same and on the further ground that the said article is not enforceable by virtue of the declaration in Article 37. Does not the passage of 44 years—more than four times the period stipulated in Article 45—convert the obligation created by the article into an enforceable right? In this context, we feel constrained to say that allocation of available funds to different sectors of education in India discloses an inversion of priorities indicated by the Constitution. The Constitution contemplated a crash programme being undertaken by the State to achieve the goal set out in Article 45.

It is relevant to notice that Article 45 does not speak of the "limits of its economic capacity and development" as does Article 41, which inter alia speaks of right to education. What has actually happened is more money is spent and more attention is directed to higher education than to—and at the cost of—primary education. (By primary education, we mean the education which a normal child receives by the time he completes 14 years of age.) Neglected more so are the rural sectors, and the weaker sections of the society referred to in Article 46. We clarify, we are not seeking to lay down the priorities for the Government—we are only emphasizing the constitutional policy as disclosed by Articles 45, 46 and 41. Surely the wisdom of these constitutional provisions is beyond question.

The court then proceeded to examine how this right would be enforceable and to what extent. It clarified the issue thus: The right to education further means that a citizen has a right to call upon the State to provide educational facilities to him within the limits of its economic capacity and development. By saying so, we are not transferring Article 41 from Part IV to Part III—we are merely relying upon Article 41 to illustrate the content of the right to education flowing from Article 21. We cannot believe that any State would say that it need not provide education to its people even within the limits of its economic capacity and development. It goes without saying that the limits of economic capacity are, ordinarily speaking, matters within the subjective satisfaction of the State.

More caution followed. The court's apprehension clearly was that recognition of such a right might open the flood gates for other claims. It clarified: We must hasten to add that just because we have relied upon some of the directive principles to locate the parameters of the right to education implicit in Article 21, it does not follow automatically that each and every obligation referred to in Part IV gets automatically included within the purview of Article 21. We have held the right to education to be implicit in the right to life because of its inherent fundamental importance. As a matter of fact, we have referred to Articles 41, 45 and 46 merely to determine the parameters of the said right.

In fact, the court had broken new ground in the matter of justiciability and enforceability of the DPSP. The decision in Unnikrishnan case has been applied by the court in formulating broad parameters for compliance by the government in the matter of eradication of child labour. This it did in a PIL where it said:

Now, strictly speaking a strong case exists to invoke the aid of Article 41 of the Constitution regarding the right to work and to give meaning to what has been provided in Article 47 relating to raising of standard of living of the population, and Articles 39 (e) and (f) as to non-abuse of tender age of children and giving opportunities and facilities to them to develop in a healthy manner, for asking the State to see that an adult member of the family, whose child is in employment in a factory or a mine or in other hazardous work, gets a job anywhere, in lieu of the child. This would also see the fulfillment of the wish contained in Article 41 after about half a century of its being in the paramount parchment, like primary education desired by Article 45, having been given the status of fundamental right by the decision in Unnikrishnan. We are, however, not asking the State at this stage to ensure alternative employment in every case covered by Article 24, as Article 41 speaks about right to work "within the limits of the economic capacity and development of the State".

The very large number of child labour in the aforesaid occupations would require giving of job to a very large number of adults, if we were to ask the appropriate Government to assure alternative employment in every case, which would strain the resources of the State, in case it would not have been able to secure job for an adult in a private sector establishment or, for that matter, in a public sector organisation. We are not issuing any direction to do so presently. Instead, we leave the matter to be sorted out by the appropriate Government. In those cases where it would not be possible to provide job as above mentioned, the appropriate Government would, as its contribution/grant, deposit in the aforesaid Fund a sum of Rs. 5000/- for each child employed in a factory or mine or in any other hazardous employment. M.C.Mehta v. State of Tamil Nadu (1996) 6 SCC 772, para. 31

The court, while recognising the importance of declaring the child's negative right against exploitation and positive right to education, chose a pragmatic approach when it came to enforceability. Earlier the court would have shrugged off the whole issue as not being within its domain. That has now changed as is clear from the recent trend of cases.

It is here the Supreme Court read into our Constitution several provisions of International Covenants. The Judges also considered DPSP and how the same could be read together with the Fundamental Rights. As stated in the case of Unnikrishnan v/s. State of AP [(1993)1 SCC 645, para 165] "In order to treat a right as fundamental right, it is not necessary that it should be expressly stated as one in Part III of the Constitution. The provisions of Part III and Part IV are supplementary and complementary to each other." That is why very often the court reads the two together. There is no conflict between the two. It is wrong to assume that fulfillment of obligations relating to social and economic human rights would impair fundamental rights. That is why we incorporated Article 31-C (25th Amendment Act 1971) which says, "Notwithstanding anything contained in Article 13, no law giving effect to the policy of the State towards securing all or any of the principles laid down in Part IV shall be deemed to be void on the ground that it is inconsistent with, or takes away or abridges any of the rights conferred by Article 14 or Article 19." As Glanville Austin says: "The core of the commitment to the social revolution lies in Part III and IV in the Fundamental Rights and in the

Directive Principles of State Policy. These are the conscience of the Constitution." This is what Bhagwati J. said in Minerva Mills case (AIR 1980 SC 1789 at 1846): "The core of the commitment of the social revolution lies in the Fundamental Rights and directive principles of state policy."

The Directive Principles also urge the nation to develop a uniform civil code and offer free legal aid to all citizens. They urge measures to maintain the separation of the judiciary from the executive and direct the government to organise village panchayats to function as units of self-government. This latter objective was advanced by the Seventy-third Amendment and the Seventy-fourth Amendment in December 1992. The Directive Principles also order that India should endeavour to protect and improve the environment and protect monuments and places of historical interest.

The Forty-second Amendment, which came into force in January 1977, attempted to raise the status of the Directive Principles by stating that no law implementing any of the Directive Principles could be declared unconstitutional on the grounds that it violated any of the Fundamental Rights. The amendment simultaneously stated that laws prohibiting "antinational activities" or the formation of "antinational associations" could not be invalidated because they infringed on any of the Fundamental Rights. It added a new section to the constitution on "Fundamental Duties" that enjoined citizens "to promote harmony and the spirit of common brotherhood among all the people of India, transcending religious, linguistic and regional or sectional diversities."

However, the amendment reflected a new emphasis in governing circles on order and discipline to counteract what some leaders had come to perceive as the excessively freewheeling style of Indian democracy. After the March 1977 general election ended the control of the Congress (Congress (R) from 1969) over the executive and legislature for the first time since independence in 1947, the new Janata-dominated Parliament passed the Forty-third Amendment (1977) and Forty-fourth Amendment (1978). These amendments revoked the Forty-second Amendment's provision that Directive

Principles take precedence over Fundamental Rights and also curbed Parliament's power to legislate against "antinational activities.

RIGHT TO HEALTH

The right to health has been perhaps the least difficult area for the court in terms of justiciability, but not in terms of enforceability. Article 47 of DPSP provides for the duty of the state to improve public health. However, the court has always recognised the right to health as being an integral part of the right to life Francis Coralie Mullin, note 3 above; Parmanand Katara v. Union of India (1989) 4 SCC 286. The principle got tested in the case of an agricultural labourer whose condition, after a fall from a running train, worsened considerably when as many as seven government hospitals in Calcutta refused to admit him as they did not have beds vacant. The Supreme Court did not stop at declaring the right to health to be a fundamental right and at enforcing that right of the labourer by asking the Government of West Bengal to pay him compensation for the loss suffered. It directed the government to formulate a blue print for primary health care with particular reference to treatment of patients during an emergency (Paschim Banga Khet Majoor Samity v. State of West Bengal (1996) 4 SCC 37).

State of Punjab v. Ram Lubhaya Bagga (1998) 4 SCC 117, para. 29. A note of caution was struck when government employees protested against the reduction of their entitlements to medical care.

The court said: No State or country can have unlimited resources to spend on any of its projects. That is why it only approves its projects to the extent it is feasible. The same holds good for providing medical facilities to its citizens including its employees. Provision on facilities cannot be unlimited. It has to be to the extent finances permit. If no scale or rate is fixed then in case private clinics or hospitals increase their rate to exorbitant scales, the State would be bound to reimburse the same. The principle of fixation of rate and scale under the new policy is justified and cannot be held to be violative of article 21 or article 47 of the Constitution

FUNDAMENTAL DUTIES

Fundamental Duties of citizens serve a useful purpose. In particular, no democratic polity can ever succeed where the citizens are not willing to be active participants in the process of governance by assuming responsibilities and discharging citizenship duties and coming forward to give their best to the country. Some of the fundamental duties enshrined in article 51A have been incorporated in separate laws. For instance, the first duty includes respect for the National Flag and the National Anthem. Disrespect is punishable by law. To value and preserve the rich heritage of the mosaic that is India should help to weld our people into one nation but much more than article 51A will be needed to treat all human beings equally, to respect each religion and to confine it to the private sphere and not make it a bone of contention between different communities of this land. In sum, the Commission believes that article 51A has travelled a great distance since it was introduced in the Forty-second Amendment and further consideration should be given to ways and means to popularise the knowledge and content of the Fundamental Duties and effectuate them.

The most important task before us is to reconcile the claims of the individual citizen and those of the civic society. To achieve this, it is important to orient the individual citizen to be conscious of his social and citizenship responsibilities and so shape the society that we all become solicitous and considerate of the inalienable rights of our fellow citizens. Therefore, awareness of our citizenship duties is as important as awareness of our rights. Every right implies a corresponding duty but every duty does not imply a corresponding right. Man does not live for himself alone. He lives for the good of others as well as of himself. It is this knowledge of what is right and wrong that makes a man responsible to himself and to the society and this knowledge is inculcated by imbibing and clearly understanding one's citizenship duties. The fundamental duties are the foundations of human dignity and national character. If every citizen performs his duties irrespective of considerations of caste, creed, colour and language, most of the malaise of the present day polity could be contained, if not eradicated, and the society as a whole uplifted. Rich or poor, in power or out of power, obedience to citizenship duty, at all costs and risks, is the essence of civilized life.

Spirit of Harmony and Dignity of Women Some further thought needs to be given to clauses (e) and (f) of article 51A. Article 51A(e) desires the promotion of harmony and the spirit of common brotherhood among all the people of India transcending religious, linguistic and regional or sectional diversities and renunciation of practices derogatory to the dignity of women. It is couched in broad terms but it should be clear that attacks on minority communities or minority opinions are frowned upon. Respect for both are essential and the wording lends support to a broad humanism to cover such differences as may exist or better still, co-exist. Two thoughts can be distilled. The first is that the objective will not be reached unless there is a determined effort to restrict religious practices to the home on the justified premise that one's religion is a personal matter and is not conducive to mass assertiveness. The other is the status of women.

Lip service is being paid to the doctrine of gender equality. The fact remains that generally women are still regarded as inferior both home and workplace although the Commission has noticed an improvement, however dissatisfied it may be with the degree of the at improvement. It is necessary to separate religious precepts from civil law. Civil law as the name implies is a matter for society not for religious leaders and it would seem to us to be axiomatic that in matters of civil rights, laws of property and inheritance and marriage and divorce, although practices may differ, legal rights that accrue must be the same. For example, a marriage may be solemnised according to religious or social custom but the rights of a woman in the case of divorce must be the same no matter what her religion is. Clause (e) of article 51A also seems to cover the need to regard all human beings equally. In this connection, it is necessary to consider the question of the upliftment of the Scheduled Castes and other disadvantaged sections of our society. The scourge must be eradicated. The Constitution gave us ten years to do the job; the provision has been extended to fifty years and we are in our sixth ten-year period but we are no nearer the goal. The discrimination is two fold. It is economic-condemning whole sections of our society numbering millions to menial jobs as part of the evil of treating them as sub-human. We have provided for reservation of jobs to these people, we have even given them separate constituencies to represent them. It has created a vested interest in backwardness. The other adverse result is that it has had no effect on their status in society, which continues to be determined by birth and not human worth and human personality. It is this social stigma which still plagues our people and the struggle to restore to them basic human dignity has made no significant progress. While the Commission appreciates the context in which affirmative action became necessary, it feels that reservation of jobs and seats in the legislatures will not help this aspect of the matter.

It is quite clear to the Commission that the disease of considering human beings as high or low based on the accident of birth is a disease rooted in the mind and it is in the mind that the defences of a society based on human dignity and equality must be constructed. Logically this leads directly to the conclusion that the key lies in education. The time to begin training our young people to respect the National flag and sing the National anthem, to respect women, to hold all religions equal and deserving of as much respect as one's own, to accept that all human beings are born equal and are entitled to equal treatment are among principles best taught by examples when the child is too young to understand but not too young to obey. The focus must, therefore, shift to education which has suffered from serious neglect. Schools restrict admissions on unacceptable criteria, teachers themselves are untrained and often politicised, as is the curriculum. Despite these hardships, many of our young people have done well.

COMPOSITE CULTURE

Clause (f) of article 51A requires us to value and preserve the rich heritage of our composite culture. It follows that we may not break each other's places of worship, set fire to religious texts, or beat up one another's priests or obstruct those who exercise their Fundamental Right under article 25 to profess, practice and propagate religion. Composite culture means culture drawn from many strands. Here again education in its broadest and best sense can provide the corrective to the aberrations that have occurred. Education is not confined only to the time spent in schools and colleges. Education begins at birth in the subconscious and continues till death. Anyone who says that he has nothing more to learn is already brain-dead. It follows that the influences that play on a child at home are of great importance. Parents should understand that education begins at home, the examples they set, the environment of enlightenment and tolerance that is necessary to produce good citizens cannot be sub-contracted to formal schooling important though this is. Schemes should, therefore, be framed that include parents in social activities that have as their objective the country's age-old traditions, its welcome to the persecuted of every faith, its virtues of tolerance of and respect for all religions and a certain pride in belonging to this land and in being considered as Indian. The highest office in our democracy is the office of citizen; this is not only a platitude, it must translate into reality.

The distinction is not illusory. This country has given far too much indulgence to an attitude of mind that acts on the question - what is there in it for me? Education and the process of inculcating unselfishness and a sense of obligation to one's fellowmen should inspire the question – where does my duty lie? The transformation has the potential to make our nation strong, invincible and able to command the respect of the world.

(i) The Commission recommends that the first and foremost step required by the Union and State Governments is to sensitise the people and to create a general awareness of the provisions of fundamental duties amongst the citizens on the lines recommended by the Justice Verma Committee on the subject. Consideration should be given to the ways and means by which Fundamental Duties could be popularised and made effective;

(ii) right to freedom of religion and other freedoms must be jealously guarded and rights of minorities and fellow citizens respected;

(iii) reform of the whole process of education is an immediate but immense need, as is the need to free it from governmental or political control; it is only through education that will power to adhere to our Fundamental Duties as citizens can be inculcated; and

(iv) duty to vote at elections, actively participate in the democratic process of governance and to pay taxes should be included in article 51A. The Commission fully endorses the other recommendations of the Justice Verma Committee on operationalisation of Fundamental Duties of Citizens and strongly suggests their early implementation.

The Commission also recommends that the following should be incorporated as fundamental duties in article 51A of the Constitution:

- To fosters a spirit of family values and responsible parenthood in the matter of education, physical and moral well-being of children.
- Duty of industrial organisations to provide education to children of their employees.

REFERENCES

- Goldman, H.: *Co-ordination of Computerization of the Criminal Justice System*, London, Home Office, 1986.
- Austin, Granville: *The Indian Constitution: Cornerstone of a Nation*, Oxford, Clarendon Press, 1966.
- Howard McIlwain: *Constitutionalism: Ancient and Modern*, N.Y., Cornell University Press, 1958.
- Rosenbloom, H. : *Handbook of Regulation and Administrative Law*, New York, Marcel Dekker, 1994.

3

History of Indian Constitution and its Acts

GOVERNMENT OF INDIA ACT 1858

The Government of India Act 1858 is an Act of the Parliament of the United Kingdom (21 & 22 Vict. c. 106) passed on August 2, 1858. Its provisions called for the liquidation of the British East India Company (who had up to this point been ruling British India under the auspices of Parliament) and the transference of its functions to the British Crown. Lord Palmerston, then-Prime Minister of the United Kingdom, introduced a bill for the transfer of control of the Government of India from the East India Company to the Crown, referring to the grave defects in the existing system of the government of India.

The main provisions of the bill were:

- The Company's territories in India were to be vested in the Queen, the Company ceasing to exercise its power and control over these territories. India was to be governed in the Queen's name.
- The Queen's Principal Secretary of State received the powers and duties of the Company's Court of Directors. A council of fifteen members was appointed to assist the Secretary of State for India. The council became an advisory body in India affairs. For all the communications between Britain and India, the Secretary of State became the real channel.

- The Secretary of State for India was empowered to send some secret despatches to India directly without consulting the Council. He was also authorised to constitute special committees of his Council.
- The Crown was empowered to appoint a Governor-General and the Governors of the Presidencies.
- Provision for the creation of an Indian Civil Service under the control of the Secretary of State.
- All the property of the East India Company was transferred to the Crown. The Crown also assumed the responsibilities of the Company as they related to treaties, contracts, and so forth.

The Act ushered in a new period of Indian history, bringing about the end of Company rule in India. The era of the new British Raj would last until Partition of India in August 1947, at which time all of the territory of the Raj was granted dominion status within the Dominion of Pakistan and the Union of India.

INDIAN COUNCILS ACT 1861

The Indian Councils Act 1861 was an Act of the Parliament of the United Kingdom that transformed the Viceroy of India's executive council into a cabinet run on the portfolio system. This cabinet had six "ordinary members" who each took charge of a separate department in Calcutta's government: home, revenue, government, law, finance, and (after 1874) public works. The military Commander-in-Chief sat in with the council as an extraordinary member. The Viceroy was allowed, under the provisions of the Act, to overrule the council on affairs if he deemed it necessary - as was the case in 1879, during the tenure of Lord Lytton.

The Secretary of State for India at the time the Act was passed, Sir Charles Wood, believed that the Act was of immense importance: "the act is a great experiment. That everything is changing in India is obvious enough, and that the old autocratic government cannot stand unmodified is indisputable."

The 1861 Act restored the legislative power taken away by the Charter Act of 1833. The legislative council at Calcutta was given extensive authority to pass laws for British India as a whole, while the legislative councils at Bombay and Madras were given the power to make laws for the "Peace and good Government" of their respective presidencies.

INDIAN COUNCILS ACT 1892

The Indian Councils Act 1892 was an Act of the Parliament of the United Kingdom that authorised an increase in the size of the various legislative councils in British India. Enacted due to the demand of the Indian National Congress to expand legislative council, the number of non-official members was increased both in central and provincial legislative councils. The universities, district board, municipalities, zamindars and chambers of commerce were empowered to recommend members to provincial councils. Thus was introduced the principle of representation. It also relaxed restrictions imposed by the Indian Councils Act 1861, thus allowing the councils to discuss each year's annual financial statement. They coud also put questions within certain limts to the government on the matter of public interest after giving six days' notice. Thus it prepared the base of Indian Democracy.

GOVERNMENT OF INDIA ACT 1935

The Government of India Act 1935 was originally passed in August 1935 (25 & 26 Geo. 5 c. 42), and is said to have been the longest (British) Act of Parliament ever enacted by that time. Because of its length, the Act was retroactively split by the Government of India (Reprinting) Act 1935 (26 Geo. 5 & 1 Edw. 8 c. 1) into two separate Acts:

1. The Government of India Act 1935 (26 Geo. 5 & 1 Edw. 8 c. 2)
2. The Government of Burma Act 1935 (26 Geo. 5 & 1 Edw. 8 c. 3)

References in literature on Indian political and constitutional history are usually to the shortened Government of India Act 1935 (i.e. 26 Geo. 5 & 1 Edw. 8 c. 2), rather than to the text of the Act as originally enacted.

Overview

The most significant aspects of the Act were:

- the grant of a large measure of autonomy to the provinces of British India (ending the system of dyarchy introduced by the Government of India Act 1919)
- provision for the establishment of a "Federation of India", to be made up of both British India and some or all of the "princely states"
- the introduction of direct elections, thus increasing the franchise from seven million to thirty-five million people
- a partial reorganization of the provinces:
  - o Sind was separated from Bombay
  - o Bihar and Orissa was split into the separate provinces of Bihar and Orissa
  - o Burma was completely separated from India
  - o Aden was also detached from India, and established as a separate colony
- membership of the provincial assemblies was altered so as to include more elected Indian representatives, who were now able to form majorities and be appointed to form governments
- the establishment of a Federal Court.

However, the degree of autonomy introduced at the provincial level was subject to important limitations: the provincial Governors retained important reserve powers, and the British authorities also retained a right to suspend responsible government.

The parts of the Act intended to establish the Federation of India never came into operation, due to opposition from rulers of the princely states. The remaining parts of the Act came into force in 1937, when the first elections under the Act were also held.

THE ACT

Background to the Act

Indians had increasingly been demanding a greater role in the government of their country since the late 19th century. The Indian contribution to the British war effort during the

First World War meant that even the more conservative elements in the British political establishment felt the necessity of constitutional change, resulting in the Government of India Act 1919. That Act introduced a novel system of government known as provincial "dyarchy", i.e., certain areas of government (such as education) were placed in the hands of ministers responsible to the provincial legislature, while others (such as public order and finance) were retained in the hands of officials responsible to the British-appointed provincial Governor. While the Act was a reflection of the demand for a greater role in government by Indians, it was also very much a reflection of British fears about what that role might mean in practice for India (and of course for British interests there).

The experiment with dyarchy proved unsatisfactory. A particular frustration for Indian politicians was that even for those areas over which they had gained nominal control, the "purse strings" were still in the hands of British officialdom.

The intention had been that a review of India's constitutional arrangements and those princely states that were willing to accede to it. However, division between Congress and Muslim representatives proved to be a major factor in preventing agreement as to much of the important detail of how federation would work in practice.

Against this practice, the new Conservative-dominated National Government in London decided to go ahead with drafting its own proposals (the white paper). A joint parliamentary select committee, chaired by Lord Linlithgow, reviewed the white paper proposals at great length. On the basis of this white paper, the Government of India Bill was framed. At the committee stage and later, to appease the diehards, the "safeguards" were strengthened, and indirect elections were reinstated for the Central Legislative Assembly (the central legislature's lower house). The bill duly passed into law in August 1935.

As a result of this process, although the Government of India Act 1935 was intended to go some way towards meeting Indian demands, both the detail of the bill and the lack of Indian involvement in drafting its contents meant that the Act met with a lukewarm response at best in India, while still proving too radical for a significant element in Britain.

SOME FEATURES OF THE ACT

No Preamble – The Ambiguity of the British Commitment to Dominion Status

While it had become uncommon for British Acts of Parliament to contain a preamble, the absence of one from the Government of India Act 1935 contrasts sharply with the 1919 Act, which set out the broad philosophy of that Act's aims in relation to Indian political development.

The 1919 Act's preamble quoted, and centered on, the statement of the Secretary of State for India, Edwin Montagu (17 July 1917 – 19 March 1922) to the House of Commons on 20 August 1917, which pledged:

...the gradual development of self-governing institutions, with a view to the progressive realization of responsible government in India as an integral Part of the British Empire.

Indian demands were by now centering on British India achieving constitutional parity with the existing Dominions such as Canada and Australia, which would have meant complete autonomy within the British Commonwealth. A significant element in British political circles doubted that Indians were capable of running their country on this basis, and saw Dominion status as something that might, perhaps, be aimed for after a long period of gradual constitutional development, with sufficient "safeguards".

This tension between and within Indian and British views resulted in the clumsy compromise of the 1935 Act having no preamble of its own, but keeping in place the 1919 Act's preamble even while repealing the remainder of that Act. Unsurprisingly, this was seen in India as yet more mixed messages from the British, suggesting at best a lukewarm attitude and at worst suggesting a "minimum necessary" approach towards satisfying Indian desires.

No Bill of Rights

In contrast with most modern constitutions, but in common

with Commonwealth constitutional legislation of the time, the Act does not include a "bill of rights" within the new system that it aimed to establish. However, in the case of the proposed Federation of India there was a further complication in incorporating such a set of rights, as the new entity would have included nominally sovereign (and generally autocratic) princely states.

A different approach was considered by some, though, as the draft outline constitution in the Nehru Report included such a bill of rights.

Relationship to a Dominion Constitution

In 1947, a relatively few amendments in the Act made it the functioning interim constitutions of India and Pakistan.

Safeguards

The Act was not only extremely detailed, but it was riddled with 'safeguards' designed to enable the British Government to intervene whenever it saw the need in order to maintain British responsibilities and interests. To achieve this, in the face of a gradually increasing Indianization of the institutions of the Government of India, the Act concentrated the decision for the use and the actual administration of the safeguards in the hands of the British-appointed Viceroy and provincial governors who were subject to the control of the Secretary of State for India.

'In view of the enormous powers and responsibilities which the Governor-General must exercise in his discretion or according to his individual judgment, it is obvious that he (the Viceroy) is expected to be a kind of superman. He must have tact, courage, and ability and be endowed with an infinite capacity for hard work. "We have put into this Bill many safeguards," said Sir Robert Horne... "but all of those safeguards revolve about a single individual, and that is the Viceroy. He is the linch-pin of the whole system.... If the Viceroy fails, nothing can save the system you have set up." This speech reflected the point of view of the die-hard Tories who were horrified by the prospect that some day there might be a Viceroy appointed by a Labour government.'

Reality of Responsible Government Under the Act

A close reading of the Act reveals that the British Government equipped itself with the legal instruments to take back total control at any time they considered this to be desirable. However, doing so without good reason would totally sink their credibility with groups in India whose support the act was aimed at securing. Some contrasting views:

"In the federal government... the semblance of responsible government is presented. But the reality is lacking, for the powers in defence and external affairs necessarily, as matters stand, given to the governor-general limit vitally the scope of ministerial activity, and the measure of representation given to the rulers of the Indian States negatives any possibility of even the beginnings of democratic control. It will be a matter of the utmost interest to watch the development of a form of government so unique; certainly, if it operates successfully, the highest credit will be due to the political capacity of Indian leaders, who have infinitely more serious difficulties to face than had the colonial statesmen who evolved the system of self-government which has now culminated in Dominion status."

Lord Lothian, in a talk lasting forty-five minutes, came straight out with his view on the Bill: "I agree with the diehards that it has been a surrender. You who are not used to any constitution cannot realise what great power you are going to wield. If you look at the constitution it looks as if all the powers are vested in the Governor-General and the Governor. But is not every power here vested in the King? Everything is done in the name of the King but does the King ever interfere? Once the power passes into the hands of the legislature, the Governor or the Governor-General is never going to interfere. ...The Civil Service will be helpful. You too will realise this. Once a policy is laid down they will carry it out loyally and faithfully... We could not help it. We had to fight the diehards here. You could not realise what great courage has been shown by Mr. Baldwin and Sir Samuel Hoare. We did not want to spare the diehards as we had to talk in a different language... These various meetings — and in due course G.D. (Birla), before his return in September, met virtually everyone of importance in Anglo-

Indian affairs — confirmed G.D.'s original opinion that the differences between the two countries were largely psychological, the same proposals open to diametrically opposed interpretations. He had not, probably, taken in before his visit how considerable, in the eyes of British conservatives, the concessions had been... If nothing else, successive conversations made clear to G.D. that the agents of the Bill had at least as heavy odds against them at home as they had in India.

False Equivalences

"The law, in its majestic equality, forbids the rich as well as the poor to sleep under bridges, to beg in the streets, and to steal bread."

Under the Act, British citizens resident in the UK and British companies registered in the UK must be treated on the same basis as Indian citizens and Indian registered companies unless UK law denies reciprocal treatment. The unfairness of this arrangement is clear when one considers the dominant position of British capital in much of the Indian modern sector and the complete dominance, maintained through unfair commercial practices, of UK shipping interests in India's international and coastal shipping traffic and the utter insignificance of Indian capital in Britain and the non-existence of Indian involvement in shipping to or within the UK. There are very detailed provisions requiring the Viceroy to intervene if, in his unappealable view, any India law or regulation is intended to, or will in fact, discriminate against UK resident British subjects, British registered companies and, particularly, British shipping interests.

"The Joint Committee considered a suggestion that trade with foreign countries should be made by the Minister of Commerce, but it decided that all negotiations with foreign countries should be conducted by the Foreign Office or Department of External Affairs as they are in the United Kingdom. In concluding agreements of this character, the Foreign Secretary always consults the Board of Trade and it was assumed that the Governor-General would in like manner consult the Minister of Commerce in India. This may be true, but the analogy itself is false. In the United Kingdom, both departments are subject to the same legislative control, whereas in India one is responsible to the federal legislature and the other to the Imperial Parliament."

British Political Needs vs. Indian Constitutional Needs

From the moment of the Montagu statement of 1917, it was vital that the reform process stay ahead of the curve if the British were to hold the strategic initiative. However, imperialist sentiment, and a lack of realism, in British political circles made this impossible. Thus the grudging conditional concessions of power in the Acts of 1919 and 1935 caused more resentment and signally failed to win the Raj the backing of influential groups in India which it desperately needed. In 1919 the Act of 1935, or even the Simon Commission plan would have been well received. There is evidence that Montagu would have backed something of this sort but his cabinet colleagues would not have considered it. By 1935, a constitution establishing a Dominion of India, comprising the British Indian provinces might have been acceptable in India though it would not have passed the British Parliament.

'Considering the balance of power in the Conservative party at the time, the passing of a Bill more liberal than that which was enacted in 1935 is inconceivable.'

Provincial Part of the Act

The provincial part of the Act, which went into effect automatically, basically followed the recommendations of the Simon Commission. Provincial dyarchy was abolished; that is, all provincial portfolios were to be placed in charge of ministers enjoying the support of the provincial legislatures. The British-appointed provincial governors, who were responsible to the British Government via the Viceroy and Secretary of State for India, were to accept the recommendations of the ministers unless, in their view, they negatively affected his areas of statutory "special responsibilities" such as the prevention of any grave menace to the peace or tranquility of a province and the safeguarding of the legitimate interests of minorities. In the event of political breakdown, the governor, under the supervision of the Viceroy, could take over total control of the provincial government. This, in fact, allowed the governors a more untrammeled control than any British official had enjoyed in the history of the Raj. After the resignation of the congress provincial ministries in 1939, the governors did directly rule the ex-Congress provinces throughout the war.

It was generally recognized, that the provincial part of the Act, conferred a great deal of power and patronage on provincial politicians as long as both British officials and Indian politicians played by the rules. However, the paternalistic threat of the intervention by the British governor rankled.

Federal Part of the Act

Unlike the provincial portion of the Act, the Federal portion was to go into effect only when half the States by weight agreed to federate. This never happened and the establishment of the Federation was indefinitely postponed after the outbreak of the Second World War.

Terms of the Act

The Act provided for Dyarchy at the Centre. The British Government, in the person of the Secretary of State for India, through the Governor-General of India – Viceroy of India, would continue to control India's financial obligations, defence, foreign affairs and the British Indian Army and would make the key appointments to the Reserve Bank of India (exchange rates) and Railway Board and the Act stipulated that no finance bill could be placed in the Central Legislature without the consent of the Governor General. The funding for the British responsibilities and foreign obligations (e.g. loan repayments, pensions), at least 80 percent of the federal expenditures, would be non-votable and be taken off the top before any claims could be considered for (for example) social or economic development programs. The Viceroy, under the supervision of the Secretary of State for India, was provided with overriding and certifying powers that could, theoretically, have allowed him to rule autocratically.

Objectives of the British Government

The federal part of the Act was designed to meet the aims

of the Conservative Party. Over the very long term, the Conservative leadership expected the Act to lead to a nominally dominion status India, conservative in outlook, dominated by an alliance of Hindu princes and right-wing Hindus which would be well disposed to place itself under the guidance and protection of the United Kingdom. In the medium term, the Act was expected to (in rough order of importance):

- win the support of moderate nationalists since its formal aim was to lead eventually to a Dominion of India which, as defined under the Statute of Westminster 1931 virtually equalled independence;
- retain British of control of the Indian Army, Indian finances and India's foreign relations for another generation;
- win Muslim support by conceding most of Jinnah's Fourteen Points;
- convince the Princes to join the Federation by giving the Princes conditions for entry never likely to be equaled. It was expected that enough would join to allow the establishment of the Federation. The terms offered to the Princes included:
  - o The Princes would select their state's representatives in the Federal Legislature. There would be no pressure for them to democratize their administrations or allow elections for state's representatives in the Federal Legislature;
  - o The Princes would enjoy heavy weightage. The Princely States represented about a quarter of the population of India and produced well under a quarter of its wealth. Under the Act:
    - — The Upper House of the Federal Legislature, the Council of State, would consist of 260 members (156 (60%) elected from the British India and 104 (40%) nominated by the rulers of the princely states) and,
    - — The Lower House, the Federal Assembly, would consist of 375 members (250 (67%) elected by

the Legislative Assemblies of the British Indian provinces; 125 (33%) nominated by the rulers of the princely states.)

- ensuring that the Congress could never rule alone or gain enough seats to bring down the government

This was done by over-representing the Princes, giving every possible minority, the right to separately vote for candidates belonging to their respective communities, and by making the executive theoretically, but not practically, removable by the legislature.

Gambles Taken by the British Government

- Viability of the proposed Federation. It was hoped that the gerrymandered federation, encompassing units of such hugely different sizes, sophistication and varying in forms of government from autocratic Princely States to democratic provinces, could provide the basis for a viable state. However, this was not a realistic possibility. In reality, the Federation, as planned in the Act, almost certainly was not viable and would have rapidly broken down with the British left to pick up the pieces without any viable alternative.
- Princes Seeing and Acting in Their Own Long-Range Best Interests - That the Princes would see that their best hope for a future would lie in rapidly joining and becoming a united block without which no group could hope, mathematically, to wield power. However, the princes did not join, and thus exercising the veto provided by the Act prevented the Federation from coming into existence. Among the reasons for the Princes staying out were the following:
    - o They did not have the foresight to realize that this was their only chance for a future.
    - o Congress had begun, and would continue, agitating for democratic reforms within the Princely States. Since the one common concern of the 600 or so Princes was their desire to continue to rule their states without interference, this was indeed a mortal

> threat. It was on the cards that this would lead eventually to more democratic state regimes and the election of states' representatives in the Federal Legislature. In all likelihood, these representatives would be largely Congressmen. Had the Federation been established, the election of states' representatives in the Federal Legislature would amount to a Congress coup from the inside. Thus, contrary to their official position that the British would look favourably on the democratization of the Princely States, their plan required that the States remain autocratic. This reflects a deep contradiction on British views of India and its future.

'At a banquet in the princely state of Benares Hailey observed that although the new federal constitution would protect their position in the central government, the internal evolution of the states themselves remained uncertain. Most people seemed to expect them to develop representative institutions. Whether those alien grafts from Westminster would succeed in British India, however, itself remained in doubt. Autocracy was "a principle which is firmly seated in the Indian States," he pointed out; "round it burn the sacred fires of an age-long tradition," and it should be given a fair chance first. Autocratic rule, "informed by wisdom, exercised in moderation, and vitalized by a spirit of service to the interests of the subject, may well prove that it can make an appeal in India as strong as that of representative and responsible institutions." This spirited defence brings to mind Nehru's classic paradox of how the representatives of the advanced, dynamic West allied themselves with the most reactionary forces of the backward, stagnant East.'

Under the Act, 'There are a number of restrictions on the freedom of discussion in the federal legislature. For example the act forbids... any discussion of, or the asking of questions about, a matter connected with an Indian State, other than a matter with respect to which the federal legislature has power to make laws for that state, unless the Governor-General in his discretion is satisfied that the matter affects federal interests or affects a British subject, and has given his consent to the matter being discussed or the question being asked.'

-
  - o They were not a cohesive group and probably realized that they would never act as one.
  - o Each Prince seemed consumed by the desire to gain the best deal for himself were his state to join the Federation: the most money, the most autonomy.
- That enough was being offered at the Centre to win the support of moderate nationalist Hindu and Muslim support. In fact, so little was offered that all significant groups in British India rejected and denounced the proposed Federation. A major contributing factor was the continuing distrust of British intentions for which there was considerable basis in fact. In this vital area the Act failed Irwin's test:

'I don't believe that... it is impossible to present the problem in such a form as would make the shop window look respectable from an Indian point of view, which is really what they care about, while keeping your hand pretty firmly on the things that matter.' (Irwin to Stonehaven, 12 November 1928)

- That the wider electorate would turn against the Congress. In fact, the 1937 elections showed overwhelming support for Congress among the Hindu electorate.
- That by giving Indian politicians a great deal of power at the provincial level, while denying them responsibility at the Centre, it was hoped that Congress, the only national party, would disintegrate into a series of provincial fiefdoms. In fact, the congress High Command was able to control the provincial ministries and to force their resignation in 1939. The Act showed the strength and cohesion of Congress and probably strengthened it. This does not imply that Congress was not made up of and found its support in various sometimes competing interests and groups. Rather, it recognizes the ability of Congress, unlike the British Raj, to maintain the

cooperation and support of most of these groups even if, for example in the forced resignation of Congress provincial ministries in 1939 and the rejection of the Cripps Offer in 1942, this required a negative policy that was harmful, in the long run, to the prospects for an independent India that would be both united and democratic.

Indian Reaction to the Proposed Federation

No significant group in India accepted the Federal portion of the Act. A typical response was: 'After all, there are five aspects of every Government worth the name: (a) The right of external and internal defence and all measures for that purpose; (b) The right to control our external relations; (c) The right to control our currency and exchange; (d) The right to control our fiscal policy; (e) the day-to-day administration of the land.... (Under the Act) You shall have nothing to do with external affairs. You shall have nothing to do with defence. You shall have nothing to do, or, for all practical purposes in future, you shall have nothing to do with your currency and exchange, for indeed the Reserve Bank Bill just passed has a further reservation in the Constitution that no legislation may be undertaken with a view to substantially alter the provisions of that Act except with the consent of the Governor-General.... there is no real power conferred in the Centre.' (Speech by Mr Bhulabhai DESAI on the Report of the Joint Parliamentary Committee on Indian Constitutional Reform, 4 February 1935.

However, the Liberals, and even elements in the Congress were tepidly willing to give it a go:

"Linlithgow asked Sapru whether he thought there was a satisfactory alternative to the scheme of the 1935 Act. Sapru replied that they should stand fast on the Act and the federal plan embodied in it. It was not ideal but at this stage it was the only thing.... A few days after Sapru's visit Birla came to see the Viceroy. He thought that Congress was moving towards acceptance of Federation. Gandhi was not over-worried, said Birla, by the reservation of defence and external affairs to the centre, but was concentrating on the method of choosing the States' representatives. Birla wanted the Viceroy to help Gandhi by persuading a number of Princes to move towards democratic election of representatives. ...Birla then said that the only chance for Federation lay in agreement between Government and Congress and the best hope of this lay in discussion between the Viceroy and Gandhi."

The Working of the Act

The British government sent out Lord Linlithgow as the new viceroy with the remit of bringing the Act into effect. Linlithgow was intelligent, extremely hard working, honest, serious and determined to make a success out of the Act. However, he was also unimaginative, stolid, legalistic and found it very difficult to "get on terms" with people outside his immediate circle.

In 1937, after a great deal of confrontation, Provincial Autonomy commenced. From that point until the declaration of war in 1939, Linlithgow tirelessly tried to get enough of the Princes to accede to launch the Federation. In this he received only the weakest backing from the Home Government and in the end the Princes rejected the Federation *en masse*. In September 1939, Linlithgow simply declared that India was at war with Germany. Though Linlithgow's behaviour was constitutionally correct it was also offensive to much of Indian opinion. This led directly to the resignation of the Congress provincial ministries which undermined Indian unity.

From 1939, Linlithgow concentrated on supporting the war effort.

1946 CABINET MISSION TO INDIA

The British Cabinet Mission of 1946 to India aimed to discuss and plan for the transfer of power from the British Raj to Indian leadership, providing India with independence under Dominion status in the Commonwealth of Nations. Formulated at the initiative of Clement Attlee, the Prime Minister of the United Kingdom, the mission consisted of Lord Pethick-Lawrence, the Secretary of State for India, Sir Stafford Cripps, President of the Board of Trade, and A. V. Alexander, the First Lord of the Admiralty. However, Lord Wavell, the Viceroy of India, did not participate.

Purpose and proposals

The Mission's purpose was to:

1. Hold preparatory discussions with elected representatives of British India and the Indian states in order to secure agreement as to the method of framing the constitution.
2. Set up a constitution body.
3. Set up an Executive Council with the support of the main Indian parties.

The Mission held talks with the representatives of the Indian National Congress and the All-India Muslim League, the two largest political parties in the Constituent Assembly of India. The two parties planned to determine a power-sharing arrangement between Hindus and Muslims to prevent a communal dispute, and to determine whether British India would be better-off unified or divided. The Congress party under Gandhi-Nehru nexus wanted to obtain a strong central government with more powers compared to state governments. The All India Muslim League under Jinnah, wanted to keep India united but with political safeguards provided to Muslims such as 'guarantee' of 'parity' in the legislatures. This stance of the League was backed up by the wide belief of Muslims that the British Raj was simply going to be turned in to a 'Hindu Raj' once the British departed; and since the Muslim League was the sole spokesman party of Indian Muslims, it was incumbent up on it to take the matter up with the Crown. After initial dialogue, the Mission proposed its plan over the composition of the new government on May 16, 1946:

Plan of May 16

Promulgated on 16 May 1946, the plan to create a united dominion of India as a loose confederation of provinces came to be known by the date of its announcement:

1. A united Dominion of India would be given independence.
2. Muslim-majority provinces would be grouped - Baluchistan, Sind, Punjab and North-West Frontier Province would form one group, and Bengal and Assam would form another.

3. Hindu-majority provinces in central and southern India would form another group.
4. The Central government would be empowered to run foreign affairs, defence and communications, while the rest of powers and responsibility would belong to the provinces, coordinated by groups.

Plan of June 16

The plan of May 16, 1946 had envisaged a united India in line with Congress and Muslim League aspirations. But that was where the consensus between the two parties ended since Congress abhorred the idea of having groupings of Muslim majority provinces and that of Hindu majority provinces with the intention of 'balancing' each other at the Central Legislature. The Muslim League could not accept any changes to this plan since the same 'balance' or 'parity' that Congress was loath to accept formed the basis of Muslim demands of 'political safeguards' built in to post-British Indian laws so as to prevent absolute rule of Hindus over Muslims.

Reaching an impasse, the British proposed a second, alternative plan on June 16, 1946. This plan sought to arrange for India to be divided into Hindu-majority India and a Muslim-majority India that would later be renamed Pakistan, since Congress had vehemently rejected 'parity' at the Centre. A list of princely states of India that would be permitted to accede to either dominion or attain independence was also drawn up.

The Cabinet Mission arrived in India on March 23, 1946 and in Delhi on April 2, 1946. The announcement of the Plan on May 16, 1946 was preceded by the Simla Conference of 1945 in the first week of May.

Reactions and Acceptance

The approval of the plans would determine the composition of the new government. The Congress Working Committee had initially approved the plan. However, on 10 July, Jawaharlal Nehru, who later became the first prime minister of India, held a press conference in Bombay declaring that the Congress had agreed only to participate in the Constituent Assembly and "regards itself free to change or modify the Cabinet Mission

Plan as it thought best." The Congress ruled out the June 16 plan, seeing it as the division of India into small states. Moreover, the Congress was a Centralist party. Intellectuals like Kanji Dawarkadas criticized the Cabinet Plan. Congress was against decentralization and it had been under pressure from Indian capitalists who wanted a strong Center. The plan's strongest opponent was the principal Indian leader Mohandas Gandhi, due to the reason that the territories had been grouped together on the basis of religion.

The Muslim League gave its approval to the plan for 2 reasons: 1:grave issues were involved and Muslim league sincerely desirous for a peaceful solution... 2:The basic and foundation of Pakistan are inherent in the mission plan, by virtue of the compulsory grouping, of the 5 Muslim provinces (Punjab, Sindh, Balochistan, NWFP, Bengal & Assam) Jinnah, in his speech to the League Council, clearly stated that he recommended acceptance only because nothing better could be obtained. However, on declaration from the Congress President that the Congress could change the scheme through its majority in the Constituent Assembly, this meant that the minorities would be placed at the mercy of the majority. The Muslim League Council met at Bombay on 27 July. "Mr. Jinnah in his opening speech reiterated the demand for Pakistan as the only course left open to the Muslim League. After three days' discussion, the Council passed a resolution rejecting the Cabinet Mission Plan. It also decided to resort to direct action for the achievement of Pakistan."

However, the plan had its advocates. Maulana Azad, a nationalist Muslim leader, said that while the groupings were a major concession to the theme of religious separatism, it would also force the League to accept a framework for a united India. While assuring minority rights and participation, an independent India would be free to do away eventually with the groupings arrangement. Gandhi criticized the Maulana's views for ignoring practical considerations and League ambitions. Cabinet Mission plan had similar recommendations already in news and intellectual circles from 1940. Amedkar, Mollana Obid ullah Sindhi and Mollana azad already gave such recommendations. Amedkar wrote his book in 1940, Mollana Sindhi gave his manifesto of new party in 1939 based on decentralize India while Azad ABC plan was also similar to Cabinet Mission. Azad's position was very tricky yet Gandhi ji and Patel at that moment changed AZAD and installed Jawahar Lal Nehru as president. Kanji Dawarka Das in his famous book "Ten Years to freedom 1937-47" and Jaswant singh in his recent book "Jinnah India-Independence-Partition" writes all details of congress working committee debates and untimely press conference by JLN in which congress rejected the last effort to avoid partition.

Formation of a Government

The Viceroy began organizing the transfer of power to a Congress-League coalition. But League president Muhammad Ali Jinnah denounced the hesitant and conditional approval of the Congress and rescinded League approval of both plans. Thus Congress leaders entered the newly styled Viceroy's Executive Council: Jawaharlal Nehru became the head - vice president in title, but possessing the executive authority. Vallabhbhai Patel became the Home member - responsible for internal security and government agencies. Congress-led governments were formed in most provinces - including in the NWFP, in Punjab (a coalition with the Shiromani Akali Dal and the Unionist Muslim League). The League led governments in Bengal and Sind. The Constituent Assembly was instructed to begin work to write a new constitution for India.

Coalition and Breakdown

Jinnah and the League condemned the new government, and vowed to agitate for Pakistan by any means possible. Disorder arose in Punjab and Bengal, including the cities of Delhi, Bombay and Calcutta. On the League-organized Direct Action Day, over 5,000 people were killed across India, and Hindu, Sikh and Muslim mobs began clashing routinely. Viceroy Wavell stalled the Central government's efforts to stop the disorder, and the provinces were instructed to leave this to the governors, who did not undertake any major action. To end the disorder and rising bloodshed, Wavell encouraged Nehru to ask the League to enter the government. While Patel and most Congress leaders were opposed to conceding to a party that was organizing disorder, Nehru conceded in hope of preserving communal peace.

League leaders entered the council under the leadership of Liaquat Ali Khan, the future first Prime Minister of Pakistan who became the finance minister. But the council did not function in harmony - separate meetings were not held by League ministers, and both parties vetoed the major initiatives proposed by the other, highlighting their ideological differences and political antagonism. At the arrival of the new (and proclaimed as the last) viceroy, Lord Mountbatten of Burma in early 1947, Congress leaders expressed the view that the coalition was unworkable. This led to the eventual proposal, and acceptance of the partition of India. The rejection of cabinet mission plan led to a resurgence of confrontational politics beginning with the Muslim League's Direct action day and the subsequent Bihar killings. The portioning of responsibility between the League, the Congress and the British Colonial Administration for this breakdown continues to be a topic of fierce disagreement.

CONSTITUTIONAL PREDILECTIONS

On 26 November 1949, after almost three years of deliberation, the Constituent Assembly of India adopted a constitution for what remains the world's largest liberal democracy. From our vantage point 50 years later, it is instructive to reflect on how the 'founding fathers' (along with a handful of 'mothers') sought to address issues of diversity. After all, in a world in which more than a third of all states possess constitutions acquired only in the first half of the 1990s, our constitution has survived the test of time far better than most of its post-colonial counterparts.

The debate in the Assembly reflected the paradoxes of the Indian situation. To begin with, there was the problem of reconciling the political form (i.e. the liberal democratic state) of a model of modernity based upon features that were relatively weak in India – industrialisation, rationalism, the secularisation of society, individuation and democratisation – with the reality of India. This reality was of a society in which more than four-fifths of the population was illiterate and derived their livelihood from the land, 15 out of every 100 infants born died and the average life expectancy was just 32 years.

It was an especially daunting challenge to conceive of a secular state in a country that had just been partitioned on the basis of religion. Where, while there were over 50 million Muslims, Christians and Sikhs, and another 78 million belonged to Scheduled Castes or Tribes, nearly 85% of the population of 361 million was classified as 'Hindu' in the 1951 census. The nationalist movement itself had, especially under Gandhi, acquired an aura of religiosity so that the secular stance of Prime Minister Jawaharlal Nehru resembled a kind of splendid isolation.

It was scarcely surprising that the form of secularism that found expression in the Constitution was ambiguous. Leaders like Deputy Prime Minister Sardar Patel, Rajendra Prasad, the President of the Constituent Assembly, and K.M. Munshi, Patel's right-hand man in the Assembly, were sensitive, if not openly sympathetic, to the majoritarian Hindu sentiments voiced by a number of Congressmen in the Constituent Assembly. They knew that their predilections were widely shared, especially among upper caste Hindi-speaking members from the United Provinces (U.P..), the Central Provinces (C.P.) and Berar, Bihar and Punjab.

The result was that the Constitution sought to do several things. It made some allowance for the role played by religion, especially Hinduism, in Indian life. It also gave statutory recognition to minorities, thereby implicitly accepting the existence of a majority. It aimed to foster a common civic identity but then compromised this by the provision of reserved seats in legislatures to Schedule Castes and Scheduled Tribes (initially meant to last 10 years, no Parliament has contemplated doing away with this and its regular extension has become a formality).

While such measures may be regarded as having been defensible under the circumstances (i.e. the Constitution was as secular as it could have been), it meant that issues not definitively resolved by the Constitution continued to form the subject of public controversy. Cow slaughter, religious conversion, the status of Hindi as the national language, the preservation of a distinct Sikh identity, the right of religious minorities to maintain their own personal law and reservation for the low castes have all occasioned not just heated debate but violent conflict over the past five decades.

An irony of independent India's birth as a secular state was that the midwife – the Constituent Assembly – represented the final outcome of the communal politics that dominated the final years of British India. The Assembly was elected by the provincial assemblies of British India grouped into three sections – Muslim-majority areas in the north-west and north-east and the remaining Hindu-majority provinces. With each province allotted seats proportionate to its population, members were elected by legislators belonging to religious categories. The predictable outcome was that while the Muslim League claimed 73 of the 78 Muslim seats and the Panthic Akalis three of the four Sikh ones, Congress won 202 of the 210 'general' seats.

The Congress leadership sought to ensure that minority groups were adequately represented in the 'general' category. These included non-Congressmen seen as leaders of their respective communities such as B.R. Ambedkar, the Scheduled Castes spokesman, and the Anglo-Indian, Frank Anthony. In all some 30% of the post-partition Constituent Assembly (37.5% excluding the members from the former princely states) was made up of representatives of minorities. This reflected the makeup of Indian society – according to the 1951 census 37.8% of the population were either non-Hindu or belonged to the Scheduled Castes and Tribes.

However, it would not be true to assume from this that the Assembly represented a microcosm of Indian society. Most strikingly, Brahmins, who formed about 5% of the population, accounted for around a quarter of the total of 407 individuals who served in the body between 1946 and 1949 (it had 307 members in 1949). Their preponderance was especially evident among members from U.P. and Bombay – more than a third.

The Assembly also presented a contrast to society at large in other respects. Only 15 women ever got to sit in it and whereas only one in six Indians were literate, an analysis of the membership of the Provisional Parliament reveals that 68% of the members were graduates with a further 18% having attended college or high school. In a country where more than 80% of the population still lived on the land, people with a professional background formed over three-fifths of its first legislature – lawyers alone contributing almost a third.

But what was perhaps most significant about the Assembly members in terms of the task they had to undertake was the fact that almost half (200 of the 407) were serving members of other legislatures at the time of their election and nearly one in six (61) also served as ministers either at the centre or in the provinces. Since the Assembly also functioned as independent India's first Parliament, this experience tempered its nationalist fervour and Gandhian idealism with an awareness of what was practical and prudent.

Its debates revealed a range of attitudes towards secularism. Analysing the contributions of the hundred or so members who spoke on pertinent issues, they can be grouped in five broad, sometimes overlapping, categories: dogmatic secularists, those favouring 'unity in diversity', majoritarian Hindus, Gandhian critics, and minority advocates of special rights or protection. Some of the most uncompromising proponents of a secular state belonged to religious minorities – notably the Christian Minister of Health Rajkumari Amrit Kaur, the Parsi (and erstwhile socialist) Minoo Masani, the socialist economist K.T. Shah (a Jain), Tajamul Husain, a Shia Muslim landlord, and Frank Anthony. Among the others were two Congress-women (Hansa Mehta and Renuka Ray), a former leader of the defunct National Liberal Federation (H.N. Kunzru) and a newspaper editor from Madras who led the opposition to the imposition of Hindi as the sole national language (K. Santhanam). To this atypical collection can be added Babasaheb Ambedkar, whose contributions were made more circumspect by his concern for the advancement of the Scheduled Castes and his role as chairman of the drafting committee.

More influential within the Assembly were those who interpreted secularism to mean religious pluralism and the equal treatment of all religions by the state. Among those who favoured such an attitude were religious-minded members from different faiths including the Tamil Brahmin philosopher (and future President) Sarvepalli Radhakrishnan, and a Catholic Jesuit priest, Jerome D'Souza. The idea also appealed to the romantic in Nehru – 'the glory of India has been the way in which it manages to keep two things going at the same time:... infinite variety and... unity in that variety' (speech on 8 November 1948, *Constituent Assembly Debates* VII, p. 323). A report by a commission on university education chaired by Radhakrishnan held that, 'The absolute religious neutrality of the state can be preserved... if what is good and great in every religion is presented, and what is more essential, the unity of all religion.' D.E. Smith has pointed out how such an idea, to which Gandhi also subscribed, represented an unverifiable religious dogma, the propagation of which was not the proper function of a secular state, however useful it might be in strengthening it. This inconsistency, based as it was upon the assumption that Hinduism was somehow naturally secular, has caused the Indian state to be described as 'majoritarian'.

In fact many Hindu majoritarians harboured misgivings about the Constitution. While Sardar Patel and K.M. Munshi were instrumental in getting rid of separate electorates and reserved seats for religious minorities, their preparedness to accommodate minority sensitivities in religious and social matters, as well as the lack of reference in the Constitution to God, to a distinctly Hindu identity or to central tenets of Brahminical Hinduism such as the notion of *dharma*, left the majoritarians dissatisfied. Those expressing majoritarian sentiments included a sprinkling of Congressmen from eastern and southern India but were mostly upper caste Hindi speakers from U.P., Bihar, C.P. and Berar and East Punjab. The most prominent was Purushottamdas Tandon, elected Congress President with Patel's support in 1950 (he was forced to resign after Patel's death and a confrontation with Nehru the following year).

Those criticising the Draft Constitution as 'un-Gandhian' included some majoritarians but the feeling that it had abandoned Gandhian ideals was more widespread. Arun Chandra Guha, a violent revolutionary turned Gandhian from Bengal, was among the many members unhappy with the draft tabled by Ambedkar in November 1948. Responding to Ambedkar's scathing attack on village India as 'a sink of localism, a den of ignorance, narrow-mindedness and communalism' (cad vii, p.39), he regretted that the document bore 'no trace of Gandhian social and political outlook' and argued that the village be made the basis of the machinery of government (cad vii, p. 256).

After Partition, Muslims and Akali Sikhs advocating special provisions for religious minorities found themselves isolated. Members belonging to other non-Hindu groups, notably Christians and Parsis, tended to adopt either the dogmatic secularist or 'unity in diversity' viewpoints, holding that the best guarantee of equal treatment lay in the development of a common civil identity irrespective of religious differences. Though the odd Muslim or Sikh went along with this, the peculiar situation facing them left most Muslim and Sikh representatives torn between struggling for the retention of political safeguards and facing up to the new realities.

The Muslim Leaguers in the Assembly were in an unenviable position. Bereft of leadership as the most prominent left for Pakistan, the majority of north Indian Muslims eventually acquiesced in the abandonment of reserved seats while seeking to preserve religious freedoms. Only an isolated handful of members from Madras led by Mohammed Ismail decided to revive the League and continue to hold out for the maintenance of reserved seats (and even separate electorates). The position of the marginalised nationalist Muslims within Congress was not any easier and Abul Kalam Azad, the most senior Muslim Congressman and Education Minister, who has been described as forming, together with Nehru, Patel and Prasad, the 'oligarchy within the Assembly', was conspicuously silent in the debates on secularism. The case of the Sikhs of Punjab, as the community that had suffered most from Partition, was a bit different. The Akali representatives felt that they had the right to demand special protection and the seemingly grudging concessions made by Sardar Patel left them embittered (the two Akali members refused to sign the Constitution).

The debate on minority rights involved the consideration of three different kinds of rights: political representation, freedom of religion and cultural autonomy. The writers of the Constitution faced a dilemma. Underwriting any minority 'rights' could be seen as compromising the secular character of the state but if such rights were left unprotected, there was the danger that the state might be secular in form but unrestrainedly majoritarian in practice.

In the aftermath of Partition there was wide agreement among Congressmen that there was no place in an independent India for the separate communal electorates introduced by the British under the Morley-Minto reforms of 1909. Nevertheless, the Report on Minority Rights, tabled by Sardar Patel as the Chairman of the Advisory Committee, initially recommended the continued reservation of seats (on the basis of common electorates) in legislatures for Muslims, Christians and the Scheduled Castes (the case of the Sikhs was left pending owing to the dislocation occasioned by the partition of Punjab).

But behind the scenes Sardar Patel and K.M. Munshi, supported by Professor H.C. Mookerjee, the Christian Chairman of the Minorities Sub Committee, and Tajamul Husain, an ex-Muslim Leaguer who struck a stridently secular pose, sought to persuade minority representatives of the inadvisability of insisting on separate representation. Eventually, the majority of erstwhile Muslim Leaguers, demoralised by their abandonment by Jinnah following the creation of Pakistan, came around to accepting an end to reservation even before the nationalist Muslims.

In May 1949, six months before the Assembly concluded its deliberations, Sardar Patel moved the final Report of the Advisory Committee on Minorities, abandoning reservation for minority religious groups. The principle of universality was only to be diluted by the temporary retention of reservation to redress the age-old social discrimination suffered by Scheduled

Castes and Tribes (as well as to address the special problems faced by the small Anglo-Indian community) (Arts. 330-342 of the Constitution). The end of separate representation on the basis of religion was hailed by Patel, without any apparent hint of irony, as making it possible 'to lay, with the grace of God and with the blessings of the almighty, the foundations of a true secular democratic state' (26 May 1949, cad viii, p. 354).

This pious reaction was indicative of the rather different attitude taken by the makers of the Constitution when it came to dealing with the religious concerns of minorities. When Minoo Masani, together with Ambedkar and the two women members (Rajkumari Amrit Kaur and Hansa Mehta), pressed in the Fundamental Rights Sub-Committee for an enforceable commitment to a uniform civil code, this was successfully opposed by the male upper caste Hindu majority on the committee. As a result, and mainly in deference to the vocal opposition of Muslim members to any threat of state interference with their personal law, the objective of a uniform civil code for all citizens was relegated to the status of a non-justiciable directive principle of state policy (Art. 44)

A similar concern showed itself in Sardar Patel's proposal to omit a clause, vehemently opposed by Christian members and organisations, that explicitly outlawed conversion from one religion to another through coercion or undue influence. Despite the strong objections to the very idea of conversion expressed by majoritarian Hindu Congressmen such as Purushottamdas Tandon (speech of 1 May 1947, cad iii, p. 492), the Constitution's only reference to religious liberty was thus a positive one, affirming 'the right freely to profess, practice and propagate religion' (Art. 25.1). This was denounced by one majoritarian Congressman, Lokanath Misra, as 'a charter for Hindu enslavement' (3 December 1948, cad vii, p. 822).

Article 29 of the Constitution protected the right of any section 'having a distinct language, script or culture... to conserve the same,' while Article 30 enshrined the right of 'minorities, whether based on religion or language... to establish and administer educational institutions of their choice.' Like Articles 25 and 44, they reflected the distinction drawn between granting political recognition to minorities and respecting their religious and cultural autonomy. On this there was no difference between the secular-minded Nehru, desiring national cohesion but sensitive to minority fears, and Patel, who despite his majoritarian instincts, was pragmatic enough to recognise the distinction. Perhaps this was because, when considered together with some of the 'Hindu' concerns that found expression in the Constitution, it was a distinction that was central to the subdued majoritarianism of the 'unity in diversity' viewpoint.

In the Hindu majoritarian discourse, cultural and religious themes, such as caste and the reform of Hinduism and the adoption of Hindi as the sole national language, loomed large.

Inspite of the misgivings of Christian missionaries and others, the British colonial rulers had continued to act, albeit in more limited fashion, as the patrons and protectors of religious institutions. So, the immediate state tradition that the makers of the Constitution had to draw upon was not one that conformed to a Jeffersonian 'wall of separation' doctrine of secularism. In any case, scarcely any Congressmen argued that this was desirable, given the need to deal with the widespread practice of untouchability in Indian society, a concern lent urgency by Gandhi's struggle to eliminate it and Ambedkar's fight to win political recognition for the untouchables.

Politically, the Hindu majoritarians, overwhelmingly caste Hindu by background, were concerned first with establishing the 'Hindu' identity of out-castes. In August 1947, Sardar Patel accepted an amendment to the first Minority Rights Report from K.M. Munshi that explicitly referred to the Scheduled Castes as a 'section of the Hindu Community' (cad v, p. 234). The Constitution prohibited the practice of untouchability in any form (Art. 17), further empowering the state to make any law 'providing for social welfare and reform or the throwing open of Hindu religious institutions of a public character to all classes and sections of Hindus' (Art. 25.2b). Significantly, an explanation was added that the reference to 'Hindus' included Sikhs, Jains and Buddhists.

The wide powers granted to the state in pursuit of the reform of Hindu social practices sharply contrasted with the concern not to be seen as interfering with the religious practices of Muslims or Christians. By associating the Indian state with the reform of the social practices of people belonging to a particular religious tradition, it placed the state in a unique position in relation to that tradition.

Of all the majoritarian themes that found expression in the Assembly debate, the most contentious was the adoption of Hindi as the sole national language, discussion of which was postponed almost to the very end of the deliberations. Fears of Hindi domination among both Urdu-speaking Muslim members and non-Hindi speakers, especially from the South, contributed to an imperfect congruence of the pro and anti-camps in the debates over secularism and language.

In an uncompromising speech (delivered in Hindi, unlike the majority of speeches which were in English), Seth Govind Das, the foremost spokesman for the Hindi enthusiasts, described Urdu (written in Arabic script and strongly influenced by Arabic and Persian) as drawing 'inspiration from outside this country' and supported by people who were communal in their outlook. Rejecting the notion that the acceptance of a secular state implied the acceptance of cultural heterogeneity, he declared that, 'For thousands of years one and the same culture has all along been obtaining here.... It is in order to maintain this tradition that we want one language and one script for the whole country.' (12 September 1949, cad ix, p. 1328)

But what the language debate actually did was highlight the fact that religious identity represented only one of the potential fissures in the Indian body politic. Recognising this, even some erstwhile Hindi enthusiasts like K.M. Munshi became convinced of the need for compromise. A committee assigned to find a way out of the impasse evolved a formula by which Hindi in the Devanagari script would become the official language of the Union and international (rather than Nagari) numerals be used for official purposes (Art. 343). The proviso was that English would continue to be used for official purposes for 15 years with Parliament allowed to provide for its continued use thereafter.

As with minorities and separate electorates, the one attempt to unambiguously define political identity along majoritarian lines also failed. In August 1949, P.S. Deshmukh, a Congressman from the Central Provinces, proposed an amendment giving all Hindus and Sikhs the right to become citizens of India, arguing that, 'Here we are an entire nation with a history of thousands of years and we are going to discard it, in spite of the fact that neither the Hindu nor the Sikh has any other place in the wide world to go to... But we are a secular state and do not want to recognise the fact... If the Muslims want an exclusive place for themselves called Pakistan, why should not Hindus and Sikhs have India as their home?' (cad ix, p. 356)

The reference to a secular state drew an exasperated response from Nehru who asked, 'May I beg with all humility those gentlemen who use this word often to consult some dictionary before they use it?... it is brought in all contexts, as if by saying that we are a secular state we have done something amazingly generous.... We have only done something which every country does except a very few misguided and backward countries in the world.' (cad ix, p. 401)

Attracting the support of only a handful of members, the amendment was easily defeated. However, the fact that such a proposal could have been made by someone like Deshmukh, who held a doctorate from Oxford and had served as a provincial minister, is significant as is the fact that he went on to serve under Nehru for 10 years as a Union minister of state. Clearly, the majoritarian discourse was one shared by a large number of middle-ranking Congress leaders whom Nehru, despite his commanding stature, could not disregard. Could the makers of the Constitution have tackled the challenge presented by India's religious plurality any differently? It is difficult to see how. Indian secularism represented the outcome of contradictions: between the secular form of the modern state and a religious society; between contending visions of what India should be, embodied by some of the principal figures involved in drawing up the Constitution – Nehru, Patel, Prasad, Ambedkar; between the anxieties of minority religious groups and the majoritarian inclinations of many Hindu Congressmen; between the enthusiasts for Hindi and the fears of the non-Hindi speaking majority; and between the demands of a putative nation and the pressures of a diverse federal polity. These contradictions have not disappeared.

Obscured for a time by being internalised within the Congress Party, over the past two decades the rise of Hindu nationalism and the growing political strength of regional and low caste parties have helped expose the tears in the fabric. But the fact that the cloth has not been rent testifies to the lasting utility of the deliberately ambiguous concept of 'unity in diversity'.

EVOLUTION OF THE INDIAN CONSTITUTION

Acts of British Parliament before 1935

After the Indian Rebellion of 1857, the British Parliament passed the Government of India Act 1858, which abolished the role of the East India Company in the government of India, and transferred British India to the direct rule of the Crown. The Act also established in England the office of the Secretary of State for India through whom Parliament would exercise its rule (along with a Council of India to aid him), as well as establishing the office of Viceroy of India (along with an Executive Council in India, consisting of high officials of the British Government). The Indian Councils Act 1861 provided for a Legislative Council consisting of the members of the Executive council and non-official members. The Indian Councils Act 1892 established provincial legislatures and increased the powers of the Legislative Council. Although these Acts increased the representation of Indians in the government, their power still remained limited. The Indian Councils Act 1909 and the Government of India Act 1919 further expanded participation of Indians in the government.

Government of India Act 1935

The provisions of the Government of India Act 1935, though never implemented fully, had a great impact on the Constitution of India. Many key features of the constitution are directly taken from this Act: the federal structure of government, provincial autonomy, a bicameral central legislature consisting of a federal assembly and a Council of States, and the separation of legislative powers between the centre and provinces, are some of the provisions of the Act which are present in the Constitution of India.

The Cabinet Mission Plan

In 1946, British Prime Minister Clement Attlee formulated a cabinet mission to India to discuss and finalise plans for the transfer of power from the British Raj to Indian leadership as well as provide India with independence under Dominion status in the Commonwealth of Nations. The Mission discussed the framework of the constitution and laid down in some detail the procedure to be followed by the constitution drafting body. Elections for the 296 seats assigned to the British Indian provinces were completed by August 1946. The Constituent Assembly of India first met and began work on 9 December 1946.

Indian Independence Act 1947

The Indian Independence Act, passed by the British Parliament on 18 July 1947, divided British India into two new independent states, India and Pakistan, which were to be dominions under the Commonwealth of Nations until they had each finished drafting and enacted a new constitution. The Constituent Assembly was divided into two for the separate states, with each new Assembly having sovereign powers transferred to it for the respective dominion. The Act also terminated British suzerainty over the princely states, each of which was expected to accede to one or other of the new dominions (rather than continue as independent states in their own right). When the Constitution of India came into force on 26 January 1950, it repealed the Indian Independence Act. India ceased to be a dominion of the British Crown and became a sovereign democratic republic. 26 November 1949 is also known as National Law Day.

Constituent Assembly

The Constitution was drafted by the Constituent Assembly.

which was elected by the elected members of the provincial assemblies. Jawaharlal Nehru, C. Rajagopalachari, Rajendra Prasad, Sardar Vallabhbhai Patel, Sandipkumar Patel, Dr Ambedkar, Maulana Abul Kalam Azad, Shyama Prasad Mukherjee, Nalini Ranjan Ghosh, and Balwant Singh Mehta were some important figures in the Assembly. There were more than 30 members of the scheduled classes. Frank Anthony represented the Anglo-Indian community, and the Parsis were represented by H. P. Modi.

The Chairman of the Minorities Committee was Harendra Coomar Mookerjee, a distinguished Christian who represented all Christians other than Anglo-Indians. Ari Bahadur Gururng represented the Gorkha Community. Prominent jurists like Alladi Krishnaswamy Iyer, B. R. Ambedkar, Benegal Narsing Rau and K. M. Munshi, Ganesh Mavlankar were also members of the Assembly. Sarojini Naidu, Hansa Mehta, Durgabai Deshmukh, Rajkumari Amrit Kaur and Vijayalakshmi Pandit were important women members. The first president of the Constituent Assembly was Dr Sachidanand Sinha. Later, Rajendra Prasad was elected president of the Constituent Assembly. The members of the Constituent Assembly met for the first time on 9 December 1946.

Drafting

In the 14 August 1947 meeting of the Assembly, a proposal for forming various committees was presented. Such committees included a Committee on Fundamental Rights, the Union Powers Committee and Union Constitution Committee. On 29 August 1947, the Drafting Committee was appointed, with Dr Ambedkar as the Chairman along with six other members. A Draft Constitution was prepared by the committee and submitted to the Assembly on 4 November 1947.

The architects of India's constitution, though drawing on many external sources, were most heavily influenced by the British model of parliamentary democracy. In addition, a number of principles were adopted from the Constitution of the United States of America, including the separation of powers among the major branches of government, the establishment of a supreme court, and the adoption, albeit in modified form, of a federal structure (a constitutional division of power between the Union (central) government and state governments). The Assembly met in sessions open to the public, for 166 days, spread over a period of 2 years, 11 months and 18 days before adopting the Constitution. After many deliberations and some modifications, the 308 members of the Assembly signed two copies of the document (one each in Hindi and English) on 24 January 1950. The original Constitution of India is handwritten with beautiful calligraphy, each page beautified and decorated by artists from Santiniketan including Beohar Rammanohar Sinha and others. Two days later, on 26 January 1950, the Constitution of India became the law of all the States and territories of India. The Constitution has undergone many amendments since its enactment.

Structure

The Constitution, in its current form (March 2011), consists of a preamble, 22 parts containing 450 articles, 12 schedules, 2 appendices and 94 amendments to date. Although it is federal in nature it also has a strong unitary bias.

Parts

The individual Articles of the Constitution are grouped together into the following Parts:

- Preamble
- Part I – Union and its Territory
- Part II – Citizenship.
- Part III – Fundamental Rights
- Part IV – Directive Principles and Fundamental Duties.
- Part V – The Union.
- Part VI – The States.
- Part VII – States in the B part of the First schedule (Repealed).
- Part VIII – The Union Territories
- Part IX – Panchayat system and Municipalities.
- Part X – The scheduled and Tribal Areas

- Part XI – Relations between the Union and the States.
- Part XII – Finance, Property, Contracts and Suits
- Part XIII – Trade and Commerce within the territory of India
- Part XIV – Services Under the Union, the States and Tribunals
- Part XV – Elections
- Part XVI – Special Provisions Relating to certain Classes.
- Part XVII – Languages
- Part XVIII – Emergency Provisions
- Part XIX – Miscellaneous
- Part XX – Amendment of the Constitution
- Part XXI – Temporary, Transitional and Special Provisions
- Part XXII – Short title, date of commencement, Authoritative text in Hindi and Repeals.

Schedules

Schedules are lists in the Constitution that categorise and tabulate bureaucratic activity and policy of the Government.

- First Schedule (Articles 1 and 4)- This lists the states and territories of India, lists any changes to their borders and the laws used to make that change.
- Second Schedule (Articles 59, 65, 75, 97, 125, 148, 158, 164, 186 and 221)- – This lists the salaries of officials holding public office, judges, and Comptroller and Auditor-General of India.
- Third Schedule (Articles 75, 99, 124, 148, 164, 188 and 219)—Forms of Oaths – This lists the oaths of offices for elected officials and judges.
- Fourth Schedule (Articles 4 and 80) – This details the allocation of seats in the *Rajya Sabha* (the upper house of Parliament) per State or Union Territory.
- Fifth Schedule (Article 244) – This provides for the administration and control of Scheduled Areas and Scheduled Tribes (areas and tribes needing special protection due to disadvantageous conditions).

- Sixth Schedule (Articles 244 and 275)— Provisions for the administration of tribal areas in Assam, Meghalaya, Tripura, and Mizoram.
- Seventh Schedule (Article 246)—The union (central government), state, and concurrent lists of responsibilities.
- Eighth Schedule (Articles 344 and 351)—The official languages.
- Ninth Schedule (Article 31-B) – Articles mentioned here are immune from judicial review.
- Tenth Schedule (Articles 102 and 191)—"Anti-defection" provisions for Members of Parliament and Members of the State Legislatures.
- Eleventh Schedule (Article 243-G)—*Panchayat Raj* (rural local government).
- Twelfth Schedule (Article 243-W)—Municipalities (urban local government).

System of Government

The basic form of the Union Government envisaged in the Constitution is as follows,

"A democratic executive must satisfy three conditions:

1. It must be a stable executive, and
2. It must be a responsible executive.

Unfortunately, it has not been possible so far to devise a system which can ensure both conditions in equal degree. The daily assessment of responsibility, which is not available in the American system is, it is felt, far more effective than the periodic assessment and far more necessary in a country like India. The Draft Constitution in recommending the parliamentary system of Executive has preferred more responsibility to stability."

Federal Structure

The Constitution provides for distribution of powers between the Union and the States. It enumerates the powers of the Parliament and State Legislatures in three lists, namely Union list, State list and Concurrent list. Subjects like national defence, foreign policy, issuance of currency are reserved to the Union list. Public order, local governments, certain taxes are examples of subjects of the State List, on which the Parliament has no power to enact laws in those regards, barring exceptional conditions. Education, transportation, criminal law are a few subjects of the Concurrent list, where both the State Legislature as well as the Parliament have powers to enact laws. The residuary powers are vested with the Union.

The upper house of the Parliament, the Rajya Sabha, which consists of representatives of States, is also an example of the federal nature of the government.

Parliamentary Democracy

The President of India is elected by the Parliament and State Legislative Assemblies, and not directly by the people. The President is the head of state, and all the business of the Executive and Laws enacted by the Parliament are in his/her name. However, these powers are only nominal, and the President must act only according to the advice of the Prime Minister and the Council of Ministers.

The Prime Minister and the Council of Ministers exercise their offices only as long as they enjoy a majority support in the Lok Sabha, the lower house of the Parliament, which consists of members directly elected by the people. The ministers are answerable to both the houses of the Parliament. Also, the Ministers must themselves be elected members of either house of the Parliament. Thus, the Parliament exercises control over the Executive.

A similar structure is present in States, where the directly elected Legislative Assembly enjoys control over the Chief Minister and the State Council of Ministers.

Independent Judiciary

The Judiciary of India is free of control from either the executive or the Parliament. The judiciary acts as an interpreter of the constitution, and as an intermediary in case of disputes between two States, or between a State and the Union. An act passed by the Parliament or a Legislative Assembly is subject to judicial review, and can be declared unconstitutional by the judiciary if it feels that the act violates the provisions of the Constitution.

Changing the Constitution

Amendments to the Constitution are made by the Parliament, the procedure for which is laid out in Article 368. An amendment bill must be passed by both the Houses of the Parliament by a two-thirds majority and voting. In addition to this, certain amendments which pertain to the federal nature of the Constitution must be ratified by a majority of state legislatures. As of September 2010, there have been 108 amendment bills presented in the Parliament, out of which 94 have been passed to become Amendment Acts. Most of these amendments address issues dealt with by statute in other democracies. However, the Constitution is so specific in spelling out government powers that many of these issues must be addressed by constitutional amendment. As a result, the document is amended roughly twice a year.

The Supreme Court has ruled in Kesavananda Bharati v. State of Kerala case that not every constitutional amendment is permissible, the amendment must respect the "basic structure" of the constitution, which is immutable. In 2000 the National Commission to Review the Working of the Constitution (NCRWC) was setup to look into updating the constitution.

Judicial Review of Laws

Judicial review is adopted in the Constitution of India from the Constitution of the United States of America. In the Indian constitution, Judicial Review is dealt with under Article 13. Judicial Review refers that the Constitution is the supreme power of the nation and all laws are under its supremacy. Article 13 states that:

1. All pre-constitutional laws, after the coming into force of constitution, if in conflict with it in all or some of its provisions then the provisions of constitution will prevail and the provisions of that pre-constitutional law which conflicts the provisions of the constitution will not be

in force until an amendment of the constitution relating to the same matter. In such situation the provision of that law will again come into force, if it is compatible with the constitution as amended. This is called the *Doctrine of Eclipse*.

2. In a similar manner, laws made after adoption of the Constitution by the Constituent Assembly must be compatible with the constitution, otherwise the laws and amendments will be deemed to be void-ab-initio.

In such situations, the Supreme Court or High Court interprets the laws as if they are in conformity with the Constitution. If such an interpretation is not possible because of inconsistency, and where a separation is possible, the provision that is inconsistent with constitution is considered to be void. In addition to article 13, articles 32, 124, 131, 219, 228 and 246 provide a constitutional basis to the Judicial review in India.

REFERENCES

- Best M.: *The New Competition. Institutions of Industrial Restructuring*, Cambridge, Polity Press, 1990.
- Chandra, R.: *Judicial System in India*, Lucknow, Print House (India), 1992.
- Derrett, J. : *Religion, Law, and the State in India*, London, Faber, 1968.
- Kenneth C. Wheare: *Modern Constitutions*, New York, Oxford University Press, 1951.

4

Indian Constitutional Amendment Acts

THE CONSTITUTION (FIRST AMENDMENT) ACT, 1951

[18th June,1951.]

An Act to amend the Constitution of India.

BE it enacted by Parliament as follows:-

1. Short title.-This Act may be called the Constitution (First Amendment) Act, 1951.

2. Amendment of article 15.-To article 15 of the Constitution, the following clause shall be added:-

"(4) Nothing in this article or in clause (2) of article 29 shall pre- vent the State from making any special provision for the advancement of any socially and educationally backward classes of citizens or for the Scheduled Castes and the Scheduled Tribes.".

3. Amendment of article 19 and validation of certain laws.-(1) In article 19 of the Constitution,-

(a) for clause (2), the following clause shall be substituted, and the said clause shall be deemed always to have been enacted in the following form, namely:---

"(2) Nothing in sub-clause (a) of clause (1) shall affect the operation of any existing law, or prevent the State from making any law, in so far as such law imposes reasonable restrictions on the exercise of the right conferred by the said sub-clause in the interests of the security of the State, friendly relations with foreign States, public order, decency or morality, or in relation to contempt of court, defamation or incitement to an offence."; (b) in clause (6), for the words beginning with the words "nothing in the said sub-clause" and ending with the words "occupation, trade or business", the following shall be substituted, namely:- "nothing in the said sub-clause shall affect the operation of any existing law in so far as it relates to, or prevent the State from making any law relating to-

(i) the professional or technical qualifications necessary for practising any profession or carrying on any occupation, trade or business, or

(ii) the carrying on by the State, or by a corporation owned or controlled by the State, of any trade, business, industry or service, whether to the exclusion, complete or partial, of citizens or otherwise".

(2) No law in force in the territory of India immediately before the commencement of the Constitution which is consistent with the provisions of article 19 of the Constitution as amended by sub-section (1) of this section shall be deemed to be void, or over to have become void, on the ground only that, being a law which takes away or abridges the right conferred by sub-clause (a) of clause (1) of the said article, its operation was not saved by clause (2) of that article as originally enacted.

Explanation.-In this sub-section, the expression "law in force" has the same meaning as in clause (1) of article 13 of the Constitution.

4. Insertion of new article 31A.-After article 31 of the Constitution, the following article shall be inserted, and shall be deemed always to have been inserted, namely:-

"31A. Saving of laws providing for acquisition of estates, etc.-(1) Notwithstanding anything in the foregoing provisions of this Part, no law providing for the acquisition by the State of any estate or of any rights therein or for the extinguishment or modification of any such rights shall be deemed to be void on the ground that it is inconsistent with, or takes away or abridges any of the rights conferred by, any provisions of this

Part: Provided that where such law is a law made by the Legislature of a State, the provisions of this article shall not apply thereto unless such law, having been reserved for the consideration of the President, has received his assent.

(2) In this article,- (a) the expression "estate" shall, in relation to any local area, have the same meaning as that expression or its local equivalent has in the existing law relating to land tenures in force in that area, and shall also include any jagir, inam or muafi or other similar grant; (b) the expression "rights", in relation to an estate, shall include any rights vesting in a proprietor, sub-proprietor, under-proprietor, tenure-holder or other intermediary and any rights or privileges in respect of land revenue.".

5. Insertion of new article 31B.-After article 31A of the Constitution as inserted by section 4, the following article shall be inserted, namely:-

"31B. Validation of certain Acts and Regulations.-Without prejudice to the generality of the provisions contained in article 31A, none of the Acts and Regulations specified in the Ninth Schedule nor any of the provisions thereof shall be deemed to be void, or ever to have become void, on the ground that such Act, Regulation or provision is inconsistent with, or takes away or abridges any of the rights conferred by, any provisions of this Part, and notwithstanding any judgment, decree or order of any court or tribunal to the contrary, each of the said Acts and Regulations shall, subject to the power of any competent Legislature to repeal or amend it, continue in force.".

6. Amendment of article 85.-For article 85 of the Constitution, the following article shall be substituted, namely:-

"85. Sessions of Parliament, prorogation and dissolution.-(1) The President shall from time to time summon each House of Parliament to meet at such time and place as he thinks fit, but six months shall not intervene between its last sitting in one session and the date appointed for its first sitting in the next session.

(2) The President may from time to time-

(a) prorogue the Houses or either House;

(b) dissolve the House of the People.".

7. Amendment of article 87.-In article 87 of the Constitution,-

(1) in clause (1), for the words "every session", the words "the first session after each general election to the House of the People and at the commencement of the first session of each year" shall be substituted;

(2) in clause (2), the words "and for the precedence of such discussion over other business of the House" shall be omitted.

8. Amendment of article 174.-For article 174 of the Constitution, the following article shall be substituted, namely:-

"174. Sessions of the State Legislature, prorogation and dissolution.-(1) The Governor shall from time to time summon the House or each House of the Legislature of the State to meet at such time and place as he thinks fit, but six months shall not intervene between its last sitting in one session and the date appointed for its first sitting in the next session.

(2) the Governor may from time to time-

(a) prorogue the House or either House;

(b) dissolve the Legislative Assembly.".

9. Amendment of article 176.-In article 176 of the Constitution,-

(1) in clause (1), for the words "every session", the words "the first session after each general election to the Legislative Assembly and at the commencement of the first session of each year" shall be substituted;

(2) in clause (2), the words "and for the precedence of such discussion over other business of the House" shall be omitted.

10. Amendment of article 341.-In clause (1) of article 341 of the Constitution, for the words "may, after consultation with the Governor or Rajpramukh of a State,", the words "may with respect to any State, and where it is a State specified in Part A or Part B of the First Schedule, after consultation with the Governor or Rajpramukh thereof," shall be substituted.

11. Amendment of article 342.-In clause (1) of article 342 of the Constitution, for the words "may, after consultation with

the Governor or Rajpramukh of a State,", the words "may with respect to any State, and where it is a State specified in Part A or Part B of the First Schedule, after consultation with the Governor or Rajpramukh thereof," shall be substituted.

12. Amendment of article 372.-In sub-clause (a) of clause (3) of article 372 of the Constitution, for the words "two years", the words "three years" shall be substituted.

13. Amendment of article 376.-At the end of clause (1) of article 376 of the Constitution, the following shall be added, namely:--- "Any such Judge shall, notwithstanding that he is not a citizen of India, be eligible for appointment as Chief Justice of such High Court, or as Chief Justice or other Judge of any other High Court.".

14. Addition of Ninth Schedule.-After the Eighth Schedule to the Constitution, the following Schedule shall be added, namely:-

"NINTH SCHEDULE [Article 31B]

1. The Bihar Land Reforms Act, 1950 (Bihar Act XXX of 1950).
2. The Bombay Tenancy and Agricultural Lands Act, 1948 (Bombay Act LXVII of 1948).
3. The Bombay Maleki Tenure Abolition Act, 1949 (Bombay Act LXI of 1949).
4. The Bombay Taluqdari Tenure Abolition Act, 1949 (Bombay Act LXII of 1949).
5. The Panch Mahals Mehwassi Tenure Abolition Act, 1949 (Bombay Act LXIII of 1949).
6. The Bombay Khoti Abolition Act, 1950 (Bombay Act VI of 1950).
7. The Bombay Paragana and Kulkarni Watan Abolition Act, 1950 (Bombay Act LX of 1950).
8. The Madhya Pradesh Abolition of Proprietary Rights (Estates, Mahals, Alienated Lands) Act, 1950 (Madhya Pradesh Act I of 1951).
9. The Madras Estates (Abolition and Conversion into Ryotwari) Act, 1948 (Madras Act XXVI of 1948).

10. The Madras Estates (Abolition and Conversion into Ryotwari) Amendment Act, 1950 (Madras Act I of 1950).
11. The Uttar Pradesh Zamindari Abolition and Land Reforms Act, 1950 (Uttar Pradesh Act I of 1951).
12. The Hyderabad (Abolition of Jagirs) Regulation, 1358F. (No. LXIX of 1358, Fasli).
13. The Hyderabad Jagirs (Commutation) Regulation, 1359F. (No. XXV of 1359, Fasli).".

THE CONSTITUTION (SECOND AMENDMENT) ACT, 1952

Statement of Objects and Reasons appended to THE CONSTITUTION (Second Amendment) Bill, 1952 which was enacted as the the Constitution (Second Amendment) Act, 1952

An Act further to amend the Constitution of India.

[1st May, 1953.]

BE it enacted by Parliament as follows:-

1. Short title.-This Act may be called the Constitution (Second Amendment) Act, 1952.

2. Amendment of article 81.-In sub-clause (b) of clause (1) of article 81 of the Constitution, the words and figures "not less than one member for every 750,000 of the population and" shall be omitted.

THE CONSTITUTION (THIRD AMENDMENT) ACT, 1954

Statement of Objects and Reasons appended to THE CONSTITUTION (Second Amendment) Bill, 1952 which was enacted as the the Constitution (Second Amendment) Act, 1952

[22nd February, 1955.]

An Act further to amend the Constitution of India.

BE it enacted by Parliament in the Fifth Year of the Republic of India as follows:-

1. Short title.-This Act may be called the Constitution (Third Amendment) Act 1954.

2. Amendment of the Seventh Schedule.-In the Seventh Schedule to the Constitution, for entry 33 of List III, the following entry shall be substituted, namely:-

"33. Trade and commerce in, and the production, supply and distribution of,-

(a) the products of any industry where the control of such industry by the Union is declared by Parliament by law to be expedient in the public interest, and imported goods of the same kind as such products;

(b) foodstuffs, including edible oil seeds and oils;

(c) cattle fodder, including oilcakes and other concentrates;

(d) raw cotton whether ginned or unginned, and cotton seeds; and

(e) raw jute.".

THE CONSTITUTION (FOURTH AMENDMENT) ACT, 1955

Statement of Objects and Reasons appended to THE CONSTITUTION (Fourth Amendment) Bill, 1954 which was enacted as the Constitution (Fourth Amendment) Act, 1954

THE CONSTITUTION (FOURTH AMENDMENT) ACT, 1955

[27th April, 1955.]

An Act further to amend the Constitution of India.

BE it enacted by Parliament in the Sixth Year of the Republic of India as follow:-

1. Short title.-This Act may be called the Constitution (Forth Amendment) Act, 1955.

2. Amendment of article 31.-In article 31 of the Constitution, for clause (2), the following clauses shall be substituted, namely:-

"(2) No property shall be compulsorily acquired or requisitioned save for a public purpose and save by authority of a law which provides for compensation for the property so acquired or requisitioned and either fixes the amount of the compensation or specifies the principles on which, and the manner in which, the compensation is to be determined and given; and no such law shall be called in question in any court on the ground that the compensation provided by that law is not adequate.

(2A) Where a law does not provide for the transfer of the ownership or right to possession of any property to the State or to a corporation owned or controlled by the State, it shall not be deemed to provide for the compulsory acquisition or requisitioning of property, notwithstanding that it deprives any person of his property.".

3. Amendment of article 31A.-In article 31A of the Constitution,- (a) for clause (1), the following clause shall be, and shall be deemed always to have been, substituted, namely:-

"(1) Notwithstanding anything contained in article 13, no law providing for-

(a) the acquisition by the State of any estate or of any rights therein or the extinguishment or modification of any such rights, or

(b) the taking over of the management of any property by the State for a limited period either in the public interest or in order to secure the proper management of the property, or

(c) the amalgamation of two or more corporations either in the public interest or in order to secure the proper management of any of the corporations, or

(d) the extinguishment or modification of any rights of managing agents, secretaries and treasurers, managing directors, directors or managers of corporations, or of any voting rights of shareholders thereof, or

(e) the extinguishment or modification of any rights accruing by virtue of any agreement, lease or licence for the purpose of searching for, or winning, any mineral or mineral oil, or the premature termination or cancellation of any such agreement, lease or licence, shall be deemed to be void on the ground that it is inconsistent with, or takes away or abridges any of the rights conferred by article 14, article 19 or article 31:

Provided that where such law is a law made by the Legislature of a State, the provisions of this article shall not apply thereto unless such law, having been reserved for the consideration of the President, has received his assent."; and (b) in clause (2),- (i) in sub-clause (a), after the word "grant", the words "and in the States of Madras and Travancore-Cochin, any janman right" shall be, and shall be deemed always to have been, inserted; and (ii) in sub-clause (b), after the word "tenure-holder", the words "raiyat, under-raiyat" shall be, and shall be deemed always to have been, inserted.

4. Substitution of new article for article 305.-For article 305 of the Constitution, the following article shall be substituted, namely:-

"305. Saving of existing laws and laws providing for State monopolies.-Nothing in articles 301 and 303 shall affect the provisions of any existing law except in so far as the President may by order otherwise direct; and nothing in article 301 shall affect the operation of any law made before the commencement of the Constitution (Fourth Amendment) Act, 1955, in so far as it relates to, or prevent Parliament or the Legislature of a State from making any law relating to, any such matter as is referred to in sub-clause (ii) of clause (6) of article 19.".

5. Amendment of the Ninth Schedule.-In the Ninth Schedule to the Constitution, after entry 13, the following entries shall be added, namely:---

"14. The Bihar Displaced Persons Rehabilitation (Acquisition of Land) Act, 1950 (Bihar Act XXXVIII of 1950).

15. The United Provinces Land Acquisition (Rehabilitation of Re- fugees) Act, 1948 (U.P. Act XXVI 1948).

16. The Resettlement of Displaced Persons (Land Acquisition) Act, 1948 (Act LX of 1948).

17. Sections 52A to 52G of the Insurance Act, 1938 (Act IV of 1938), as inserted by section 42 of the Insurance (Amendment) Act, 1950 (Act XLVII of 1950).

18. The Railway Companies (Emergency Provisions) Act, 1951 (Act LI of 1951).

19. Chapter III-A of the Industries (Development and Regulation) Act, 1951 (Act LXV of 1951), as inserted by section 13 of the Industries (Development and Regulation) Amendment Act, 1953 (Act XXVI of 1953).

20. The West Bengal Land Development and Planning Act, 1948 (West Bengal Act XXI of 1948), as amended by West Bengal Act XXIX of 1951.".

THE CONSTITUTION (FIFTH AMENDMENT) ACT, 1955

[24th December, 1955.]

An Act further to amend the Constitution of India.

BE it enacted by Parliament in the Sixth Year of the Republic of India as follows:---

1. Short title.-This Act may be called the Constitution (Fifth Amendment) Act, 1955.

2. Amendment of article 3.-In article 3 of the Constitution, for the proviso, the following proviso shall be substituted, namely:-

"Provided that no Bill for the purpose shall be introduced in either House of Parliament except on the recommendation of the President and unless, where the proposal contained in the Bill affects the area, boundaries or name of any of the States specified in Part A or Part B of the First Schedule, the Bill has been referred by the President to the Legislature of that State for expressing its views thereon within such period as may be specified in the reference or within such further period as the President may allow and the period so specified or allowed has expired.".

THE CONSTITUTION (SIXTH AMENDMENT) ACT, 1956

[11th September, 1956.]

An Act further to amend the Constitution of India. BE it enacted by Parliament in the Seventh Year of the Republic of India as follows:-

1. Short title.-This Act may be called the Constitution (Sixth Amendment) Act, 1956.

2. Amendment of the Seventh Schedule.-In the Seventh Schedule to the Constitution,- (a) in the Union List, after entry 92, the following entry shall be inserted, namely:-

"92A. Taxes on the sale or purchase of goods other than newspapers, where such sale or purchase takes place in the course of inter-State trade or commerce."; and (b) in the State List, for entry 54, the following entry shall be substituted, namely:-

"54. Taxes on the sale or purchase of goods other than newspapers, subject to the provisions of entry 92A of List I.".

3. Amendment of article 269.-In article 269 of the Constitution,- (a) in clause (1), after sub-clause (f), the following sub-clause shall be inserted, namely:-

"(g) taxes on the sale or purchase of goods other than newspapers, where such sale or purchase takes place in the course of inter-State trade or commerce."; and (b) after clause (2), the following clause shall be inserted, namely:-

"(3) Parliament may by law formulate principles for determining when a sale or purchase of goods takes place in the course of inter-State trade or commerce.".

4. Amendment of article 286.-In article 286 of the Constitution,- (a) in clause (1), the Explanation shall be omitted; and (b) for clauses (2) and (3), the following clauses shall be substituted, namely:-

"(2) Parliament may by law formulate principles for determining when a sale or purchase of goods takes place in any of the ways mentioned in clause (1).

(3) Any law of a State shall, in so far as it imposes or authorises the imposition of, a tax on the sale or purchase of goods declared by Parliament by law to be of special importance in inter-State trade or commerce, be subject to such restrictions and conditions in regard to the system of levy, rates and other incidents of the tax as Parliament may by law specify.".

THE CONSTITUTION (SEVENTH AMENDMENT) ACT, 1956

Statement of Objects and Reasons appended to the Constitution Ninth Amendment) Bill, 1956 (Bill No. 29 of 1956) which was enacted as THE CONSTITUTION (Seventh Amendment) Act, 1956

[19th October, 1956.]

An Act further to amend the Constitution of India.

BE it enacted by Parliament in the Seventh Year of the Republic of India as follows:-

Short title and commencement.-(1) This Act may be called the Constitution (Seventh Amendment) Act, 1956.

(2) It shall come into force on the 1st day of November, 1956.

2. Amendment of article 1 and First Schedule.-(1) In article 1 of the Constitution,-

(a) for clause (2), the following clause shall be substituted, namely:-

"(2) The States and the territories thereof shall be as specified in the First Schedule."; and

(b) in clause (3), for sub-clause (b), the following sub-clause shall be substituted, namely:-

"(b) the Union territories specified in the First Schedule; and".

(2) For the First Schedule to the Constitution as amended by the States Reorganisation Act, 1956, and the Bihar and West Bengal (Transfer of Territories) Act, 1956, the following Schedule shall be substituted, namely:-

The States

	Name	Territories
1.	Andhra Pradesh	The territories specified in sub-section (1) of section 3 of the Andhra State Act, 1953 and the territories specified in sub-section (1) of section 3 of the States Reorganisation Act, 1956.
2.	Assam	The territories which immediately before the commencement of this Constitution were comprised in the Province of Assam, the Khasi States and the Assam Tribal Areas, but excluding the territories specified in the Schedule to the Assam (Alteration of Boundaries) Act, 1951.
3.	Bihar	The territories which immediately before the commencement of this Constitution were either comprised in the Province of Bihar or were being administered as if they formed part of that Province, but excluding the

	territories specified in sub-section (1) of section 3 of the Bihar and West Bengal (Transfer of Territories) Act, 1956.
4. Bombay	The territories specified in sub-section (1) of section 8 of the States Reorganisation Act, 1956.
5. Kerala	The territories specified in sub-section (1) of section 5 of the States Reorganisation Act, 1956.
6. Madhya Pradesh	The territories specified in sub-section (1) of section 9 of the States Reorganisation Act, 1956.
7. Madras	The territories which immediately before the commencement of this Constitution were either comprised in the Province of Madras or were being administered as if they formed part of that Province and the territories specified in section 4 of the States Reorganisation Act, 1956, but excluding the territories specified in sub-section (1) of section 3 and sub-section (1) of section 4 of the Andhra State Act, 1953 and the territories specified in clause (b) of sub-section (1) of section 5, section 6 and clause (d) of sub-section (1) of section 7 of the States Reorganisation Act, 1956.
8. Mysore	The territories specified in sub-section (1) of section 7 of the States Reorganisation Act, 1956.
9. Orissa	The territories which immediately before the commencement of this Constitution were either comprised in the Province of Orissa or were being administered as if they formed part of that Province.
10. Punjab	The territories specified in section 11 of the States Reorganisation Act, 1956.
11. Rajasthan	The territories specified in section 10 of the States Reorganisation Act, 1956.
12. Uttar Pradesh	The territories which immediately before the commencement of this Constitution were either comprised in the Province known as

		the United Provinces or were being administered as if they formed part of that Province.
13.	West Bengal	The territories which immediately before the commencement of this Constitution were either comprised in the Province of West Bengal or were being administered as if they formed part of that Province and the territory of Chandernagore as defined in clause (c) of section 2 of the Chandernagore (Merger) Act, 1954, and also the territories specified in sub-section (1) of section 3 of the Bihar and West Bengal (Transfer of Territories) Act, 1956.
14.	Jammu & Kashmir	The territory which immediately before the commencement of this Constitution was comprised in the Indian State of Jammu and Kashmir.

The Union Territories

	Name	**Extent**
1.	Delhi	The territory which immediately before the commencement of this Constitution was comprised in the Chief Commissioner's Province of Delhi.
2.	Himachal Pradesh	The territories which immediately before the commencement of this Constitution were being administered as if they were Chief Com- missioner's Provinces under the names of Himachal Pradesh and Bilaspur.
3.	Manipur	The territory which immediately before the commencement of this Constitution was being administered as if it were a Chief Com- missioner's Province under the name of Manipur.
4.	Tripura	The territory which immediately before the commencement of this Constitution was being administered as if it were a Chief Commissioner's Province under the name of Tripura.
5.	The Andaman & Nicobar Islands	The territory which immediately before the commencement of this Constitution was

	comprised in the Chief Commissioner's Province of the Andaman and Nicobar Islands.
6. The Laccadive	The territory specified in section 6 of the Minicoy and States Reorganisation Act, 1956.". Amindivi Islands.

3. Amendment of article 80 and Fourth Schedule.-(1) In article 80 of the Constitution,- (a) in sub-clause (b) of clause (1), after the word "States", the words "and of the Union territories" shall be added; (b) in clause (2), after the words "of the States", the words "and of the Union territories" shall be inserted; (c) in clause (4), the words and letters "specified in Part A or Part B of the First Schedule" shall be omitted; and (d) in clause (5), for the words and letter "States specified in Part of the First Schedule", the words "Union territories" shall be substituted. (2) For the Fourth Schedule to the Constitution as amended by the States Reorganisation Act, 1956, and the Bihar and West Bengal (Transfer of Territories) Act, 1956, the following Schedule shall be substituted, namely:-

"FOURTH SCHEDULE
[ARTICLES 4(1) AND 80(2)]

Allocation of Seats in the Council of States

To each State or Union territory specified in the first column of the following table, there shall be allotted the number of seats specified in the second column thereof opposite to that State or that Union territory, as the case may be.

TABLE

1.	Andhra Pradesh	.18
2.	Assam	7
3.	Bihar	22
4.	Bombay	27
5.	Kerala	9
6.	Madhya Pradesh	16
7.	Madras	17
8.	Mysore	12
9.	Orissa	10

10.	Punjab	11
11.	Rajasthan	10
12.	Uttar Pradesh	34
13.	West Bengal	16
14.	Jammu and Kashmir	4
15.	Delhi	3
16.	Himachal Pradesh	2
17.	Manipur	1
18.	Tripura	1
	Total	220".

4. Substitution of new articles for articles 81 and 82.-For articles 81 and 82 of the Constitution, the following articles shall be substituted, namely:-

"81. Composition of the House of the People.-(1) Subject to the provisions of article 331, the House of the People shall consist of- (a) not more than five hundred members chosen by direct election from territorial constituencies in the States, and (b) not more than twenty members to represent the Union territories, chosen in such manner as Parliament may by law provide.

(2) For the purposes of sub-clause (a) of clause (1),- (a) there shall be allotted to each State a number of seats in the House of the People in such manner that the ratio between that number and the population of the State is, so far as practicable, the same for all States; and (b) each State shall be divided into territorial constituencies in such manner that the ratio between the population of each constitu- ency and the number of seats allotted to it is, so far as practicable, the same throughout the State.

(3) In this article, the expression "population" means the population as ascertained at the last preceding census of which the relevant figures have been published.

82. Readjustment after each census.-Upon the completion of each census, the allocation of seats in the House of the People to the States and the division of each State into territorial constituencies shall be readjusted by such authority and in such manner as Parliament may by law determine:

Provided that such readjustment shall not affect representation in the House of the People until the dissolution of the then existing House.".

5. Amendment of article 131.-In article 131 of the Constitution, for the proviso, the following proviso shall be substituted, namely:-

"Provided that the said jurisdiction shall not extend to a dispute arising out of any treaty, agreement, covenant, engagement, sanad or other similar instrument which, having been entered into or executed before the commencement of this Constitution, continues in operation after such commencement, or which provides that the said jurisdiction shall not extend to such a dispute.".

6. Amendment of article 153.-To article 153 of the Constitution, the following proviso shall be added, namely:-

"Provided that nothing in this article shall prevent the appointment of the same person as Governor for two or more States.".

7. Amendment of article 158.-In article 158 of the Constitution, after clause (3), the following clause shall be inserted, namely:-

"(3A) Where the same person is appointed as Governor of two or more States, the emoluments and allowances payable to the Governor shall be allocated among the States in such proportion as the President may by order determine.".

8. Amendment of article 168.-(1) in clause (1) of article 168 of the Constitution, in sub-clause (a), after the word "Madras", the word "Mysore" shall be inserted. (2) In the said sub-clause, as from such date as the President may, by public notification, appoint, after the word "Bombay", the words "Madhya Pradesh" shall be inserted.

9. Substitution of new article for article 170.-For article 170 of the Constitution, the following article shall be subsituted, namely:-

"170. Composition of the Legislative Assemblies.-(1) Subject to the provisions of article 333, the Legislative Assembly of each State shall consist of not more than five hundred, and not less than sixty, members chosen by direct election from territorial constituencies in the State.

(2) For the purposes of clause (1), each State shall be divided into territorial constituencies in such manner that the ratio between the population of each constituency and the number of seats allotted to it shall, so far as practicable, be the same throughout the State.

Explanation.-In this clause, the expression "population" means the population as ascertained at the last preceding census of which the relevant figures have been published.

(3) Upon the completion of each census, the total number of seats in the Legislative Assembly of each State and the division of each State into territorial constituencies shall be readjusted by such authority and in such manner as Parliament may by law determine:

Provided that such readjustment shall not affect representation in the Legislative Assembly until the dissolution of the then existing Assembly.".

10. Amendment of article 171.-In clause (1) of article 171 of the Constitution, for the word "one-fourth", the word "one-third" shall be substituted.

11. Amendment of article 216.-In article 216 of the Constitution, the proviso shall be omitted.

12. Amendment of article 217.-In article 217 of the Constitution, in clause (1), for the words "shall hold office until he attains the age of sixty years", the following words and figures shall be substituted, namely:- "shall hold office, in the case of an additional or acting Judge, as provided in article 224, and in any other case, until he attains the age of sixty years".

13. Substitution of new article for article 220.-For article 220 of the Constitution, the following article shall be substituted, namely:-

"220. Restriction on practice after being a permanent Judge.- No person who, after the commencement of this Constitution, has held office as a permanent Judge of a High Court shall plead or act in any court or before any authority in India except the Supreme Court and the other High Courts.

Explanation.-In this article, the expression "High Court" does not include a High Court for a State specified in Part B of the First Schedule as it existed before the commencement of the Constitution (Seventh Amendment) Act, 1956.".

14. Amendment of article 222.-In article 222 of the Constitution,--- (a) in clause (1), the words "within the territory of India" shall be omitted; and (b) clause (2) shall be omitted.

15. Substitution of new article for article 224.-For article 224 of the Constitution, the following article shall be substituted, namely:-

"224. Appointment of additional and acting Judges.-(1) If by reason of any temporary increase in the business of a High Court or by reason of arrears of work therein, it appears to the President that the number of the Judges of that Court should be for the time being increased, the President may appoint duly qualified persons to be additional Judges of the Court for such period not exceeding two years as he may specify. (2) When any Judge of a High Court other than the Chief Justice is by reason of absence or for any other reason unable to perform the duties of his office or is appointed to act temporarily as Chief Justice, the President may appoint a duly qualified person to act as a Judge of that Court until the permanent Judge has resumed his duties. (3) No person appointed as an additional or acting Judge of a High Court shall hold office after attaining the age of sixty years.".

16. Substitution of new articles for articles 230, 231 and 232.- For articles 230, 231 and 232 of articles the Constitution, the following shall be substituted, namely:-

"230. Extension of jurisdiction of High Courts to Union territories.- (1) Parliament may by law extend the jurisdiction of a High Court to, or exclude the jurisdiction of a High Court from, any Union territory. (2) Where the High Court of a State exercises jurisdiction in relation to a Union territory,- (a) nothing in this Constitution shall be construed as empowering the Legislature of the State to increase, restrict or abolish that jurisdiction; and (b) the reference in article 227 to the Governor shall, in relation to any rules, forms or tables for subordinate courts in that territory, be construed as a reference to the President.

231. Establishment of a common High Court for two or more States.- (1) Notwithstanding anything contained in the preceding provisions of this Chapter, Parliament may by law establish a common High Court for two or more States or for two or more States and a Union territory. (2) In relation to any such High Court,- (a) the reference in article 217 to the Governor of the State shall, be construed as a reference to the Governors of all the States in relation to which the High Court exercises jurisdiction; (b) the reference in article 227 to the Governor shall, in relation to any rules, forms or tables for subordinate courts, be construed as a reference to the Governor of the State in which the subordinate courts are situate; and (c) the references in articles 219 and 229 to the State shall be construed as a reference to the State in which the High Court has its principal seat:

Provided that if such principal seat is in a Union territory, the references in articles 219 and 229 to the Governor, Public Service Commission,. Legislature and Consolidated Fund of the State shall be construed respectively as references to the President, Union Public Service Commission, Parliament and Consolidated Fund of India.".

17. Amendment of Part VIII.-In Part VIII of the Constitution,- (a) for the heading "THE STATES IN PART C OF THE FIRST SCHEDULE", the heading "THE UNION TERRITORIES" shall be substituted; and (b) for articles 239 and 240, the following articles shall be substituted namely:-

"239. Administration of Union territories.-(1) Save as otherwise provided by Parliament by law, every Union territory shall be administered by the President acting, to such extent as he thinks fit, through an administrator to be appointed by him with such designa- tion as he may specify.

(2) Notwithstanding anything contained in Part VI, the President may appoint the Governor of a State as the

administrator of an adjoining Union territory, and where a Governor is so appointed, he shall exercise his functions as such administrator independently of his Council of Ministers.

240. Power of President to make regulations for certain Union territories.- (1) The President may make regulations for the peace, progress and good government of the Union territory of- (a) the Andaman and Nicobar Islands; (b) the Laccadive, Minicoy and Amindivi Islands. (2) Any regulation so made may repeal or amend any Act made by Parliament or any existing law which is for the time being ap- plicable to the Union territory and, when promulgated by the President, shall have the same force and effect as an Act of Parliament which applies to that territory.".

18. Insertion of new article 258A.- After article 258 of the Constitution, the following article shall be inserted, namely:-

"258A Power of the States to entrust functions to the Union.- Not- withstanding anything in this Constitution, the Governor of a State may, with the consent of the Government of India, entrust either conditionally or unconditionally to that Government or to its officers functions in relation to any matter to which the executive power of the State extends.".

19. Insertion of new article 290A.-After article 290 of the Constitution, the following article shall be inserted, namely:-

"290A. Annual payment to certain Devaswom Funds.-A sum of forty-six lakhs and fifty thousand rupees shall be charged on, and paid out of, the Consolidated Fund of the State of Kerala every year to the Travan- core Devaswom Fund; and a sum of thirteen lakhs and fifty thousand rupees shall be charged on, and paid out of, the Consolidated Fund of the State of Madras every year to the Devaswom Fund established in that State for the maintenance of Hindu temples and shrines in the territories transferred to that State on the 1st day of November, 1956, from the State of Travancore-Cochin.".

20. Substitution of new article for article 298.- For article 298 of the Constitution, the following article shall be substituted, namely:-

"298. Power to carry on trade, etc.-The executive power of

the Union and of each State shall extend to the carrying on of any trade or business and to the acquisition, holding and disposal of property and the making of contracts for any purpose:

Provided that- (a) the said executive power of the Union shall, in so far as such trade or business or such purpose is not one with respect to which Parliament may make laws, be subject in each State to legislation by the State; and (b) the said executive power of each State shall, in so far as such trade or business or such purpose is not one with respect to which the State Legislature may make laws, be subject to legislation by Parliament.".

21. Insertion of new articles 350A and 350B.-After article 350 of the Constitution, the following articles shall be inserted, namely:-

"350A. Facilities for instruction in mother-tongue at primary stage.-It shall be the endeavour of every State and of every local authority within the State to provide adequate facilities for instruction in the mother-tongue at the primary stage of education to children belonging to linguistic minority groups; and the President may issue such directions to any State as he considers necessary or proper for securing the provision of such facilities.

350B. Special Officer for linguistic minorities.-(1) There shall be a Special Officer for linguistic minorities to be appointed by the President. (2) It shall be the duty of the Special Officer to investigate all matters relating to the safeguards provided for linguistic minorities under this Constitution and report to the President upon those matters at such intervals as the President may direct, and the President shall cause all such reports to be laid before each House of Parliament, and sent to the Governments of the States concerned.".

22. Substitution of new article for article 371.-For article 371 of the Constitution, the following article shall be substituted, namely:-

"371. Special provision with respect to the States of Andhara Pradesh, Punjab and Bombay.-(1) Notwithstanding anything in this Constitution, the President may, by order made with respect to the State of Andhra Pradesh or Punjab, provide for the constitution and functions of regional committees of the Legislative Assembly of the State, for the modifications to be made in the rules of business of the Government and in the rules of procedure of the Legislative Assembly of the State and for any special responsibility of the Governor in order to secure the proper functioning of the regional committees.

(2) Notwithstanding anything in this Constitution, the President may by order made with respect to the State of Bombay, provide for any special responsibility of the Governor for- (a) the establishment of separate development boards for Vidarbha, Marathwada. the rest of Maharashtra, Saurashtra, Kutch and the rest of Gujarat with the provision that a report on the working of each of these boards will be placed each year before the State Legislative Assembly; (b) the equitable allocation of funds for developmental expenditure over the said areas, subject to the requirements of the State as a whole; and (c) an equitable arrangement providing adequate facilities for technical education and vocational training, and adequate opportunities for employment in services under the control of the State Government, in respect of all the said areas, subject to the requirements of the State as a whole.".

23. Insertion of new article 372A.-After article 372 of the Constitution, the following article shall be inserted, namely:-

"372A. Power of the President to adapt laws.-(1) For the purposes of bringing the provisions of any law in force in India or in any part thereof, immediately before the commencement of the Constitution (Seventh Amendment) Act, 1956, into accord with the provisions of this Constitution as amended by that Act, the President may by order made before the 1st day of November, 1957, make such adaptations and modifications of the law, whether by way of repeal or amendment, as may be necessary or expedient, and provide that the law shall, as from such date as may be specified in the order, have effect subject to the adaptations and modifications so made, and any such adaptation or modification shall not be questioned in any court of law. (2) Nothing in clause (1) shall be deemed to prevent a competent legislature or other competent authority from repealing or amending any law adapted or modified by the President under the said clause.".

24. Insertion of new article 378A.-After article 378 of the Constitution, the following article shall be inserted, namely:-

"378A. Special provision as to duration of Andhra Pradesh Legislative Assembly.- Notwithstanding anything contained in article 172, the Legislative Assembly of the State of Andhra Pradesh as constituted under the provisions of sections 28 and 29 of the State Reorganisation Act, 1956, shall, unless sooner dissolved, continue for a period of five years from the date referred to in the said section 29 and no longer and the expiration of the said period shall operate as a dissolution of that Legislative Assembly.".

25. Amendment of Second Schedule.-In the Second Schedule to the Constitution,- (a) in the heading of Part D, the words and letter "in States in Part A of the First Schedule" shall be omitted; (b) in sub-paragraph (1) of paragraph 9, for the words "shall be reduced by the amount of that pension", the following shall be substituted, namely:-

"shall be reduced- (a) by the amount of that pension, and (b) if he has, before such appointment, received in lieu of a portion of the pension due to him in respect of such previous service the commuted value thereof, by the amount of that portion of the pension, and (c) if he has, before such appointment, received a retirement gratuity in respect of such previous service, by the pension equivalent of that gratuity"; and (c) in paragraph 10- (i) for sub-paragraph (1), the following sub-paragraph shall be substituted, namely:-

"(1) There shall be paid to the Judges of High Courts, in respect of time spent on actual service, salary at the following rates per mensem, that is to say,-

The Chief Justice.. 4,000 rupees

Any other Judge.. 3,500 rupees:

Provided that if a Judge of a High Court at the time of his appointment is in receipt of a pension (other than a disability or wound pension) in respect of any previous service under the Government of India or any of its predecessor Governments or under the Government of a State or any of its predecessor Governments, his salary in respect of service in the High Court shall be reduced- (a) by the amount of that pension, and (b) if he has, before such appointment, received in lieu of a portion of the pension due to him in respect of such previous service the commuted value thereof, by the amount of that portion of the pension, and (c) if he has, before such appointment, received a retirement gratuity in respect of such previous service, by the pension equivalent of that gratuity."; and (ii) for sub-paragraphs (3) and (4), the following sub-paragraph shall be substituted, namely:-

"(3) Any person who, immediately before the commencement of the Constitution (Seventh Amendment) Act, 1956 was holding office as the Chief Justice of the High Court of a State specified in Part B of the First Schedule and has on such commencement become the Chief Justice of the High Court of a State specified in the said Schedule as amended by the said Act, shall, if he was immediately before such commencement drawing any amount as allowance in addition to his salary, be entitled to receive in respect of time spent on actual service as such Chief Justice, the same amount as allowance in addition to the salary specified in sub-paragraph (1) of this paragraph.".

26. Modification of entries in the Lists relating to acquisition and requisitioning of property.-In the Seventh Schedule to the Constitution, entry 33 of the Union List and entry 36 of the State List shall be omitted and for entry 42 of the Concurrent List, the following entry shall be substituted, namely:-

"42. Acquisition and requisitioning of property. .

27. Amendment of certain provisions relating to ancient and historical monuments, etc.-In each of the following provisions of the Constitution, namely:-

(i) entry 67 of the Union List,

(ii) entry 12 of the State List,

(iii) entry 40 of the Concurrent List, and

(iv) article 49, for the words "declared by Parliament by law", the words "declared by or under law made by Parliament" shall be substituted.

28. Amendment of entry 24 of State List.-In the Seventh Schedule to the Constitution, in entry 24 of the State List, for the word and figures "entry 52", the words and figures "entries 7 and 52" shall be substituted.

29. Consequential and minor amendments and repeals and savings.- (1) The consequential and minor amendments and repeals directed in the Schedule shall be made in the Constitution and in the Constitution (Removal of Difficulties) Order, No. VIII, made under article 392 of the Constitution.

(2) Notwithstanding the repeal of article 243 of the Constitution by the said Schedule, all regulations made by the President under that article and in force immediately before the commencement of this Act shall continue in force until altered or repealed or amended by a competent Legislature or other competent authority.

THE CONSTITUTION (NINTH AMENDMENT) ACT, 1960

Statement of Objects and Reasons appended to the Constitution (Ninth Amendment) Bill, 1960 (Bill No. 90 of 1960) which was enacted as THE CONSTITUTION (Ninth Amendment) Act, 1960

[28th December, 1960.]

An Act further to amend the Constitution of India to give effect to the transfer of certain territories to Pakistan in pursuance of the agreements entered into between the Governments of India and Pakistan.

BE it enacted by Parliament in the Eleventh Year of the Republic of India as follows:-

1. Short title.-This Act may be called the Constitution (Ninth Amendment) Act, 1960.

2. Definitions.- In this Act,-

(a) "appointed day" means such date_661 as the Central Government may, by notification in the Official Gazette, appoint as the date for the transfer of territories to Pakistan in pursuance of the Indo-Pakistan agreements, after causing the territories to be so transferred and referred to in the First Schedule demarcated for the purpose, and different dates1 may be appointed for the transfer of such territories from different States and from the Union territory of Tripura;

(b) "Indo-Pakistan agreements" mean the Agreements dated the 10th day of September, 1958, the 23rd day of October, 1959 and the 11th day of January, 1960, entered into between the Governments of India and Pakistan, the relevant extracts of which are set out in the Second Schedule;

(c) "transferred territory" means so much of the territories comprised in the Indo-Pakistan agreements and referred to in the First Schedule as are demarcated for the purpose of being transferred to Pakistan in pursuance of the said agreements.

3. Amendment of the First Schedule to the Constitution.- As from the appointed day, in the First Schedule to the Constitution,-

(a) in the paragraph relating to the territories of the State of Assam the words, brackets and figures "and the territories referred to in Part I of the First Schedule to the Constitution (Ninth Amendment) Act, 1960" shall be added at the end;

(b) in the paragraph relating to the territories of the State of Punjab, the words, brackets and figures "but excluding the territories referred to in Part II of the First Schedule to the Constitution (Ninth Amendment) Act, 1960" shall be added at the end;

(c) in the paragraph relating to the territories of the State of West Bengal, the words, brackets and figures "but excluding the territories referred to in Part III of the First Schedule to the Constitution (Ninth Amendment) Act, 1960" shall be added at the end;

(d) in the paragraph relating to the extent of the Union territory of Tripura, the words, brackets and figures "but excluding the territories referred to in Part IV of the First Schedule to the Constitution (Ninth Amendment) Act, 1960" shall be added at the end.

[See Sections 2(a), 2(c) and 3]

PART I

The transferred territory in relation to item (7) of paragraph

2 of the Agreement dated the 10th day of September, 1958, and item (i) of paragraph 6 of the Agreement dated the 23rd day of October, 1959.

PART II

The transferred territory in relation to item (i) and item (iv) of paragraph 1 of the Agreement dated the 11th day of January, 1960.

PART III

The transferred territory in relation to item (3), item (5) and item (10) of paragraph 2 of the Agreement dated the 10th day of September, 1958, and paragraph 4 of the Agreement dated the 23rd day of October, 1959.

PART IV

The transferred territory in relation to item (8) of paragraph 2 of the Agreement dated the 10th day of September, 1958.

THE SECOND SCHEDULE

[SEE SECTION 2(B)]

1. EXTRACTS FROM THE NOTE CONTAINING THE AGREEMENT DATED THE 10TH DAY OF SEPTEMBER, 1958

2. As a result of the discussions, the following agreements were arrived at:-

(3) Berubari Union No. 12

This will be so divided as to give half the area to Pakistan the other half adjacent to India being retained by India. The division of Berubari Union No. 12 will be horizontal, starting from the north-east corner of Debiganj thana.

The division should be made in such a manner that the Cooch Behar enclaves between Pachagar thana of East Pakistan and Berubari Union No. 12 of Jalpaiguri thana of West Bengal will remain connected as at present with Indian territory and will remain with India. The Cooch Behar enclaves lower down between Boda thana of East Pakistan and Berubari Union No. 12 will be exchanged alongwith the general exchange of enclaves and will go to Pakistan.

(5) 24 Parganas---Khulna 24 Parganas---Jessore Boundary disputes.

It is agreed that the mean of the two respective claims of India and Pakistan should be adopted, taking the river as a guide, as far as possible, in the case of the latter dispute (Ichhamati river).

(7) Piyain and Surma river regions to be demarcated in accordance with the relevant notifications, cadastral survey maps and, if necessary, record of rights. Whatever the result of this demarcation might be, the nationals of both the Governments to have the facility of navigation on both these rivers.

(8) Government of India agree to give in perpetual right to Pakistan the land belonging to Tripura State to the west of the railway line as well as the land appurtenant to the railway line at Bhagalpur.

(10) Exchange of old Cooch Behar enclaves in Pakistan and Pakistan enclaves in India without claim to compensation for extra area going to Pakistan, is agreed to.

(Sd.) M. S. A. BAIG, Foreign Secretary, Ministry of Foreign Affairs and Commonwealth Relations, Government of Pakistan.

(Sd.) M. J. DESAI, Commonwealth Secretary, Ministry of External Affairs, Government of India.

NEW DELHI, THE SEPTEMBER 10, 1958.

2. EXTRACTS FROM AGREEMENT ENTITLED "AGREED DECISIONS AND PRO- CEDURES TO END DISPUTES AND INCIDENTS ALONG THE INDO-EAST PAKISTAN BORDER AREAS", DATED THE 23RD DAY OF OCTOBER, 1959.

4. West Bengal-East Pakistan Boundary Over 1,200 miles of this boundary have already been demarcated. As regards the boundary between West Bengal and East Pakistan in the areas of Mahananda, Burung and Karatoa rivers, It was agreed that demarcation will be made in accordance with the latest cadastral survey maps supported by relevant notifications and record-of-rights.

6. Assam-East Pakistan Boundary.

(i) The dispute concerning Bagge Award III has been settled by adopting the following rational boundary in the Patharia Forest Reserve region:

From a point marked X (H522558) along the Radcliffe Line BA on the old Patharia Reserve Boundary as shown in the topographical map sheet No. 83D/5, the boundary line shall run in close proximity and parallel to the cart road to its south to a point A (H531554); thence in a southerly direction up the spur and along the ridge to a hill top marked B (H523529); thence in a south-easterly direction along the ridge down the spur across a stream to a hill top marked C (H532523); thence in a southerly direction to a point D (H530517); thence in a south-westerly direction to a flat top E (H523507); thence in a southerly direction to a point F (H524500); thence in a south-easterly direction in a straight line to the mid-stream point of the Gandhai Nala marked G (H540494); thence in south-westerly direction up the mid-stream of Gandhai Nala to point H (H533482); thence in a south-westerly direction up a spur and along the ridge to a point I (H517460); thence in a southerly direction to a point on the ridge marked J (H518455); thence in a south-westerly direction along the ridge to a point height 364 then continues along the same direction along the same ridge to a point marked K (H500428); thence in a south and south-westerly direction along the same ridge to a point marked L (H496420); thence in a south- easterly direction along the same ridge to a point marked M (H499417); thence in a south-westerly direction along the ridge to a point on the bridle path with a height 587; then up the spur to the hill top marked N (H487393); then in a south-easterly and southerly direction along the ridge to the hill top with height 692; thence in a southerly direction down the spur to a point on Buracherra marked O (H484344); thence in a south-westerly direction up the spur along the ridge to the trigonometrical survey station with height 690; thence in a southerly direction along the ridge to a point height 490 (H473292); thence in a straight line due south to a point on the eastern boundary of the Patharia Reserve Forest marked Y (H473263); along the Radcliffe Line BA

The line described above has been plotted on two copies of topographical map sheets Nos. 83D/5, 83D/6 and 83D/2.

The technical experts responsible for the ground demarcation will have the authority to make minor adjustments in order to make the boundary alignment agree with the physical features as described.

The losses and gains to either country as a result of these adjustments with respect to the line marked on the map will be balanced by the technical experts.

(Sd.) J. G. KHARAS, Acting Foreign Secretary, Ministry of Foreign Affairs and Commonwealth Relations, Karachi.

(Sd.) M. J. DESAI, Commonwealth Secretary, Ministry of External Affairs, New Delhi.

NEW DELHI; OCTOBER 23, 1959.

3. EXTRACTS FROM THE AGREEMENT ENTITLED "AGREED DECISIONS AND PROCEDURES TO END DISPUTES AND INCIDENTS ALONG THE INDO-WEST PAKISTAN BORDER AREAS", DATED THE 11TH DAY OF JANUARY, 1960.

1. West Pakistan-Punjab border.-Of the total of 325 miles of the border in this sector, demarcation has been completed along about 252 miles. About 73 miles of the border has not yet been demarcated due to differences between the Governments of India and Pakistan regarding interpretation of the decision and Award of the Punjab Boundary Commission presented by Sir Cyril Radcliffe as Chairman of the Commission. These differences have been settled along the lines given below in a spirit of accommodation:

(i) The Sarja Marja, Rakh Hardit Singh and Pathanke (Amritsar- Lahore border).-The Governments of India and Pakistan agree that the boundary between West-Pakistan and India in the this region should follow the boundary between the Tehsils of Lahore and Kasur as laid down under Punjab Government Notification No. 2183-E, dated 2nd June, 1939. These three villages will in consequence, fall within the territorial jurisdiction of the Government of Pakistan.

(iv) Suleimanke (Ferozepur-Montgomery border).-The Governments of India and Pakistan agree to adjust the district boundaries in this region as specified in the attached Schedule and as shown in the map appended thereto as Annexure I.

(Sd.) M. J. DESAI, Commonwealth Secretary, Ministry of External Affairs, Government of India.

(Sd.) J. G. KHARAS, Joint Secretary, Ministry of Foreign Affairs and Commonwealth Relations, Government of Pakistan.

NEW DELHI; JANUARY 11, 1960.

THE CONSTITUTION (TENTH AMENDMENT) ACT, 1961

Statement of Objects and Reasons appended to the Constitution (Tenth Amendment) Bill, 1961 (Bill No. 43 of 1961) which was enacted as THE CONSTITUTION (Tenth Amendment) Act,1961

STATEMENT OF OBJECTS AND REASONS

The people and the Varishta Panchayat of Free Dadra and Nagar Haveli have repeatedly affirmed their request to the Government of India for integration of their territories with the Union of India to which they rightly belong. Their request was recently embodied in a formal Resolution adopted by the Varishta Panchayat on the 12th June, 1961. In deference to the desire and request of the people of Free Dadra and Nagar Haveli for integration of their territories with the Union of India, the Government of India have decided that these territories should form part of the Union of India.

It is proposed to specify these areas expressly as the Union territory of Dadra and Nagar Haveli by amending the First Schedule to the Constitution. It is further proposed to amend clause (1) of article 240 of the Constitution to include therein the Union territory of Dadra and Nagar Haveli in order to enable the President to make regulations for the peace, progress and good government of the territory.

The Bill seeks to give effect to these proposals.

NEW DELHI. JAWAHARLAL NEHRU.

Statement of Objects and Reasons appended to the

Constitution (Tenth Amendment) Bill, 1956 (Bill No. 35 of 1956) which was enacted as THE CONSTITUTION (Sixth Amendment) Act, 1956

STATEMENT OF OBJECTS AND REASONS

While "taxes on the sale or purchase of goods other than newspapers" is an entry in the State List, article 286 of the Constitution subjects the States' power to impose such taxes to four restrictions, of which two are total and two are partial. Under clause (1) of the article, a State is debarred from imposing such a tax when the sale or purchase takes place outside the State or in the course of import into, or export from, the country. With regard to the first restriction, namely, the non-taxability of sales outside the State, an explanation is given in the clause that "a sale or purchase shall be deemed to have taken place in the State in which goods have actually been delivered as a direct result of such sale or purchase for the purpose of consumption in that State". Then, under clause (2), a State is debarred from imposing the tax on inter-State sales except in so far as Parliament may otherwise provide. Lastly, under clause (3), Parliament is authorised to declare the goods which are essential to the life of the community, and when such a declaration has been made, any law made by a State legislature imposing a tax on the sale or purchase of those goods has to receive the President's assent in order to be effective.

High judicial authorities have found the interpretation of the article a difficult task and expressed divergent views as to the scope and effect, in particular, of the explanation in clause (1) and of clause (2). The majority view of the Supreme Court in the State of Bombay v. the United Motors (India) Ltd., (1953) S.C.R. 1069, was that sub-clause (a) and the explanation in clause (1) prohibited the taxation of a sale involving inter-State elements by all States except the State in which the goods are delivered for the purpose of consumption therein, and further more, that clause (2) did not affect the power of that State to tax the inter-State sale even though Parliament had not made a law removing the ban imposed by that clause. This resulted in dealers resident in one State being subjected to the sales tax jurisdiction and procedure of several other States with which they had dealings in the normal course of their business. Two-and-a-half years later, the second part of this decision was reversed by the Supreme Court in the Bengal Immunity Company Ltd. v. the State of Bihar. (1955) S.C.A. 1140 but here too the Court was not unanimous.

In pursuance of clause (3) of the article, Parliament passed an Act in 1952 declaring a number of goods like foodstuffs of various kinds, cloth, raw cotton, cattle feeds, iron and steel, coal, etc., to be essential to the life of the community. Since this declaration could not affect pre-existing State laws imposing sales tax on these goods, the result was a wide disparity from State to States, not only in the range of exempted goods, but also in the rates applicable to them.

The Taxation Enquiry Commission, after examining the problem with great care and throughness, have made certain recommendations which may be summarised as follows. In essence, sales tax must continue to be a State source of revenue and its levy and administration must substantially pertain to the State Governments.

The sphere of power and responsibility of the State may, however, be said to end, and that of the Union to begin, when the sales tax of one State impinges, administratively on the dealers, and fiscally on the consumers, of another State. Broadly, therefore, inter-State sales should be the concern of the Union, but the responsibilities pertaining to the Union could be exercised through the State Governments, and in any case, the revenue should appropriately devolve on them.

Intra-State sales, on the other hand, should be left to the States, but with one important exception. Where, for instance, raw material produced in a State is important from the point of view of the consumer or the industry of another State, certain restrictions have to be placed on the taxing power of the State Government, as otherwise it can effect an increase in the cost of the manufactured article, whether such manufacture takes place in the State which produces the raw material, or in another State which imports the material from that State.

In either case, to the extent that the finished goods are consumed in a State other than the one which taxes the raw materal, the increase in cost on account of the tax is a matter of direct concern to the consumer of another State. Such cases of intra-State sales should apropriately be brought under the full control of the Union. These recommendations of the Commission have been generally accepted by all the State Governments.

The object of this Bill is to give effect to the recommendations of the Commission as regards the amendment of the constitutional provisions relating to sales tax.

In clause 2, it is proposed to add a new entry 92A in the Union List placing taxes on inter-State sales and purchases within the exclusive legislative and executive power of the Union, and to make entry 54 of the State List "subject to the provisions" of this new entry.

In clause 3, it is proposed to add these taxes to the list given in clause (1) of article 269, so that, although they will be levied and collected in accordance with an Act of Parliament, they will not form part of the Consolidated Fund of India, but will accrue to the States themselves in accordance with such principles of distribution as may be formulated by Parliament by law. A further provision is proposed in article 269 expressly empowering Parliament to formulate by law principles for determining when a sale or purchase of goods takes place in the course of inter-State trade or commerce.

It is proposed in clause 4 to omit from clause (1) of article 286 the explanation which has given rise to a great deal of legal controversy and practical difficulty. In view of the centralisation of inter-State sales tax proposed in clause 2 of this Bill clause (2) of article 286 in its present form will cease to be appropriate. In its place it is proposed to insert a provision empowering Parliament to formulate principles for determining when a sale or purchase of goods takes place (a) outside a State, or (b) in the course of import of the goods into the territory of India or (c) in the course of export of the goods out of the territory of India.

It is further proposed to replace clause (3) of article 286 by a new clause on the lines recommended by the Taxation Enquiry Commission. Under this revised clause Parliament will have the power to declare by law the goods which are of special importance in inter-State trade or commerce and also to specify the restrictions and conditions to which any State law (whether made before or after the Parliamentary law) will be subject in regard to the system of levy, rates and other incidents of the tax on the sale or purchase of those goods.

[BW DELHI; MANILAL SHAH.

The 30th April, 1956.

THE CONSTITUTION (TENTH AMENDMENT) ACT, 1961

[16th August, 1961.]

An Act further to amend the Constitution of India. BE it enacted by Parliament in the Twelfth Year of the Republic of India as follows:-

1. Short title and commencement.-(1) This Act may be called the Constitution (Tenth Amendment) Act, 1961.

(2) It shall be deemed to have come into force on the 11th day of August, 1961.

2. Amendment of the First Schedule to the Constitution.- In the First Schedule to the Constitution, under the heading "THE UNION TERRITORIES", after entry 6, the following entry shall be inserted, namely:-

"7. Dadra and Nagar Haveli	The territory which immediately before the eleventh day of August, 1961 was comprised in Free Dadra and Nagar Haveli.".

3. Amendment of article 240.-In article 240 of the Constitution, in clause (1), after entry (b), the following entry shall be inserted, namely:-

"(c) Dadra and Nagar Haveli.".

THE CONSTITUTION (ELEVENTH AMENDMENT) ACT, 1961

Statement of Objects and Reasons appended to the

Constitution (Eleventh Amendment) Bill, 1961 which was enacted as the Constitution (Eleventh Amendment) Act, 1961

[19th December,1961.]

An Act further to amend the Constitution of India.

BE it enacted by Parliament in the Twelfth Year of the Republic of India as follows:-

1. Short title.-This Act may be called the Constitution (Eleventh Amendment) Act, 1961.

(2) Amendment of article 66.-In article 66 of the Constitution, in clause (1), for the words "members of both Houses of Parliament assembled at a joint meeting", the words "members of an electoral college consisting of the members of both Houses of Parliament" shall be substituted.

3. Amendment of article 71.-In article 71 of the Constitution, after clause (3), the following clause shall be inserted, namely:- "(4) The election of a person as President or Vice-President shall not be called in question on the ground of the existence of any vacancy for whatever reason among the members of the electoral college electing him.".

THE CONSTITUTION (TWELFTH AMENDMENT) ACT, 1962

Statement of Objects and Reasons appended to the Constitution (Twelfth Amendment) Bill, 1962 which was enacted as the Constitution (Twelfth Amendment) Act, 1962

[27th March, 1962.]

An Act further to amend the Constitution of India.

BE it enacted by Parliament in the Thirteenth Year of the Republic of India as follows:-

1. Short title and commencement.-(1) This Act may be called the Constitution (Twelfth Amendment) Act, 1962.

(2) It shall be deemed to have come into force on the 20th day of December 1961.

2. Amendment of the First Schedule to the Constitution.- In the First Schedule to the Constitution, under the heading

"THE UNION TERRITORIES", after entry 7, the following entry shall be inserted, namely:-

8. Goa, Daman and Diu	The territories which immediately before the twentieth day of December, 1961 were comprised in Goa, Daman and Diu.".

3. Amendment of article 240.-In article 240 of the Constitution, in clause (1), after entry (c), the following entry shall be inserted, namely:-

"(d) Goa, Daman and Diu.".

THE CONSTITUTION (THIRTEENTH AMENDMENT) ACT, 1962

Statement of Objects and Reasons appended to the Constitution (Thirteenth Amendment) Bill, 1962 which was enacted as the Constitution (Thirteenth Amendment) Act, 1962

[28th December, 1962.]

An Act further to amend the Constitution of India.

BE it enacted by Parliament in the Thirteenth Year of the Republic of India as follows:--

1. Short title and commencement.-(1) This Act may be called the Constitution (Thirteenth Amendment) Act, 1962.

(2) It shall come into force on such date_662 as the Central

Government may, by notification in the Official Gazette, appoint.

2. Amendment of Part XXI.-In PART XXI of the Constitution,- (a) for the heading, the following beading shall be substituted, namely:- "TEMPORARY, TRANSITIONAL AND SPECIAL PROVISIONS";

(b) after article 371, the following article shall be inserted, namely:-

Special provision with respect to the State of Nagaland.

(b) Special provision with respect to the State of Nagaland.-
`371A. (1) Notwithstanding anything in this Constitution,-

(a) no Act of Parliament in respect of-

(i) religious or social practices of the Nagas,

(ii) Naga customary law and procedure,

(iii) administration of civil and criminal justice involving decisions according to Naga customary law,

(iv) ownership and transfer of land and its resources, shall apply to the State of Nagaland unless the Legislative Assembly of Nagaland by a resolution so decides;

(b) the Governor of Nagaland shall have special responsibility with respect to law and order in the State of Nagaland for so long as in his opinion internal disturbances occurring in the Naga Hills-Tuensang Area immediately before the formation of that State continue therein or in any part thereof and in the discharge of his functions in relation thereto the Governor shall, after consulting the Council of Ministers, exercise his individual judgment as to the action to be taken:

Provided that if any question arises whether any matter is or is not a matter as respects which the Governor is under this sub-clause required to act in the exercise of his individual judgment, the decision of the Governor in his discretion shall be final, and the validity of anything done by the Governor shall not be called in question on the ground that he ought or ought not to have acted in the exercise of his individual judgment: Provided further that if the President on receipt of a report from the Governor or otherwise is satisfied that it is no longer necessary for the Governor to have special responsibility with respect to law and order in the State of Nagaland, he may by order direct that the Governor shall cease to have such responsibility with effect from such date as may be specified in the order;

(c) in making his recommendation with respect to any demand for a grant, the Governor of Nagaland shall ensure that any money provided by the Government of India out of the Consolidated Fund of India for any specific service or purpose is included in the demand for a grant relating to that service or purpose and not in any other demand;

(d) as from such date as the Governor of Nagaland may by public notification in this behalf specify, there shall be established a regional council for the Tuensang district consisting of thirty-five members and the Governor shall in his discretion make rules providing for-

(i) the composition of the regional council and the manner in which the members of the regional council shall be chosen:

Provided that the Deputy Commissioner of the Tuensang district shall be the Chairman ex officio of the regional council and the Vice-Chairman of the regional council shall be elected by the members thereof from amongst themselves;

(ii) the qualifications for being chosen as, and for being, members, of the regional council;

(iii) the term of office of, and the salaries and allowances, if any, to be paid to members of, the regional council;

(iv) the procedure and conduct of business of the regional council;

(v) the appointment of officers and staff of the regional council and their conditions of services; and

(vi) any other matter in respect of which it is necessary to make rules for the constitution and proper functioning of the regional council.

(2) Notwithstanding anything in this Constitution, for a period of ten years from the date of the formation of the State of Nagaland or for such further period as the Governor may, on the recommendation of the regional council, by public notification specify in this behalf,-

(a) the administration of the Tuensang district shall be carried on by the Governor;

(b) where any money is provided by the Government of India to the Government of Nagaland to meet the requirements of the State of Nagaland as a whole, the Governor shall in his discretion arrange for an equitable allocation of that money between the Tuensang district and the rest of the State;

(c) no Act of the Legislature of Nagaland shall apply to the Tuensang district unless the Governor, on the recommendation of the regional council, by public notification so directs and the Governor in giving such direction with respect to any such Act may direct that the Act shall in its application to the Tuensang district or any part thereof have effect subject to such exceptions or modifications as the Governor may specify on the recommendation of the regional council: Provided that any direction given under this sub-clause may be given so as to have retrospective effect;

(d) the Governor may make regulations for the peace progress and good government of the Tuensang district and any regulations so made may repeal or amend with retrospective effect, if necessary, any Act of Parliament or any other law which is for the time being applicable to that district;

(e) (i) one of the members representing the Tuensang district in the Legislative Assembly of Nagaland shall be appointed Minister for Tuensang affairs by the Governor on the advice of the Chief Minister and the Chief Minister in tendering his advice shall act on the recommendation of the majority of the members as aforesaid;

(ii) the Minister for Tuensang affairs shall deal with, and have direct access to the Governor on, all matters relating to the Tuensang district but he shall keep the Chief Minister informed about the same;

(f) notwithstanding anything in the foregoing provisions of this clause, the final decision on all matters relating to the Tuensang district shall be made by the Governor in his discretion;

(g) in articles 54 and 55 and clause (4) of article 80, references to the elected members of the Legislative Assembly of a State or to each such member shall include references to the members or member of the Legislative Assembly of Nagaland elected by the regional council established under this article;

(h) in article 170- (i) clause (1) shall, in relation to the Legislative Assembly of Nagaland, have effect as if for the word `sixty', the words `forty-six' had been substituted; (ii) in the said clause the reference to direct election from territorial constituencies in the State shall include election by the members of the regional council established under this article; (iii) in clauses (2) and (3), references to territorial constituencies shall mean references to territorial constituencies in the Kohima and Mokokchung districts.

(3) If any difficulty arises in giving effect to any of the foregoing provisions of this article, the President may by order do anything (including any adaptation or modification of any other article) which appears to him to be necessary for the purpose of removing that difficulty:

Provided that no such order shall be made after the expiration of three years from the date of the formation of the State of Nagaland. Explanation.-In this article, the Kohima, Mokokchung and Tuensang districts shall have the same meanings as in the State of Nagaland Act, 1962.

THE CONSTITUTION (FOURTEENTH AMENDMENT) ACT, 1962

Statement of Objects and Reasons appended to the Constitution (Fourteenth Amendment) Bill, 1962 which was enacted as THE CONSTITUTION (Fourteenth Amendment) Act, 1962

[28th December, 1962.]

An Act further to amend the Constitution of India

BE it enacted by Parliament in the Thirteenth Year of the Republic of India as follows:-

1. Short title.-This Act may be called the Constitution (Fourteenth Amendment) Act, 1962.

2. Amendment of article 81.-In article 81 of the Constitution, in sub-clause (b) of clause (1), for the words "twenty members", the words "twenty-five members" shall be substituted.

3. Amendment of the First Schedule.-In the First Schedule to the Constitution, under the heading "II. THE UNION TERRITORIES", after entry 8, the following entry shall be inserted, namely:-

"9. Pondicherry The territories which immediately before the sixteenth day of August, 1962, were comprised in the French Establishments in India known as Pondicherry, Karikal, Mahe and Yanam.".

4. Insertion of new article 239A.-After article 239 of the Constitution, the following article shall be inserted, namely:- "239A. Creation of local Legislatures or Council of Ministers or both for certain Union territories.-(1) Parliament may by law

create for any of the Union territories of Himachal Pradesh, Manipur, Tripura, Goa, Daman and Diu, and Pondicherry-

(a) a body, whether elected or partly nominated and partly elected, to function as a Legislature for the Union territory, or

(b) a Council of Ministers, or both with such constitution, powers and functions, in each case, as may be specified in the law.

(2) Any such law as is referred to in clause (1) shall not be deemed to be an amendment of this Constitution for the purposes of article 368 notwithstanding that it contains any provision which amends or has the effect of amending this Constitution.".

5. Amendment of article 240.-In article 240 of the Constitution, in clause (1),-

(a) after entry (d), the following entry shall be inserted, namely:- "(e) Pondicherry:";

(b) the following proviso shall be inserted at the end, namely:- "Provided that when any body is created under article 239A to function as a Legislature for the Union territory of Goa, Daman and Diu or Pondicherry, the President shall not make any regulation for the peace, progress and good government of that Union territory with effect from the date appointed for the first meeting of the Legislature.".

6. Amendment of the Fourth Schedule.-In the Fourth Schedule to the Constitution, in the Table,-

(a) after entry 20, the entry "21. Pondicherry........1" shall be inserted; (b) for the figures "225", the figures "226" shall be substituted.

7. Retrospective operation of certain provisions.-Section 3 and clause (a) of section 5 shall be deemed to have come into force on the 16th day of August, 1962.

EXTRACTS FROM THE CONSTITUTION (FORTY-FOURTH AMENDMENT) ACT, 1978

1. Short title and commencement.- (1) (2) It shall come into force on such date as the Central Government may, by notification in the Official Gazette, appoint and different dates may be appointed for different provisions of this Act.

3. Amendment of article 22.- In article 22 of the Constitution,- (a) for clause (4), the following clause shall be substituted, namely:- '(4) No law providing for preventive detention shall authorise the detention of a person for a longer period than two months unless an Advisory Board constituted in accordance with the recommendations of the Chief Justice of the appropriate High Court has reported before the expiration of the said period of two months that there is in its opinion sufficient cause for such detention:

Provided that an Advisory Board shall consist of a Chairman and not less than two other members, and the Chairman shall be a serving Judge of the appropriate High Court and the other members shall be serving or retired Judges of any High Court:

Provided further that nothing in this clause shall authorise the detention of any person beyond the maximum period prescribed by any law made by Parliament under sub-clause (a) of clause (7).

Explanation.- In this clause, "appropriate High Court" means,- (i) in the case of the detention of a person in pursuance of an order of detention made by the Government of India or an officer or authority subordinate to that Government, the High Court for the Union territory of Delhi; (ii) in the case of the detention of a person in pursuance of an order of detention made by the Government of any State (other than a Union territory), the High Court for that State; and (iii) in the case of the detention of a person in pursuance of an order of detention made by the administrator of a Union territory or an officer or authority subordinate to such administrator, such High Court as may be specified by or under any law made by Parliament in this behalf.'; (b) in clause (7),- (i) sub-clause (a) shall be omitted; (ii) sub-clause (b) shall be re-lettered as sub-clause (a); and (iii) sub-clause (c) shall be re-lettered as sub-clause (b) and in the sub-clause as so re-lettered, for the words, brackets, letter and figure "sub-clause (a) of clause (4)", the word, brackets and figure "clause (4)" shall be substituted.

THE CONSTITUTION (EIGHTY-SIXTH AMENDMENT) ACT, 2002

[12th December, 2002]

An Act further to amend the Constitution of India.

BE it enacted by Parliament in the Fifty-third year of the Republic of India as follows:-

1. Short title and commencement.-
   (1) This Act may be called the Constitution (Eighty-sixth Amendment) Act, 2002.
   (2) It shall come into force on such date* as the Central Government may, by notification in the Official Gazette, appoint.
2. Insertion of new article 21A.-After article 21 of the Constitution, the following article shall be inserted, namely:--

   "21A. Right to education.-The State shall provide free and compulsory education to all children of the age of six to fourteen years in such manner as the State may, by law, determine.".
3. Substitution of new article for article 45.-For article 45 of the Constitution, the following article shall be substituted, namely:-

   "45. Provision for early childhood care and education to children below the age of six years.-The State shall endeavour to provide early childhood care and education for all children until they complete the age of six years.".
4. Amendment of article 51A.-In article 51A of the Constitution, after clause (j), the following clause shall be added, namely:--

   "(k) who is a parent or guardian to provide opportunities for education to his child or, as the case may be, ward between the ago of six and fourteen years.".

THE CONSTITUTION (EIGHTY-EIGHTH AMENDMENT) ACT, 2003

[15th January, 2004.]

An Act further to amend the Constitution of India.

BE it enacted by Parliament in the Fifty-fourth Year of the Republic of India as follows:--

1. Short title and Commencement.-(1) This Act may be called the Constitution (Eighty-eighth Amendment) Act, 2003.

(2) It shall come into force on such date* as the Central Government may, by notification in the Official Gazette, appoint.

2. Insertion of new article 268A.-After article 268 of the Constitution, the following article shall be inserted, namely:-

"268A. Service tax levied by Union and collected and appropriated by the Union and the States.-(1) Taxes on services shall be levied by the Government of India and such tax shall be collected and appropriated by the Government of India and the States in the manner provided in clause (2).

(2) The proceeds in any financial year of any such tax levied in accordance with the provisions of clause (1) shall be-

(a) collected by the Government of India and the States;

(b) appropriated by the Government of India and the States, in accordance with such principles of collection and appropriation as may be formulated by Parliament by law.".

3. Amendment of article 270.-In article 270 of the Constitution, in clause (1), for the words and figures "articles 268 and 269", the words, figures and letter "articles 268, 268A and 269" shall be substituted.

4. Amendment of Seventh Schedule.-In the Seventh Schedule to the Constitution, in List I-Union List, after entry 92B, the following entry shall be inserted, namely:--

"92C. Taxes on services.".

REFERENCES

- Howard McIlwain: *Constitutionalism: Ancient and Modern*, N.Y., Cornell University Press, 1958.
- Austin, Granville: *The Indian Constitution: Cornerstone of a Nation*, Oxford, Clarendon Press, 1966.
- Goldman, H.: *Co-ordination of Computerization of the Criminal Justice System*, London, Home Office, 1986.
- Friedrich, J.: *Constitutional Government and Democracy*, Boston, Ginn, 1950.

5

Attitude of the Constituent Assembly

Divergent views and attitudes were seen in the framing of the Constitution. The members of the Assembly had a variety of perceptions about the future Indian polity. Their divergent views on the major issue of the political system Were quite interesting.

Adult Franchise: Should adult franchise be introduced, involving an increase in the electorate from 35 million to 170 million? Maulana Azad advocated its deferment for 15 years. Prasad and Nehru plumped for adult franchise as an act of faith. The vote favouring it was carried amidst acclamation.

Jammu and Kashmir: Nehru favoured incorporation of a section establishing a special relationship with the state of Jammu and Kashmir, thus inferentially recognising the state's right to frame its own constitution within the Indian Union. Patel wanted the state to be fully integrated with the Union. The "Cabinet was divided on the issue and the trend in the Constituent Assembly favoured Sardar's stand. But when the matter came before the Assembly, Patelput the unity and solidarity of the, Government before everything else and backed the Nehru formula.

Reservation for Minorities: The most delicate issue related to safeguards for minorities. Azad wanted reservation of seats for the Muslims and other minorities within the framework of general electorates. Patel opposed such safeguards. Nehru left it to Patel to jump the hurdle as Chairman of the Advisory Committee on Minorities. Two women members played a key role in this high-strung drama. Amrit Kaur, speaking for the Indian Christians, said that reservation of seats and weightage based on religion or sect would lead to fragmentation of the Indian Union. The Sikhs demanded the same treatment as given to the Muslims.. After the Committee had-wrestled with the problem for weeks, Patel decided to clinch the issue at its final meeting. He called on Begum Aizaz Rasul of Lucknow to state the Muslim view. She was a zealous leader of Muslim League before partition and had even gone to the length of giving up Saree and adopting the costume worn by the Begums of Oudh. The Muslims left behind. in India, she said nervously, were an integral part of the nation and needed no safeguards.. Patel seized this crucial movement to declare that the Muslims-were unanimously in favour of joint electorates and adjourned the meeting.

Office of the President and Governors: Much heat was generated on _ whether the President of the Republic and Governors of the Constituent States should be elected by popular vote and whether they should have discretionary powers. Legal luminaries and constitutional experts had a field day, but Nehru and Patel brought a practical approach to bear on the issue. They opposed popularly elected heads. Indeed, Nehru as Prime Minister took steps to see that; the Union President even though chosen by an electoral college consisting of all the members of the Central and State Legislatures, would be a constitutional figure head. Patel as Home Minister made sure that Governor of a State was the nominee of the Union Government and had enough discretionary powers to act as the executive agent of the Centre in an emergency.

Link Language: The question of a national link language posed the most (j difficult hurdle. Swami Dayanand and Mahatma Gandhi, both from Gujarat and Tilak and Savarkar, from Maharashtra had zealously pleaded for Hindi as the symbol of nationhood. Prasad and Patel strongly supported Hindi, while Nehru left it to the Hindi lobby to work out a formula acceptable to the non-Hindi regions, especially Madras and

Bengal. Finally, the formula providing for replacement of English by Hindi in fifteen years was embodied in the Constitution, along with each side did it with mental reservation.

Fundamental Rights: A great deal of excitement caused over the issue; should the Fundamental Right to be embodied in the Constitution guarantee fair payment for private property acquired by the state and should the right be made justiciable? Nehru was against making the right justiciable. Patel stood rocklike for the Fundamental Rights adopted by the Congress Party under his Presidentship in 1931 in Karachi. After a prolonged tug-of-war Patel won because he had the backing of the distinguished lawyers, who were fashioning the Constitution, and of the overwhelming majority of members of the Constituent Assembly.

Secular State: Another issue which the Assembly faced was about secular or non-secular character of the Constitution. There was a strong view point that after the partition of country secularism had no meaning. If the Muslims all over the world can have theocratic state, where they could preach and propagate their own faith, then why the Hindus of India cannot have their own Hindu State. On the other hand, there was predominantly Congress section in the Assembly which firmly believed that India should be a secular state.

Socialism: It was principally Patel's conservative influence that kept the Constitution from having a greater socialist content than it has; perhaps it was in deference to his wishes that Nehru omitted the world 'socialism' from the _Objective Resolutions.

Village Panchayat: The word Panchayat did not once appear in the Draft Constitution. Within a few months a reaction to this omission set in as Assembly members had time to consider the Draft. President Prasad was the most prominent among the critics. On 10 May, 1948, Prasad wrote to B. N. Rau that "I like the idea of making the Constitution begin with the village and go up to the Centre. The village has been and will ever continue to be our unit in this country." Prasad believed that the necessary articles could be redrafted, making the village Panchayats the electoral college for electing representatives to the Provinces and the Centre. But Rau rejected Prasad's suggestion. In his reply Rau said that the Assembly had already decided on direct election of Lower Houses both at the Centre and the Provinces and that he was doubtful. If the vote could be reversed a remark that indicated the general popularity of a Parliamentary constitution.

The Constituent Assembly (Legislative). When the Assembly met for purposes of ordinary law-making it was called the Legislative wing of the Constituent Assembly or the Constituent Assembly (Legislative), Presided over by the Speaker, it functioned as the Legislature of the country with the secretariat of the pre-independence Legislative Assembly as its Secretariat. The first meeting of the first session of the Constituent Assembly (Legislative) was held in the Assembly Chamber of the Council House (now called the Lok Sabha-Chamber of the Parliament House) on November 17,1947 at-11 a.m. with the I president of the. Constituent Assembly in the chair. G. V Mavalankar was declared duly elected for the office of the Speaker. Dr. Rajendra Prasad vacated the chair which was then occupied by Speaker Mavalankar. The Constituent Assembly in its capacity as Dominion Legislature was in existence for nearly two years and one month. Between November 17, 1947 and December 24, 1949 it had in all six sessions consisting of 226 days.

SALIENT FEATURES OF THE WORKING PROCESS OF THE CONSTITUENT ASSEMBLY

According to Granville Austin the success of the constitution lies principally in its having been framed by Indians, and in the excellence of the framing process itself. The members of the Assembly drafted a constitution that expressed the aspirations of the nation. They skilfully selected and modified the provisions that they borrowed, helped by the 'experts' among their number and the advice given by ministries of the Union and Provincial Governments. The Assembly members also applied to their task with great effectiveness two wholly Indian concepts, consensus and; accommodation. Accommodation was applied to the principles to be embodied in the Constitution. Consensus was the aim of the decision-making process, the single most important source of the, Constituent Assembly's effectiveness.

Decision-making by Consensus

Consensus is a manner of making decisions by unanimity. It is a recognition that majority rule may not be a successful way to decide political conflicts. Assembly leaders understood this well and bent their energies towards this goal in the hope and expectation that the constitution, framed by consensus, would work effectively and thus prove durable. According to Austin, "Consensus thus had a general appeal in the Assembly; to the leadership an ethical and effective way of reaching lasting agreement and to the rank and file as an indigenous institution that suited the framing of an Indian Constitution.

Consensus approach was adopted in a variety of ways. Most important; among them were the Congress Assembly Party meetings where each provision of the Constitution was subjected to frank and searching debates and whose approval was in fact as important as that of the Assembly itself. Everyone elected to the Assembly on the Congress ticket could attend meetings, from party stalwarts to non-congressmen like Ayyar, Ambedkar and N. G. Ayyangar, who were brought into the Assembly because the leadership believed that their talents should not be wasted. Also a part of this' process was the Assembly's committee system, the dialogue between provincial and Union. Government leaders in the Assembly, the many inter-governmental communications and the off the record discussions between Assembly leaders and dissidents among the members.

The primary, examples of decision-making by consensus were perhaps the federal and language provisions. The language question strained the Assembly's decision-making machinery to the utmost. For nearly three years the members searched for a generally acceptable solution. The Munshi-Ayyangar formula was drafted almost in desperation. Opening the final Assembly debate on language, Prasad announced that he would not put the issue to a vote. If an agreement was not acceptable to the whole country it would be most difficult to implement.

The Principle of Accommodation

According to Austin, the second of India's original contribution to constitution-making was the principle of Accommodation-the ability to reconcile apparently incompatible concepts. India's constitutional structure is a good example of the principle of accommodation on matters of substance. It has reconciled the federal and unitary system, membership of commonwealth and republican status of Government, Provisions for Panchayati Raj with the need for a strong Central Government.

The Art of Selection and Modification

According to Austin, the Constituent Assembly had discovered a new principle-the art of selection and modification. The Assembly was not merely imitative, the borrowing from different political systems did not relieve the Assembly of choice and that the borrowed provisions had to be adopted to suit Indian conditions. One example of selection and modification is the method of Constitutional amendment. The three mechanisms of the method devised by the Assembly have made the Constitution flexible while at the same time protecting the rights of the States. They have worked better than has the amending process any other country where federalism and the British Parliamentary System jointly form the bases of the Constitution. In brief, the Assembly selected and modified the provisions from other constitutions with a great deal of professional help.

COMPOSITION OF THE CONSTITUENT ASSEMBLY

In all, the Constituent Assembly was to have 389 members. As many as 296 of them were to be elected from British India and 93 were to be representatives of the native states. The Muslim League boycotted the Assembly, hence out of 296 members only 211 attended its first meeting on December 9, 1946.

The electoral process itself could not have produced a representative body because it was based on the restricted franchise established by the Sixth Schedule of the 1935 Act, which excluded the mass of peasants, the majority of small shopkeepers and traders and countless others from the rolls through tax, property and educational qualifications. Only 28.5 per cent of the adult population of the provinces could vote in the provincial assembly elections of early 1946.

WORKING OF THE CONSTITUENT ASSEMBLY

The Constituent Assembly duly opened on the appointed day Monday, the day of December, 1946.

It was truly a unique occasion in India's long history; the first time the representatives of the people were meeting to determine future Constitution of India. During its first four sittings on December 9, 11 and 12, the Assembly was involved with matters like the presentation of credentials and signing of the register, electing the permanent chairman, constituting a Committee for Rules of Procedure etc. On the 5th day of the First session of the Constituent Assembly-December 13, 1946-Nehru moved the historic Objectives Resolution. The Resolution said: "This Constituent Assembly declares its firm and solemn resolve to proclaim India as an Independent Sovereign Republic and to draw up for her future governance a constitution." Nehru's Objectives Resolution gave to the Assembly its guiding principles and the philosophy that was to permeate its task of constitution making.

The Assembly met in its Second plenary session from 20-26 January, 1947, and adopted the objective Resolution moved by Nehru. The Third plenary session was held from April 28 to May 2. It discussed the reports submitted by the Union Powers Committee and of the Advisory Committee on Fundamental Rights. On August 29, the Assembly adopted a resolution setting up a Drafting Committee to prepare a constitution in accordance with the decisions taken by it on the reports of the various committees. Dr. Ambedkar was appointed chairman of this Committee. The Second Draft was placed before the Assembly on February 21, 1948. After nearly three years the Assembly finally adopted the Constitution on November 26, 1949. In all, it held 11 sessions, covering 2965 days out of which 114 days were devoted to consideration of the draft Constitution.

COMMITTEES OF THE CONSTITUENT ASSEMBLY

The Constituent Assembly had a total of more than fifteen committees with a membership of greater than eighty individuals. Seven of them, such as the House and Staff Committee, had minor functions. The brick and mortar of the structure were provided by the reports of the Union Powers Committee, the Union Constitution Committee, the Advisory Committee on Minorities and Fundamental Rights, the Committee on Chief Commissioner's Provinces, the Committee on Financial Provisions of the Union Constitution and the Advisory Committee on Tribal Areas. These committees submitted their reports between April-August 1947, which were considered by the Constituent Assembly. On the basis of these decisions, the final shape and form were given by Dr. Ambedkar and his colleagues in the Drafting Committee.

Drafting Committee

The Assembly appointed a Drafting Committee on 29th August, 1947 to consider the Draft Constitution. Dr. Ambedkar was appointed Chairman and it had six other members. They were Sir Krishnaswami Ayyangar, N. Gopala': swami Ayyangar, K.M. Munshi, Saiyed Mohammed Sadulla, Sir B. L. Mittar and D.P. Khaitan. After the first meeting Sir B. L. Mittar ceased to be a member and in his place N. Madhava Rao was nominated by the President on December 5, 1947. The Drafting Committee, under the Chaimanship of Dr. Ambedker embodied the decision of the Assembly, with alternative and additional proposals in the form "Of a 'Draft Constitution of India' which was published in February 1948. The Drafting Committee took less than six months to prepare its Draft. In all it sat only for 141 days.

FRAMERS OF THE CONSTITUTION

The members of the Constituent Assembly were not selected purely on a party basis, but were drawn from all walks of life and represented almost every section of the Indian people. They included some of the most leading personalities of Indian public life. The moving spirit of the assembly was Jawahar Lal Nehru, the first Prune Minister of free India. Rajendra Prasad was its President. Vallabhbhai Patel was one of the most important among the leading lights. While these leaders had contributed more than all others for the formulation of the basic principles of the Constitution, it was the Drafting Committee, headed by B.R. Ambedkar, which was in charge of its drafting. Dr. Ambedkar chaired the Drafting Committee and steered the document through nearly a year of debate over its various provisions. Ambedkar was ably assisted, in the task of Constitution making by the other members of the Drafting Committee among whom Alladi Krishnaswami Aiyer, N. Gopalaswami Ayyangar, K.M. Munshi and T.T Krishnamachari were the most prominent. In the words of Granville Austin, "Four leaders, Nehru, Patel, Prasad and the Congress Muslim leader Maulana Abul Kalam Azad, through their commanding grip on the Congress (Assembly Party and the Assembly's eight committees) constituted a virtual oligarchy within the Assembly. Issues were openly debated, but the influence of the Congress leaders was nearly irresistible."

In the words of Dr. Subhash Kashyap, "Nevertheless, while others fashioned its structure and shape, most significantly, Nehru gave to the Constitution of India its spirit and soul, its philosophy and its vision." At the very outset he laid down its' general outlines and he continued to influence what the Constituent Assembly did. In this, the Constitution was his handwork. Nehru was the Assembly's philosopher and its prime constitutional thinker. The President of the Constituent Assembly, Dr. Rajendra Prasad also gave credit to Nehru and Patel for the fundamentals of the Constitution. Between the two, as Austin puts it, each had his special interests-Patel was more interested in the Princely States, the public services and the working of the Home Ministry, and Nehru in Fundamental Rights, Protection of minority rights, and the social reform aspects of the Constitution and each let the other have almost free rein in these areas.

The Constituent Assembly had eight major committees-Rules, Steering, Advisory, Drafting, Union Subjects, Union Constitution, Provincial Constitution and States-with a total membership of approximately three dozen. Either, Nehru, Patel or Prasad chaired each of these committees, and in many cases the other two or Azad were also present. Nehru personally invited Ambedkar to become a member of his Cabinet. Ambedkar joined Cabinet because he could serve the cause of Scheduled Castes better from within the Government. One more individual, B. N. Rau, must be paced among those important in the framing of the Constitution. As Constitutional Adviser, his advice was heard in the Assembly's inner councils, although he was not an Assembly member.

Under the Rules of Procedure, the Assembly elected Dr. Rajendra Prasad as its permanent President,. and V. T. Krishnamachari and H. C. Mookheijee as Vice Presidents unanimously. Dr. Rajendra Prasad, as the President of Constituent Assembly, was indeed "a very happy choice". As a veteran political leader, he was respected by all, and was very considerate towards every member of the Assembly. While conducting the proceedings of the Assembly he never allowed "legalism to defeat the work of constitution making." He, how ever, was a more active President of the Constituent Assembly than George Washington.

CONTROVERSIAL ISSUES IN THE CONSTITUENT ASSEMBLY

A ticklish constitutional problem arose on 15th August, 1947 and Nehru put in jokingly: Mavalankar has vanished into thin air." He was referring to the provision in the Indian Independence Act under which the Legislative Assembly, of which G.V. Mavalankar was President, automatically dissolved on Independence Day and the Constituent Assembly became the supreme sovereign and legislative body. The question arose how Rajendra Prasad, a member of. the Cabinet as. well as the President of the Constituent Assembly could preside over the deliberations of that body when it functioned as a legislature.

Both Nehru and Patel felt that Prasad should continue in the Cabinet and another President should be chosen for the Constituent Assembly, when Nehru took the stand that it would be intolerable in a democracy for a Minister to preside, B. N. Rau proposed that a Deputy Speaker be elected to preside over the Assembly in the name of President of the Constituent

Assembly. This led a tension between Patel and Prasad and resulted in a sharp exchange in the cabinet. A civil servant who attended the meeting observed: "These men whom we adored as giants quarrelled like children." The dispute' was referred to Gandhi, a bare week before his assassination. Prasad wanted to make a statement in the Constituent Assembly: Gandhi sent for it and modified it. Prasad accepted the changes, saying: "I stand for harmony and therefore do not press my point," Gandhi's terse comment was: "Even Rajen Babu is lured by power. I feel disillusioned."

At this point another issue was raised: "What would be Prasad's position on " the legislative side and Mavalankar's as speaker?" Reluctantly Prasad agreed to the election of another speaker, provided he was subordinate to the President of the Constituent Assembly. Mavalankar demanded equality of status and full control over his secretariat. Prasad yielded after a hard struggle, retaining the Presidentship of the Constituent Assembly, and Mavalankar took over as Speaker of the Legislative Assembly.

But the squabble' did not end there, at the instance of Gandhi, Nehru suggested that Prasad should become President of the Congress Party. Prasad objected strongly to what appeared to him an attempt to push him out of the Cabinet and Presidentship of the Constituent Assembly. For some time it appeared as though he would repudiate the agreement over Mavalankar's appointment. When Nehru dropped the proposal and Prasad's ruffed feelings had been soothed, still more difficulties were encountered. Rau took away the Legislative Assembly Secretariat, and Prasad ruled that the new staff could not be appointed without his sanction. The matter was referred to Nehru who then got Prasad to delegate to Mavalankar the authority to appoint staff. Later, a provision was written into the constitution making the Parliament Secretariat independent of the Government.

CENTRAL LEGISLATIVE ASSEMBLY

The Central Legislative Assembly was a legislature for India created by the Government of India Act 1919 from the former Imperial Legislative Council, implementing the Montagu-Chelmsford Reforms. It was also sometimes called the Indian Legislative Assembly and the Imperial Legislative Assembly. As a result of Indian independence, the Legislative Assembly was dissolved on 14 August 1947 and its place taken by the Constituent Assembly of India and the Constituent Assembly of Pakistan.

1920-1935

The new Assembly was the lower house of a bicameral parliament, with a new Council of State as the upper house, reviewing legislation passed by the Assembly. However, both its powers and its electorate were limited. Initially, of its 144 members, 103 were elected and 41 were nominated. Of the 103 elected members, fifty-one came from general constituencies, thirty were elected by Muslims, two by Sikhs, nine by Europeans, seven by landlords, and four by business men

A new "Council House" was conceived in 1919 as the seat of the future Legislative Assembly, the Council of State, and the Chamber of Princes. The foundation stone was laid on 12 February 1921 and the building was opened on 18 January 1927 by Lord Irwin, the Viceroy and Governor-General. The Council House later changed its name to Parliament House, or *Sansad Bhavan*, and is the present-day home of the Parliament of India. The first elections to the new legislatures took place in November 1920 and proved to be the first significant contest between the Moderates and the Non-cooperation movement, whose aim was for the elections to fail. The Non-cooperators were at least partly successful in this, as out of almost a million electors for the Assembly, only some 182,000 voted. The Assembly, the Council of State, and the Chamber of Princes were officially opened in 1921 by King George V's uncle, the Duke of Connaught and Strathearn

In 1923, Motilal Nehru, the father of Jawaharlal Nehru, was elected to the Assembly and became leader of the Opposition. In that role, he was able to secure the defeat, or at least the delay, of Finance bills and other legislation. He agreed to join a Committee with the object of promoting the recruitment of Indian officers into the Indian Army, but this decision contributed to others going further and joining the Government itself. In March 1926, Nehru demanded a representative conference to draft a constitution conferring full Dominion status on India, to be enacted by the parliament. When this demand was rejected by the Assembly, Nehru and his colleagues walked out and returned to the Congress.

In September 1923, Muhammad Ali Jinnah was elected as Muslim member of the Assembly for Bombay. He organized many Indian Independent members to work with the Swaraj Party and helped to press demands for full responsible government. He was so active that when Lord Reading retired as Viceroy in 1925 he offered Jinnah a knighthood, which was declined.

On 8 April 1929, Bhagat Singh and Batukeshwar Dutt threw a bomb into the corridors of the Assembly, followed by a shower of leaflets, shouting "*Inquilab Zindabad!*" ("Long Live the Revolution!"). No one was injured, and on June 12 1929 they were sentenced to Penal transportation for the bombing. Singh was executed in 1931 for other offences.

In 1934, the Congress ended its boycott of the existing legislatures and contested the elections to the fifth Central Legislative Assembly held that year. Following this move, there was a sharp increase in the number of government defeats in the Assembly. In a British House of Commons debate on 4 April 1935, the Secretary of State for India, Samuel Hoare, stated that "The number of divisions in the Legislative Assembly since the recent elections and up to the 25th March in which Government have been successful is five. The number of adverse divisions in the same period is seventeen." Henry Page Croft then asked "Can the right hon. Gentleman say whether the Government would have been successful on any occasion without the support of the nominated members?" Hoare replied "I could not answer that question without looking into the figures, but in any case I see no reason to differentiate between one class of member and another."

Many resolutions put forward by the Congress in opposition to the Government of India were passed only with the support of the Muslims of Jinnah's Independents, and an unspoken alliance between the two groupings electrified the atmosphere of the Assembly on great occasions. Indeed, there were reports of jubilant scenes of mutual embracing on occasions when the combination of the two succeeded.

1937-1947

The Government of India Act 1935 introduced further reforms. The Assembly continued as the lower chamber of a central Indian parliament based in Delhi, with two chambers, both containing elected and appointed members. The Assembly increased in size to 250 seats for members elected by the constituencies of British India, plus a further 125 seats for the Indian Princely states. The first elections to the reformed Assembly were held in 1937, and the Indian National Congress won 205 seats, with the Muslim League winning 73. With the situation in Palestine worsening, Indian troops were sent there. In the Assembly, the Viceroy, Lord Linlithgow, disallowed all questions and resolutions which asked him to express the concern of Indian Muslims about the position of Arabs in Palestine.

On 27 February 1942, during the Second World War, the Assembly held a secret session to discuss the war situation.

The electorate of the Assembly was never more than a very small fraction of the population of India. In the British House of Commons on 10 November 1942, the Labour MP Seymour Cocks asked the Secretary of State for India Leo Amery "What is the electorate for the present Central Legislative Assembly?" and received the written answer "The total electorate for the last General Election (1934) for the Central Legislative Assembly was 1,415,892." Under the provisions of the Indian Independence Act 1947, the Central Legislative Assembly was replaced in August 1947 by the Constituent Assembly of India, which became a fully sovereign body at midnight on 14/15 August, and by the Constituent Assembly of Pakistan.

Presidents of the Assembly

The presiding officer (or speaker) of the Assembly was called the President. While the Government of India Act 1919 provided for the President to be elected, it made an exception in the case of the first President, who was to be appointed by the Government, and the Governor-General's choice fell on Frederick Whyte, a former Liberal member of the British House of Commons who had been a parliamentary private secretary to Winston Churchill. Whyte was succeeded on 24 August 1925 by Vithalbhai Patel, who was elected for a second time in 1927. He succeeded in laying down clearly defined practices and procedures for the business of the Assembly and defended members' rights and privileges. In 1928, he was able to create for the first time a separate office for the Assembly, independent of the administration of the Government of India. Patel established the convention that the President would neither take part in debates nor vote, except to use his casting vote in favour of the *status quo*.

Sir Muhammad Yakub was the deputy president of the Assembly from 1927 until 1930 and became President in 1930. Yakub's deputy president from 1931 to 1933, R. K. Shanmukham Chetty, was President from 1933 to 1934. In 1935, Sir Abdur Rahim KCSI was elected as second Muslim President of the Assembly, serving until 1945. He was a former Chief Justice of the Madras High Court and professor of law in the University of Calcutta.

Ganesh Vasudev Mavlankar became the last President of the Assembly in January 1946 and remained in office until the Assembly came to an end on 14 August 1947. (Mavlankar became the first Speaker of the Constituent Assembly of India, and in 1952 the first Speaker of the *Lok Sabha*, the lower house of the Parliament of India.)

MEMBER OF THE LEGISLATIVE ASSEMBLY (INDIA)

A Member of Legislative Assembly, or MLA, is a representative elected by the voters of an electoral district to the Legislature of a State in the Indian system of government. Each state has between four and nine MLAs for every Member of Parliament (MP) that it has in the Lok Sabha. A Member of Legislative Council, or MLC, is a representative indirectly elected through an electoral college to the Legislature of a State having a bicameral legislature.

State Legislature

The state legislature in Indian States is either bicameral or unicameral type. In most cases, states legislature is unicameral. In unicameral state legislature the (only) house is called Legislative Assembly. In states where there are two houses there is a Legislative Council along with Legislative Assembly. In such a case, the Legislative Council is the Upper House, while Legislative Assembly is the Lower House of the State Legislature.

Governor is an integral part of the State Legislature.

The Legislative Assembly consists of not more than 500 members and not less than 60. The biggest state like Uttar Pradesh has 425 members in its Assembly. States which have small population and are small in size have a provision for having even lesser number of members in the Legislative Assembly. Pondicherry, Mizoram, Arunachal Pradesh have only 30 members each. Sikkim has 32 members. All members of the Legislative Assembly are elected on the basis of adult franchise, and one member is elected from one constituency. Just as the President has the power to nominate 2 Anglo Indians to the Lok Sabha, similarly, the Governor also has the power to nominate a certain number of members from the Anglo Indian community as he deems fit, if he is of the opinion that they are not adequately represented in the Assembly.

The Legislative Council consists of not more than 1/3rd of the total strength of the Legislative Assembly of the state and not less than 40. The members of the Legislative Council are elected as well as nominated. Broadly speaking, 5/6th of the total members of the Council are indirectly elected and 1/6th are nominated by the Governor. The composition is as follows:

i) 1/3 of the total members of the Council are elected by electorates consisting of members of local bodies such as corporations, municipalities and zila parishads.

ii) 1/3 are elected by members of Legislative Assembly from among the persons who are not members of the Assembly.

iii) 1/12 are elected by electorates consisting of persons who are graduates of three years standing, residing in that state.

iv) 1/12 are elected by electorates consisting of persons engaged for at least three years in teaching in educational institutions within the state, not lower in standard than secondary schools.

v) The remainder 1/6 are nominated by the Governor from persons having knowledge or practical experience in fields such as legislature, science, arts, co-operative movement and social service.

Qualification

The qualifications to be a member of the state Legislature are largely similar to the qualifications to be the members of Parliament. A person can become a member of the Legislative Assembly of the state if he or she is i) a citizen of India ii) not less than 25 years of age to be member of the Legislative Assembly and not less than 30 to be a member of the Legislative Council. No person can become a member of the Legislative Assembly or the Legislative Council of any state, unless he himself is a voter from any constituency of the state. Those who cannot become members of Parliament can also not become members of state Legislature.

Term

The term of the Legislative Assembly is five years. But it may be dissolved even earlier than five years by the Governor on the request of Chief Minister. The term of the Legislative Assembly may be extended during an Emergency, but not more than six months at a time. The Legislative Council is the Upper House in the State. Just like the Rajya Sabha it is a permanent House and cannot be dissolved. The term of each member is 6 years and 1/3rd members of the House retire after every two years.

Presiding officers

Similar to the Presiding officers of the Lok Sabha and the Rajya Sabha, the Legislative Assembly and the Legislative Council also have Presiding Officers. The Legislative Assembly has a Speaker and a Deputy Speaker. They are elected from among the members of the House. The Legislative Council has a Chairman and a Deputy Chairman who are elected in a similar fashion. The functions performed by these presiding officers are similar to the function of presiding officers of the two Houses of Parliament. The Speaker of the Assembly can decide whether a bill is a money bill or not. Presiding Officers of both the Houses have the right to exercise casting vote in case of tie.

Powers

The most important function of the Legislature is law making. The State Legislature has the power to make laws on all items on which Parliament cannot legislate. Some of these items are police, prisons, irrigation, agriculture, local governments, public health, pilgrimages, burial grounds etc. Some items on which both Parliament and states can make laws are education, marriage and divorce, forests, protection of wild animals and birds etc. As regards Money Bill, the position is the same. Bills can originate only in the Legislative Assembly. The Legislative Council can either pass the bill within 14 days from the date of the receipt of the Bill or suggest changes in it within 14 days. But these changes may or may not be accepted by the Assembly.

The State Legislature besides making laws also has one electoral power in electing the President of India. Elected members of the Legislative Assembly along with the elected members of Parliament are involved in this process. We have seen that some parts of the Constitution can be amended by Parliament with the approval of half of State Legislatures. Thus the State legislatures take part in the process of amendment of our Constitution.

Ministers in the state governments are responsible to the Vidhan Sabha (Legislative Assembly) of the state. Like Lok Sabha at the centre, state Assembly also keeps constant vigil over state's Council of Ministers. This is done through questions, supplementary questions and adjournment motions. The Assembly may force the Chief Minister and the Council of

Minister to resign if it adopts a vote of no confidence against the government, or if a government proposal, bill or budget is rejected by the Assembly.

POLITICS OF CONSTITUTIONAL AMENDMENTS IN INDIA

A Constitution is a dynamic document. It should grow with a growing' nation and should suit the changing needs and circumstances of a growing a changing people. Sometimes under the impact of new powerful social and economic forces, the pattern of government will require major changes. If the Constitution stands as a stumbling block to such desirable changes, it may under extreme pressure, be destroyed. A Constitution, as such, cannot have an: claim to permanence; nor should it, because it has been adopted and has been working ever since, claim absolute sanctity. Mulford has rightly said: ", unamendable constitution is the worst tyranny of time or rather the very tyranny of time.".

Herman Finer defined constitution as the process of amendment, for in his view, to amend is to deconstitute or reconstitute. W. Munro has rightly observed: "....... it is impossible to conceive of an unamendable constitution as any thing but a contradiction in terms."

A Constitution is a fundamental document of the land. It is a document which defines the position and power of the three organs of the State--the Executive, the Legislature and the Judiciary. It also defines the powers of the Executive and the Legislature as against the citizens. In fact, the purpose of a Constitution is not merely to create the organs of the state but also to limit their authority, because if no limitation is imposed upon the authority of the organs, there will be tyranny and oppression. Naturally, such a fundamental document as a constitution should not undergo too frequent and easy changes as that would undermine the confidence of the citizens in the abiding nature of the Constitution. Jawahar Lal Nehru has rightly said, "......The Constitution cannot and should not be changed frequently. Obviously also, it can and must be changed when the situation requires it to be changed." A Constitution to be living must be growing; must be adaptable; must be flexible, must be changeable. Indeed, any amendment of the constitution should be justified by compelling reasons and circumstances.

AMENDMENT PROCESS IN THE INDIAN CONSTITUTION

Federal Constitutions as a rule are rigid as most of them have extremely difficult and even complicated procedures of amendment. Amending a federal constitution like that of the U.S.A. and Australia is perhaps the most difficult.

In contrast, the Constitution of India presents a much simpler process. As Ambedkar pointed out in the Constituent Assembly, "The provisions for amendment while they embodied in certain measure of rigidity with regard to some parts of the Constitution, were flexible and afforded facilities for a simple process of amendment with regard to others." Pointing out the details of the scheme he stated: 'We propose to divide the various articles of the Constitution into three categories. In First category we have placed certain articles which would be open to amendment by Parliament by simple majority. The Second set of articles requires a two-thirds majority of Parliament. The Third category requires a two-thirds majority of Parliament plus ratification by the States. The States are given an important voice in the amendment of these matters. These are fundamental matters where States have important powers under the Constitution and any unilateral amendment by Parliament may vitally affect the fundamental basis of the system built up by the Constitution." The procedure for amendment is detailed under Article 368 of the Constitution. According to this, there are three ways of amending the Constitution:

Amendment by Simple Majority: There are a good number of Articles in Constitution which are of transitory nature. Though they can be changed by Parliament by passing a law by simple majority technically speaking changes made therein, are not to be considered as amendment of the Constitution. By simple majority is meant, simple majority of the members present and voting. For example, changes in the names and boundaries of the States, creation or abolition of the Legislative Councils in the States, salaries and allowances of the President, Governors and Judges of the Supreme Court and High Courts, etc., can be made by Parliament by passing a law by simple majority.

The following provisions of the Constitution also fall under this category:

1. Second Schedule of the Constitution.
2. Article 100(3) of the Constitution which fixes quorum of the transaction of business in the Parliament.
3. Article 105 of the Constitution which deals with powers, privileges and immunities of Members of Parliament.
4. Article 11 regarding acquisition and termination of citizenship.
5. Article 124 which deals with the appointment of Judges in the Supreme Court.
6. Article 135 which deals with conferring more jurisdictions on the Supreme Court.
7. Article 81 relating to the delimitation of Constituencies.
8. Article 137 of the Constitution which deals with Supreme Court's powers to review its own judgment.

Amendment by Special Majority: An amendment of the Constitution may be initiated only by the introduction of a Bill for the purpose in either House of Parliament. When the Bill is passed in each House by a majority of the total membership of that House and by a majority of not less than two-thirds of the members of that House present and voting, it shall be presented to the President for his assent. When the President gives his assent, the Constitution stands amended in accordance with the terms of the Bill.

Ratification by the State Legislatures: For the amendment of certain other provisions of the Constitution, a Bill has to be passed by each House of Parliament by a majority of the total membership of that House and by a majority of not less than two-thirds of the members present and voting, then the amendment must be ratified by the Legislatures of not less than one-half of the States by resolutions to that effect is required before the amendment Bill is presented to the President for assent. The following provisions of the' Constitution fall under this category:

1. Election of President (Article 57);
2. Extent of the Executive power of the Union (Article 73);
3. Extent of the Executive power of States (Article 162);
4. Union Judiciary (Chapter IV of Part V);
5. High Courts in the States (Chapter V of Part VI);
6. Any of the Lists in the Seventh Schedule;
7. The representation of States in Parliament; and
8. Provisions dealing with amendment of the Constitution.

SALIENT FEATURES OF THE AMENDMENT PROCESS

The salient features of the Amendment Process are:

1. *Introduction only in either House of Parliament*: The Bill for the amendment of the Constitution can be introduced in either House of parliament and not in any State Assembly.
2. *Both Houses of Parliament must pass it separately*: An Amendment Bill should be passed by both the Houses of Parliament separately. The Constitution cannot be amended in case of a deadlock between the two. Houses. There is no provision for a joint sitting if both Houses differ. For example, in 1970, the Rajya Sabha rejected the 24th Constitutional Amendment Bill which provided for the derecognition of the Princes and again in 1978, as many as five out of forty-nine clauses of the 45th Constitution Amendment Bill were rejected by the Rajya Sabha and as a result there of, the Lok Sabha had no alternative but to dele these five clauses.
3. *Meaning of majority of total membership*: The expression 'majority Of total membership' means that it is not the majority of the actual membership of the House but the majority of the total prescribed strength of the House notwithstanding the vacancies therein.
4. *Special majority at every stage of the passing of the Bill*: Whether this 'special majority' mentioned above is

needed at the time of final voting on the Bill or even on the earlier stages of the Bill. The Constitution Amendment Bill even at its introduction stage must be supported by a two-thirds majority of members present and voting which should not be less than 50 per cent of the total strength. In 1969, the 24th Constitution Amendment Bill regarding abolition of Privy Purses could not be introduced because the requisite majority did not support it. It means special majority is needed at the passing of every stage of the Bill.

5. *Ratification by the Legislatures of not less than one-half of the States.* The amendment of the articles mentioned in the provision of Article 368, must be ratified by one-half of the State Legislatures by passing resolutions in that of, respect. The expression 'State Legislature' does not include the legislatures of the Union Territories. Wherever the State Legislature is bicameral, the resolutions must be passed by both Houses separately and the resolutions so passed do not require the signature or the assent of the Governor.
6. *Presidential assent.* In the final stage, the Constitution Amendment Bill is presented to the President for his assent which the President cannot refuse. But there is no time limit within which the President must give his assent. He can keep it pending for some time in the first instance, though ordinarily it is expected that he would give his assent as soon as possible.

Thus, the Constitution is partly rigid and partly flexible document. "There; is hardly another federal constitution which provides a comparable example, winning rigidity and flexibility. In the words of Jawahar Lal Nehru: "While 'we want this Constitution to be as solid and as permanent a structure as we make it, nevertheless there is no permanence in constitutions. There should be a certain flexibility. If you make anything rigid and permanent, you stop a nation's growth, the growth of a living vital organic people. Therefore, it has to, be flexible." K.C. Where are, keeping in view the 'wide variety of the amending, process, has commented that it strikes a good balance by protecting the rights of the States while leaving the remainder of the Constitution easy to amend. But-we must bear the testimony of the fact that this 'ease' in amending process of the Indian Constitution was due to the one-party dominance both at the centre and in the State for nearly thirty years.

The practical limitations of ending process are for the first time being experienced by the Janata Government at the Centre, where it was lacking a two-thirds majority in Rajya Sabha. Under such situation, the Janata Government was unable to remove the controversial clauses of the 42nd amendment without seeking, the cooperation of the Congress Party. The 64th Constitutional Amendment Bill also had fallen through on March 30, 1990 in, the Lok Sabha for want of the requisite two-thirds majority, even though all parties had declared their support for the measure. The bill was related to extend President's rule in Punjab for six months. The 75th amendment bill, for the same purpose, also fell through (in October 1990) because the Congress (I) declined to back it. At the same time, another feature which strikes the minds of critics, is that the units or States, like those of the American States, have no Jurisdiction to Initiate any formal constitutional amendment neither there is any provision for referendum as 'such. It should appear, thus, that although the States say in the formal amendment of the Constitution is not considerable, their vital interests have been shielded by the Constitution.

THE AMENDING POWER AND THE DOCTRINE OF BASIC STRUCTURE

The Golak Nath case judgment and the amendments which sought to nullify its effect, when came up for the Supreme Court's scrutiny in the case of Kesavananda Bharti against the State of Kerala and other allied petitions In 1973, it propounded the doctrine of implied powers and the doctrine of basic structure, which were hitherto unknown in India. In Kesavananda Bharti vs. State of Kerala, the Supreme Court reasonably upheld the validity of the 24th Amendment. It was, however, held by the majority that Parliament's power of Amendment was subject to implied limitation, namely, Parliament could not amend the Constitution to bring about change in the basic features of the Constitution. In this case the Supreme Court invalidated the following portion of Article 31(c) which was inserted through 25th Amendment Act.

> *".....and now law containing a declaration that it is for giving effect to such policy be called in question in any court on the ground that it does not give effect to such policy." The Court through its decision in Kesavananda's case tried to protect its right of judicial review and exposed the nefarious intention of the government in " excluding judicial review, when the law did not give effect to the policy involving Articles 39(b) and (c).*

In the Kesavananda Bharti's case, the majority of judges held that the amending power was a limited one even though they knew that the legislature was bent upon giving unlimited amending power to itself. This courageous and independent stand was taken on the basis of the principle called 'inherent and implied limitation'.

No doubt, the Constitution does not have any provision for drafting a new_ Constitution but that does not mean that the legislature can destroy, reshape of" or restructure the Constitution. It is, therefore, logical to assume that the implied limitation restricts the legislature in changing the Constitution unidentifiably. An argument stating that Parliament's will is people's will and therefore, Parliament still have an unlimited amending power, is preposterous because the electorate does not take into account the constitutional amendments while voting in the Parliamentary elections. Had people's will been Parliament's will, the Australian electorate would not have approved only five out of thirty-two changes in the Constitution proposed by Parliament in 74 years.

So, what has to be understood clearly is that Article 368 allows the legislature to make amendments only to the extent that the Constitution does not lose its identity. Parliament by passing the 24th amendment, altered Article, 368 to' enlarge the ambit of its amending power under that very article. This is a clear violation of the principle of implied limitation. A creature of the Constitution, however, vast its power, cannot regard itself superior to the Constitution. N.A. Palkhivala is very right when he says that "It cannot itself as the master and make the Constitution subservient; it cannot convert con_ trolled constitution into an uncontrolled one.

In Kesvananda Bharti's case" six senior judges of the Supreme Court an C.J., S.M. Sikri held as follows:

(i) *Parliament's amending power is limited.* While Parliament is entitled' to a bridge any Fundamental Right or amend any provision of the Constitution, the amending power does not extend to damaging or destroying any of the essential features of the Constitution fundamental Rights are among the essential features of the Constitution; therefore, while they may be abridged. The abridgement cannot attend to the limit of damage to or destruction of their core.

(ii) Article 31C is void since it takes many invaluable Fundamental Rights even those unconnected with property.

To sum, the Supreme Court held that the Constitution is not made to suffer a loss of identity through the amending process. The identity of the Constitution is the sum of its essential features. Article 368 cannot be read as expressing the, death wish of the Constitution or as a provision for its legal suicide.

THE PHILOSOPHY OF THE INDIAN CONSTITUTION AND THE NEED TO REVIEW IT

The concepts of democracy, representative institutions, limitations on the arbitrary powers of the rulers, and rule of law were not alien to India in the hoary past. The concept of the supremacy of Dharma was hardly different from the rule of law or limited government. The rulers in ancient India were bound by Dharma, no one was above Dharma. Enough evidence has come to light to show that republican forms of government, representative deliberative bodies and local self-government institutions existed in many parts of ancient India and democratic thinking and practices permeated different aspects of the life of the people right from the Vedic age (circa 3000-

1000 B.C.). The Rigveda and the Atharvaveda mention the Sabha (General Assembly) and the Samiti (House of Elders). The Aitareya Brahmana, Panini's Ashtadhyayi, Kautilya's Arthashastra, the Mahabharata, inscriptions on Ashoka's pillars, the Budhhist and Jain texts of the period and the Manuśmriti all bear witness to the existence of several functioning republics during the post-Vedic period of Indian history. After the Mahabharata particularly, large empires gave way to a number of small republican states. Jatakas make many references to how these republics functioned.

The members met in Santhagar. Representatives were elected in open assembly. They selected their gopa who became King and ruled with the help of a Council of Ministers.

In the 4th century B.C. the republican federation known as the Kshudrak Malla Sangha offered strong resistance to Alexander. Near Patliputra (Patna), there, was Vaishali, the Capital of Lichchavis. The state was a republic governed by an assembly with an elected President called Nayak. Unfortunately, we know little of the details of the constitution of these republics. The Greek scholar Megasthenes has left records of popular assemblies that were preserved in the South and which restrained the power of Kings. Kautilya's Arthashastra also records that autocracy or the Divine Right of Kings had no place in ancient Indian polity. The power of the Indian King was hedged in by safeguards against abuse and limited by liberties and powers of other public authorities and interests. He was, in fact, a limited or a constitutional monarch. Manu and the Mahabharata say that an unjust and oppressive ruler should be killed by his own subjects like a street dog gone mad. Nitisara (Science of Polity) of Shukracharya written in the tenth century is a book on constitution. It deals with the organization of the central government as well as village and town life, of the King's Council and of various departments of government. The King was to act on the opinion of the majority of the people. Independent Sovereign Republic and to draw up for her future governance a Constitution:

WHEREIN the territories that now comprise British India, the territories that now form the Indian States, and such other parts of India as are outside British India and the States as well as such other territories as are willing to be constituted into the Independent Sovereign India, shall be a Union of them all; and

WHEREIN the said territories, whether with their present boundaries or with such others as may be determined by the Constituent Assembly and thereafter according to the law of the constitution, shah possess and retain the status of autonomous units, together with residuary powers, and exercise all powers and functions of Government and administration, save and except such powers and functions as are vested in or assigned to the Union, or as are inherent or implied in the Union or resulting therefrom; and

WHEREIN all power and authority of the Sovereign Independent India, its constituent parts and organs of Governments are derived from the people; and

WHEREIN shall be guaranteed and secured to all the people of India justice, social, economic and political; equality of status, of opportunity, and before the law; freedom of thought, expression, belief, faith, worship, vocation, association and action, subject to law and public morality; and

WHEREIN adequate safeguards shall be provided for minorities, backward and tribal areas, and depressed and other backward classes; and

WHEREIN shall be maintained the integrity of the territory of the Republic and its sovereign rights' on land, sea, and air according to justice and the law of civilise, nations; and

The ancient land attain its rightful and honoured place in the world and make its full and fulfilling contribution to the promotion of world peace and the welfare of mankind."

In the words of Pandit Nehru, the aforesaid Resolution was "something more than a resolution. It is a declaration, a firm resolve, a pledge, an undertaking and for all of us a dedication".

Constitutional Review

The framing and adoption of an acceptable Constitution and political system for a country of India's past, size and nature was no easy task. Our founding fathers were some of the wisest men and women. They gave us an excellent Constitution which has stood the test of time. It envisaged a cohesive and vibrant modern polity with emphasis on democracy, egalitarianism, secularism and rule of law. With a view to ushering in a socialistic pattern of society, emphasis was laid on planned development. Under successive five-year plans, efforts were made to ameliorate the lot of the poor and the downtrodden, build a scientific and technological infrastructure, revolutionize agriculture, diversify industry and raise industrial capacity and output.

There were scores of achievements-integration of some 600-odd states, resettlement of refugees, abolition of zamindari and other land reforms, liberation of Portuguese and French possessions in India, accession of the States of Hyderabad and Jammu and Kashmir, withstanding of several aggressions from our two neighbours, development of a meaningful foreign policy with the cardinal principles of nonalignment and peaceful coexistence (with over a hundred nations at one time accepting India's philosophy and leadership), conducting of thirteen general elections in the largest democracy on earth and peaceful transfer of power more than once from one party to another party or alliance, surviving many pressures, stresses and strains inflicted on our body politic by malevolent forces, both internal and external.

Without going into the details, it can be safely asserted that on the political plane, by far our greatest achievements have been (i) to bring about and maintain the unity and integrity of the nation and the secular character of the polity, and (ii) preserve the system of representative parliamentary democracy, ensuring the freedom and dignity of the individual. When we see all around us, these achievements appear still greater since there are very few nations in the world where really functioning democracy and freedom have survived. Not only are we a functioning democracy, we are also the largest on earth. We can take legitimate pride in the fact that-some temporary aberrations notwithstanding-whatever problems we faced, we have solved or sought to solve them within the existing system.

But there is a negative side also. The present is not very exhilarating, particularly when we think of the decline of values in all spheres and all professions, rampant corruption, terrorist activities, the use of money and muscle power in elections "the politicization of criminals" and "criminalisation of politics", the goings-on in some legislatures and the many fissiparous and divisive tendencies like casteism and communalism raising their ugly heads here and there. The noble aims and objectives enshrined in the Preamble have not been achieved. Instead of being based on some self-sacrifice and motivated by spirit of public service, politics has become a lucrative profession for sharing spoils of office. We have not been able to solve the basic problems of poverty, population, illiteracy, drinking water and development generally.

In any representative democracy, as Dr. Ambedkar had said, the root concerns are two, viz. stability and responsibility. The government that the system throws up should enjoy the strength and stability necessary for the security, development and welfare of the people and those called upon to govern should remain responsible to the people and their representatives.

Our founding fathers had the background of their sad experiences of the arbitrary colonial rule which was neither representative of the people nor responsive to their urges, aspirations and needs. It was not responsible or accountable to any representative body of the people in India. It was natural for the founding fathers to prize 'responsibility' of the executive and accountability of the administration above everything else.

They therefore adopted the parliamentary system with its concept of ministerial responsibility. In the Presidential system of Government of the U.S. type, the Executive is known to be more stable inasmuch as the President as the Chief Executive and head of the State is elected for a four year period and cannot be removed except by impeachment. Though not responsible to either House of the U.s. Congress, the Executive in the United Stales is directly responsible to the people once in four years. The French have tried to combine different models and establish what may be a parliamentary system of ministerial responsibility with a Presidential system of irremovable Chief Executive superimposed. While the Ministers with the Prime Minister at the head are responsible to the National Assembly, the President is elected by the people for a seven-year period and in order to win, he must secure more than 50 per cent votes.

The latest developments in India affecting the economy of the nation, however further underline the need for greater responsibility and accountability of the political Executive and the administrators to the people through the representative institutions. On the other hand, the spectacle of unethically engineered or defection manipulated majorities or of several successive hung Parliaments and State Legislatures and minority Governments and frequent General Elections naturally cause grave concern for stability. It is obvious that we in India would not like to dilute the element of responsibility. The choice, therefore, is to find ways and means of ensuring greater stability within the existing parliamentary system. It has also to be remembered that what is most important is the stability of the polity, of the democratic system and society and not the stability of the government of the day. All seem agreed that the country can ill-afford frequent general elections which, apart from other implications, cost collosal amounts of money. But, in a democracy, stability of the Government may not be the highest virtue. On 26 January 2000, the Constitution and the Republic of India completed half-a-century of their life. In an age when events move and developments take place at the speed of a tropical cyclone, this was not a short period in the life of a nation to take stock of our achievements and failures and attempt a self-appraisal of the working of our Constitution and the democratic institutions established thereunder.

Our Constitution is a living, dynamic process, always evolving, constantly in the making through amendments, judicial interpretations, and its actual working. It has been amended 83 times. Wide-ranging amendments followed the Swaran Singh Committee appointed by the Congress to review the Constitution. There have been numerous other amendments which have changed the Constitution without those being technically constitutional amendments. Some of the Supreme Court judgements have brought about fundamental changes. In the process there have been modifications, distortions and reversals of the intention of the framers of the Constitution. In this scenario, one has to consider whether there was anything wrong in having a look back at our experience of working the Constitution to find out if any of the problems have their source in systemic constraints or in faulty working or improper interpretation of constitutional provisions and if any remedial changes were called for. A case for review was not necessarily a case for constitutional amendments or systemic changes or for altering the basic features of the Constitution.

We have to consider what changes-legal, administrative, or other-are imperative to solve our main national problems. We have to ensure our nation's socioeconomic development and quality of life for all citizens, more particularly the deprived sections of society. Areas requiring immediate attention and separate in-depth analysis are those of Union-State relations (decentralization of powers including financial powers to the State and down to the grass roots levels), corruption (ensuring greater probity, integrity and transparency in all walks of life), reforming the political party system and the electoral processes, providing reasonable stability to society and the system without altering the parliamentary system or eroding responsibility and accountability of the government to the people, making the governance clean, efficient, less costly and citizen-friendly.

Various concrete suggestions have emerged. Not all of them may be compatible with each other or be fully acceptable. Also, they may not call for any constitutional amendments as such. But, all these may be useful as stimulants to our thinking on constitutional matters and may deserve to be considered. Some of these suggestions may be summed up here:

1. The Lok Sabha-particularly when it is a hung house with no leader commanding clear majority support should be called upon by the President to elect its Leader. The person so elected may be appointed Prime Minister. This will keep the President above unsavoury controversies.

2. Following the German practice, we could provide for a constructive vote of no-confidence in the Council of Ministers. This would make it essential for the House to select a successor simultaneously with the throwing out of the incumbent Prime Minister.
3. There may be a trend towards developing a system of two major federal parties. It may be possible for several broadly like-minded parties to come together on the basis of a common minimum programme or a national agenda and form a coalition government, with another similar coalition forming the opposition. The emergence of the National Democratic Alliance Government after the thirteenth general elections in 1999 is a pointer in that direction. But, it should not preclude any party on its own occupying in future a predominant position on the basis of popular support to its policies and programmes.
4. Political parties participating in the democratic processes of a nation's governance must themselves be democratic in their internal organization. They need to be regulated by law. Party membership must be open to all citizens without any distinction, party elections must be regular, free and fair and sources of party funds must be made public and party accounts must be duly audited and open to public scrutiny.
5. All candidates for elections to houses of Parliament or State Legislatures must be obliged by law to make verifiable public declarations of their movable and immovable assets.

Some of the other suggestions offered are:

(a) a three or four-tier system of governance with limited direct elections, a strong Union and strong units; the Gandhian bottom-up instead of the present top-down approach; something like the subsidiary principle in the European Union and in German polity where maximum power belongs to the grassroot level institutions and only what cannot be handled at the lower level is entrusted to the higher;.

(b) reforming the electoral system to make it less expensive, more representative and free from money and muscle power;

(c) placing a strict ceiling on the number of ministers and equivalent posts both at the Union and State levels;

(d) disqualifying all defectors from membership and from holding any public office;

(e) downsizing the bureaucracy drastically, debureaucratization of development planning and providing a mechanism for compulsory consensus-building among people and parties on some basic issues like family planning;

(g) placing a strict ceiling on the borrowing powers of the government and making prior legislative approval necessary;

(h) transferring right to work and compulsory elementary education to the fundamental rights chapter; and

(i) finally, making the Government and the administration clean, corruption free and citizen-friendly through whatever legal, administrative, judicial or other reforms found necessary.

REFERENCES

- Best M.: *The New Competition. Institutions of Industrial Restructuring*, Cambridge, Polity Press, 1990.
- Hans J. : *Politics Among Nations: The Struggle for Power and Peace*, New York, Knopf, 1960.
- Peddleton, E.: *Public Administration and the Public Interest*, New York, McGraw-Hill, 1936.
- Sullivan, N.: *Bureaucrats and Policy Making*, New York, Holmes & Meier, 1984.

6

Powers and Functions of the Executive, Parliament and President

THE EXECUTIVE

The President and Vice-President

52. The President of India.—There shall be a President of India.

53. Executive power of the Union.—(1) The executive power of the Union shall be vested in the President and shall be exercised by him either directly or through officers subordinate to him in accordance with this Constitution.

(2) Without prejudice to the generality of the foregoing provision, the supreme command of the Defence Forces of the Union shall be vested in the President and the exercise thereof shall be regulated by law.

(3) Nothing in this article shall—

(a) be deemed to transfer to the President any functions conferred by any existing law on the Government of any State or other authority; or

(b) prevent Parliament from conferring by law functions on authorities other than the President.

54. Election of President.—The President shall be elected by the members of an electoral college consisting of—

(*a*) the elected members of both Houses of Parliament; and

(*b*) the elected members of the Legislative Assemblies of the States.

Explanation.—In this article and in article 55, "State" includes the National Capital Territory of Delhi and the Union territory of Pondicherry.

55. Manner of election of President. —

(1) As far as practicable, there shall be uniformity in the scale of representation of the different States at the election of the President.

(2) For the purpose of securing such uniformity among the States *inter se* as well as parity between the States as a whole and the Union, the number of votes which each elected member of Parliament and of the Legislative Assembly of each State is entitled to cast at such election shall be determined in the following manner:—

(*a*) every elected member of the Legislative Assembly of a State shall have as many votes as there are multiples of one thousand in the quotient obtained by dividing the population of the State by the total number of the elected members of the Assembly;

(*b*) if, after taking the said multiples of one thousand, the remainder is not less than five hundred, then the vote of each member referred to in sub-clause (*a*) shall be further increased by one;

(*c*) each elected member of either House of Parliament shall have such number of votes as may be obtained by dividing the total number of votes assigned to the members of the Legislative Assemblies of the States under sub-clauses (*a*) and (*b*) by the total number of the elected members of both Houses of Parliament, fractions exceeding one-half being counted as one and other fractions being disregarded.

(3) The election of the President shall be held in accordance with the system of proportional representation by means of the single transferable vote and the voting at such election shall be by secret ballot.

Explanation.— In this article, the expression "population" means the population as ascertained at the last preceding census of which the relevant figures have been published:

Provided that the reference in this *Explanation* to the last preceding census of which the relevant figures have been published shall, until the relevant figures for the first census taken after the year 2026 have been published, be construed as a reference to the 1971 census.

56. Term of office of President.—(1) The President shall hold office for a term of five years from the date on which he enters upon his office:

Provided that—

(a) the President may, by writing under his hand addressed to the Vice-President, resign his office;

(b) the President may, for violation of the Constitution, be removed from office by impeachment in the manner provided in article 61;

(c) the President shall, notwithstanding the expiration of his term, continue to hold office until his successor enters upon his office.

(2) Any resignation addressed to the Vice-President under clause *(a)* of the proviso to clause (1) shall forthwith be communicated by him to the Speaker of the House of the People.

57. Eligibility for re-election.—A person who holds, or who has held, office as President shall, subject to the other provisions of this Constitution, be eligible for re-election to that office.

58. Qualifications for election as President.—(1) No person shall be eligible for election as President unless he—

(a) is a citizen of India,

(b) has completed the age of thirty-five years, and

(c) is qualified for election as a member of the House of the People.

(2) A person shall not be eligible for election as President if he holds any office of profit under the Government of India

or the Government of any State or under any local or other authority subject to the control of any of the said Governments.

Explanation.—For the purposes of this article, a person shall not be deemed to hold any office of profit by reason only that he is the President or Vice- President of the Union or the Governor of any State or is a Minister either for the Union or for any State.

59. Conditions of President's office.—(1) The President shall not be a member of either House of Parliament or of a House of the Legislature of any State, and if a member of either House of Parliament or of a House of the Legislature of any State be elected President, he shall be deemed to have vacated his seat in that House on the date on which he enters upon his office as President.

(2) The President shall not hold any other office of profit.

(3) The President shall be entitled without payment of rent to the use of his official residences and shall be also entitled to such emoluments, allowances and privileges as may be determined by Parliament by law and, until provision in that behalf is so made, such emoluments, allowances and privileges as are specified in the Second Schedule.

(4) The emoluments and allowances of the President shall not be diminished during his term of office.

60. Oath or affirmation by the President.—Every President and every person acting as President or discharging the functions of the President shall, before entering upon his office, make and subscribe in the presence of the Chief Justice of India or, in his absence, the senior-most Judge of the Supreme Court available, an oath or affirmation in the following form, that is to say—

"I, A.B., do swear in the name of God that I will faithfully execute solemnly affirm

the office of President (or discharge the functions of the President) of India and will to the best of my ability preserve, protect and defend the Constitution and the law and that I will devote myself to the service and well-being of the people of India.".

61. Procedure for impeachment of the President.— (1) When a President is to be impeached for violation of the Constitution, the charge shall be preferred by either House of Parliament.

(2) No such charge shall be preferred unless—

(a) the proposal to prefer such charge is contained in a resolution which has been moved after at least fourteen days' notice in writing signed by not less than one-fourth of the total number of members of the House has been given of their intention to move the resolution, and

(b) such resolution has been passed by a majority of not less than two-thirds of the total membership of the House.

(3) When a charge has been so preferred by either House of Parliament, the other House shall investigate the charge or cause the charge to be investigated and the President shall have the right to appear and to be represented at such investigation.

(4) If as a result of the investigation a resolution is passed by a majority of not less than two-thirds of the total membership of the House by which the charge was investigated or caused to be investigated, declaring that the charge preferred against the President has been sustained, such resolution shall have the effect of removing the President from his office as from the date on which the resolution is so passed.

62. Time of holding election to fill vacancy in the office of President and the term of office of person elected to fill casual vacancy. —

(1) An election to fill a vacancy caused by the expiration of the term of office of President shall be completed before the expiration of the term.

(2) An election to fill a vacancy in the office of President occurring by reason of his death, resignation or removal, or otherwise shall be held as soon as possible after, and in no case later than six months from, the date of occurrence of the vacancy; and the person elected to fill the vacancy shall, subject to the provisions of article 56, be entitled to hold office for the full

term of five years from the date on which he enters upon his office.

63. The Vice-President of India.—There shall be a Vice-President of India.

64. The Vice-President to be *ex officio* Chairman of the Council of States.—The Vice-President shall be *ex officio* Chairman of the Council of States and shall not hold any other office of profit:

Provided that during any period when the Vice-President acts as President or discharges the functions of the President under article 65, he shall not perform the duties of the office of Chairman of the Council of States and shall not be entitled to any salary or allowance payable to the Chairman of the Council of States under article 97.

65. The Vice-President to act as President or to discharge his functions during casual vacancies in the office, or during the absence, of President.—

(1) In the event of the occurrence of any vacancy in the office of the President by reason of his death, resignation or removal, or otherwise, the Vice-President shall act as President until the date on which a new President elected in accordance with the provisions of this Chapter to fill such vacancy enters upon his office.

(2) When the President is unable to discharge his functions owing to absence, illness or any other cause, the Vice-President shall discharge his functions until the date on which the President resumes his duties.

(3) The Vice-President shall, during, and in respect of, the period while he is so acting as, or discharging the functions of, President, have all the powers and immunities of the President and be entitled to such emoluments, allowances and privileges as may be determined by Parliament by law and, until provision in that behalf is so made, such emoluments, allowances and privileges as are specified in the Second Schedule.

66. Election of Vice-President.—

(1) The Vice-President shall be elected by the members of

an electoral college consisting of the members of both Houses of Parliament in accordance with the system of proportional representation by means of the single transferable vote and the voting at such election shall be by secret ballot.

(2) The Vice-President shall not be a member of either House of Parliament or of a House of the Legislature of any State, and if a member of either House of Parliament or of a House of the Legislature of any State be elected Vice-President, he shall be deemed to have vacated his seat in that House on the date on which he enters upon his office as Vice-President.

(3) No person shall be eligible for election as Vice-President unless he—

(a) is a citizen of India;

(b) has completed the age of thirty-five years; and

(c) is qualified for election as a member of the Council of States.

(4) A person shall not be eligible for election as Vice-President if he holds any office of profit under the Government of India or the Government of any State or under any local or other authority subject to the control of any of the said Governments.

Explanation.— For the purposes of this article, a person shall not be deemed to hold any office of profit by reason only that he is the President or Vice- President of the Union or the Governor of any State or is a Minister either for the Union or for any State.

67. Term of office of Vice-President.—The Vice-President shall hold office for a term of five years from the date on which he enters upon his office:

Provided that—

(a) a Vice-President may, by writing under his hand addressed to the President, resign his office;

(b) a Vice-President may be removed from his office by a resolution of the Council of States passed by a majority of all the then members of the Council and agreed to by the House of the People; but no resolution for the

purpose of this clause shall be moved unless at least fourteen days' notice has been given of the intention to move the resolution;

(c) a Vice-President shall, notwithstanding the expiration of his term, continue to hold office until his successor enters upon his office.

68. Time of holding election to fill vacancy in the office of Vice-President and the term of office of person elected to fill casual vacancy.—

(1) An election to fill a vacancy caused by the expiration of the term of office of Vice-President shall be completed before the expiration of the term.

(2) An election to fill a vacancy in the office of Vice-President occurring by reason of his death, resignation or removal, or otherwise shall be held as soon as possible after the occurrence of the vacancy, and the person elected to fill the vacancy shall, subject to the provisions of article 67, be entitled to hold office for the full term of five years from the date on which he enters upon his office.

69. Oath or affirmation by the Vice-President.—Every Vice-President shall, before entering upon his office, make and subscribe before the President, or some person appointed in that behalf by him, an oath or affirmation in the following form, that is to say—

"I, A.B., do swear in the name of God that I will bear true faith and solemnly affirm allegiance to the Constitution of India as by law established and that I will faithfully discharge the duty upon which I am about to enter."

70. Discharge of President's functions in other contingencies.—Parliament may make such provisions as it thinks fit for the discharge of the functions of the President in any contingency not provided for in this Chapter.

71. Matters relating to, or connected with, the election of a President or Vice-President.—

(1) All doubts and disputes arising out of or in connection with the election of a President or Vice-President shall be

inquired into and decided by the Supreme Court whose decision shall be final.

(2) If the election of a person as President or Vice-President is declared void by the Supreme Court, acts done by him in the exercise and performance of the powers and duties of the office of President or Vice-President, as the case may be, on or before the date of the decision of the Supreme Court shall not be invalidated by reason of that declaration.

(3) Subject to the provisions of this Constitution, Parliament may by law regulate any matter relating to or connected with the election of a President or Vice-President.

(4) The election of a person as President or Vice-President shall not be called in question on the ground of the existence of any vacancy for whatever reason among the members of the electoral college electing him.

72. Power of President to grant pardons, etc., and to suspend, remit or commute sentences in certain cases.— (1) The President shall have the power to grant pardons, reprieves, respites or remissions of punishment or to suspend, remit or commute the sentence of any person convicted of any offence—

(a) in all cases where the punishment or sentence is by a Court Martial;

(b) in all cases where the punishment or sentence is for an offence against any law relating to a matter to which the executive power of the Union extends;

(c) in all cases where the sentence is a sentence of death.

(2) Nothing in sub-clause *(a)* of clause (1) shall affect the power conferred by law on any officer of the Armed Forces of the Union to suspend, remit or commute a sentence passed by a Court Martial.

(3) Nothing in sub-clause *(c)* of clause (1) shall affect the power to suspend, remit or commute a sentence of death exercisable by the Governor of a State under any law for the time being in force.

73. Extent of executive power of the Union.— (1)

Subject to the provisions of this Constitution, the executive power of the Union shall extend—

(a) to the matters with respect to which Parliament has power to make laws; and

(b) to the exercise of such rights, authority and jurisdiction as are exercisable by the Government of India by virtue of any treaty or agreement:

Provided that the executive power referred to in sub-clause *(a)* shall not, save as expressly provided in this Constitution or in any law made by Parliament, extend in any State to matters with respect to which the Legislature of the State has also power to make laws.

(2) Until otherwise provided by Parliament, a State and any officer or authority of a State may, notwithstanding anything in this article, continue to exercise in matters with respect to which Parliament has power to make laws for that State such executive power or functions as the State or officer or authority thereof could exercise immediately before the commencement of this Constitution.

Council of Ministers

74. Council of Ministers to aid and advise President.—

(1) There shall be a Council of Ministers with the Prime Minister at the head to aid and advise the President who shall, in the exercise of his functions, act in accordance with such advice: Provided that the President may require the Council of Ministers to reconsider such advice, either generally or otherwise, and the President shall act in accordance with the advice tendered after such reconsideration.

(2) The question whether any, and if so what, advice was tendered by Ministers to the President shall not be inquired into in any court.

75. Other provisions as to Ministers.—

(1) The Prime Minister shall be appointed by the President and the other Ministers shall be appointed by the President on the advice of the Prime Minister.

(1A) The total number of Ministers, including the Prime Minister, in the Council of Ministers shall not exceed fifteen per cent. of the total number of members of the House of the People.

(1B) A member of either House of Parliament belonging to any political party who is disqualified for being a member of that House under paragraph 2 of the Tenth Schedule shall also be disqualified to be appointed as a Minister under clause (1) for duration of the period commencing from the date of his disqualification till the date on which the term of his office as such member would expire or where he contests any election to either House of Parliament before the expiry of such period, till the date on which he is declared elected, whichever is earlier.

(2) The Ministers shall hold office during the pleasure of the President.

(3) The Council of Ministers shall be collectively responsible to the House of the People.

(4) Before a Minister enters upon his office, the President shall administer to him the oaths of office and of secrecy according to the forms set out for the purpose in the Third Schedule.

(5) A Minister who for any period of six consecutive months is not a member of either House of Parliament shall at the expiration of that period cease to be a Minister.

(6) The salaries and allowances of Ministers shall be such as Parliament may from time to time by law determine and, until Parliament so determines, shall be as specified in the Second Schedule.

The Attorney-General for India

76. Attorney-General for India.—

(1) The President shall appoint a person who is qualified to be appointed a Judge of the Supreme Court to be Attorney-General for India.

(2) It shall be the duty of the Attorney-General to give advice to the Government of India upon such legal matters, and

to perform such other duties of a legal character, as may from time to time be referred or assigned to him by the President, and to discharge the functions conferred on him by or under this Constitution or any other law for the time being in force.

(3) In the performance of his duties the Attorney-General shall have right of audience in all courts in the territory of India.

(4) The Attorney-General shall hold office during the pleasure of the President, and shall receive such remuneration as the President may determine.

Conduct of Government Business

77. Conduct of business of the Government of India.—

(1) All executive action of the Government of India shall be expressed to be taken in the name of the President.

(2) Orders and other instruments made and executed in the name of the President shall be authenticated in such manner as may be specified in rules to be made by the President, and the validity of an order or instrument which is so authenticated shall not be called in question on the ground that it is not an order or instrument made or executed by the President.

(3) The President shall make rules for the more convenient transaction of the business of the Government of India, and for the allocation among Ministers of the said business.

78. Duties of Prime Minister as respects the furnishing of information to the President, etc.—It shall be the duty of the Prime Minister—

(a) to communicate to the President all decisions of the Council of Ministers relating to the administration of the affairs of the Union and proposals for legislation;

(b) to furnish such information relating to the administration of the affairs of the Union and proposals for legislation as the President may call for; and

(c) if the President so requires, to submit for the consideration of the Council of Ministers any matter on which a decision has been taken by a Minister but which has not been considered by the Council.

PARLIAMENT

General

79. Constitution of Parliament.—There shall be a Parliament for the Union which shall consist of the President and two Houses to be known respectively as the Council of States and the House of the People.

80. Composition of the Council of States.—

(1) The Council of States shall consist of—

(a) twelve members to be nominated by the President in accordance with the provisions of clause (3); and

(b) not more than two hundred and thirty-eight representatives of the States and of the Union territories.

(2) The allocation of seats in the Council of States to be filled by representatives of the States and of the Union territories shall be in accordance with the provisions in that behalf contained in the Fourth Schedule.

(3) The members to be nominated by the President under sub-clause *(a)* of clause (1) shall consist of persons having special knowledge or practical experience in respect of such matters as the following, namely:—

Literature, science, art and social service.

(4) The representatives of each State in the Council of States shall be elected by the elected members of the Legislative Assembly of the State in accordance with the system of proportional representation by means of the single transferable vote.

(5) The representatives of the Union territories in the Council of States shall be chosen in such manner as Parliament may by law prescribe.

81. Composition of the House of the People.—

(1) Subject to the provisions of article 331, the House of the People shall consist of—

(a) not more than five hundred and thirty members chosen by direct election from territorial constituencies in the States, and

(*b*) not more than twenty members to represent the Union territories, chosen in such manner as Parliament may by law provide.

(2) For the purposes of sub-clause (*a*) of clause (1),—

(*a*) there shall be allotted to each State a number of seats in the House of the People in such manner that the ratio between that number and the population of the State is, so far as practicable, the same for all States; and

(*b*) each State shall be divided into territorial constituencies in such manner that the ratio between the population of each constituency and the number of seats allotted to it is, so far as practicable, the same throughout the State:

Provided that the provisions of sub-clause (*a*) of this clause shall not be applicable for the purpose of allotment of seats in the House of the People to any State so long as the population of that State does not exceed six millions.

(3) In this article, the expression "population" means the population as ascertained at the last preceding census of which the relevant figures have been published:

Provided that the reference in this clause to the last preceding census of which the relevant figures have been published shall, until the relevant figures for the first census taken after the year 2026 have been published, be construed, —

(*i*) for the purposes of sub-clause (*a*) of clause (2) and the proviso to that clause, as a reference to the 1971 census; and

(*ii*) for the purposes of sub-clause (*b*) of clause (2) as a reference to the 2001 census.

82. Readjustment after each census.—Upon the completion of each census, the allocation of seats in the House of the People to the States and the division of each State into territorial constituencies shall be readjusted by such authority and in such manner as Parliament may by law determine:

Provided that such readjustment shall not affect representation in the House of the People until the dissolution of the then existing House:

Provided further that such readjustment shall take effect from such date as the President may, by order, specify and until such readjustment takes effect, any election to the House may be held on the basis of the territorial constituencies existing before such readjustment:

Provided also that until the relevant figures for the first census taken after the year 2026 have been published, it shall not be necessary to readjust—

(*i*) the allocation of seats in the House of People to the States as readjusted on the basis of the 1971 census; and

(*ii*) the division of each State into territorial constituencies as may be readjusted on the basis of the 2001 census, under this article.

83. Duration of Houses of Parliament.—

(1) The Council of States shall not be subject to dissolution, but as nearly as possible one-third of the members thereof shall retire as soon as may be on the expiration of every second year in accordance with the provisions made in that behalf by Parliament by law.

(2) The House of the People, unless sooner dissolved, shall continue for five years from the date appointed for its first meeting and no longer and the expiration of the said period of five years shall operate as a dissolution of the House:

Provided that the said period may, while a Proclamation of Emergency is in operation, be extended by Parliament by law for a period not exceeding one year at a time and not extending in any case beyond a period of six months after the Proclamation has ceased to operate.

84. Qualification for membership of Parliament.—A person shall not be qualified to be chosen to fill a seat in Parliament unless he—

(a) is a citizen of India, and makes and subscribes before some person authorised in that behalf by the Election Commission an oath or affirmation according to the form set out for the purpose in the Third Schedule;

(b) is, in the case of a seat in the Council of States, not less

than thirty years of age and, in the case of a seat in the House of the People, not less than twenty- five years of age; and

(c) possesses such other qualifications as may be prescribed in that behalf by or under any law made by Parliament.

85. Sessions of Parliament, prorogation and dissolution.—

(1) The President shall from time to time summon each House of Parliament to meet at such time and place as he thinks fit, but six months shall not intervene between its last sitting in one session and the date appointed for its first sitting in the next session.

(2) The President may from time to time—

(a) prorogue the Houses or either House;

(b) dissolve the House of the People.

86. Right of President to address and send messages to Houses.—

(1) The President may address either House of Parliament or both Houses assembled together, and for that purpose require the attendance of members.

(2) The President may send messages to either House of Parliament, whether with respect to a Bill then pending in Parliament or otherwise, and a House to which any message is so sent shall with all convenient despatch consider any matter required by the message to be taken into consideration.

87. Special address by the President.—

(1) At the commencement of the first session after each general election to the House of the People and at the commencement of the first session of each year the President shall address both Houses of Parliament assembled together and inform Parliament of the causes of its summons.

(2) Provision shall be made by the rules regulating the procedure of either House for the allotment of time for discussion of the matters referred to in such address.

88. Rights of Ministers and Attorney-General as respects Houses.—Every Minister and the Attorney-General of India shall have the right to speak in, and otherwise to take part in the proceedings of, either House, any joint sitting of the Houses, and any committee of Parliament of which he may be named a member, but shall not by virtue of this article be entitled to vote.

Officers of Parliament

89. The Chairman and Deputy Chairman of the Council of States.—

(1) The Vice- President of India shall be *ex officio* Chairman of the Council of States.

(2) The Council of States shall, as soon as may be, choose a member of the Council to be Deputy Chairman thereof and, so often as the office of Deputy Chairman becomes vacant, the Council shall choose another member to be Deputy Chairman thereof.

90. Vacation and resignation of, and removal from, the office of Deputy Chairman.—A member holding office as Deputy Chairman of the Council of States—

(a) shall vacate his office if he ceases to be a member of the Council;

(b) may at any time, by writing under his hand addressed to the Chairman, resign his office; and

(c) may be removed from his office by a resolution of the Council passed by a majority of all the then members of the Council:

Provided that no resolution for the purpose of clause *(c)* shall be moved unless at least fourteen days' notice has been given of the intention to move the resolution.

91. Power of the Deputy Chairman or other person to perform the duties of the office of, or to act as, Chairman.—

(1)While the office of Chairman is vacant, or during any period when the Vice-President is acting as, or discharging the functions of, President, the duties of the office shall be performed by the Deputy Chairman, or, if the office of Deputy Chairman is also vacant, by such member of the Council of States as the President may appoint for the purpose.

(2) During the absence of the Chairman from any sitting of the Council of States the Deputy Chairman, or, if he is also absent, such person as may be determined by the rules of procedure of the Council, or, if no such person is present, such other person as may be determined by the Council, shall act as Chairman.

92. The Chairman or the Deputy Chairman not to preside while a resolution for his removal from office is under consideration.—

(1) At any sitting of the Council of States, while any resolution for the removal of the Vice-President from his office is under consideration, the Chairman, or while any resolution for the removal of the Deputy Chairman from his office is under consideration, the Deputy Chairman, shall not, though he is present, preside, and the provisions of clause (2) of article 91 shall apply in relation to every such sitting as they apply in relation to a sitting from which the Chairman, or, as the case may be, the Deputy Chairman, is absent.

(2) The Chairman shall have the right to speak in, and otherwise to take part in the proceedings of, the Council of States while any resolution for the removal of the Vice-President from his office is under consideration in the Council, but, notwithstanding anything in article 100, shall not be entitled to vote at all on such resolution or on any other matter during such proceedings.

93. The Speaker and Deputy Speaker of the House of the People.— The House of the People shall, as soon as may be, choose two members of the House to be respectively Speaker and Deputy Speaker thereof and, so often as the office of Speaker or Deputy Speaker becomes vacant, the House shall choose another member to be Speaker or Deputy Speaker, as the case may be.

94. Vacation and resignation of, and removal from, the offices of Speaker and Deputy Speaker.— A member holding office as Speaker or Deputy Speaker of the House of the People—

(a) shall vacate his office if he ceases to be a member of the House of the People;

(b) may at any time, by writing under his hand addressed, if such member is the Speaker, to the Deputy Speaker, and if such member is the Deputy Speaker, to the Speaker, resign his office; and

(c) may be removed from his office by a resolution of the House of the People passed by a majority of all the then members of the House:

Provided that no resolution for the purpose of clause *(c)* shall be moved unless at least fourteen days' notice has been given of the intention to move the resolution:

Provided further that, whenever the House of the People is dissolved, the Speaker shall not vacate his office until immediately before the first meeting of the House of the People after the dissolution.

95. Power of the Deputy Speaker or other person to perform the duties of the office of, or to act as, Speaker.—

(1) While the office of Speaker is vacant, the duties of the office shall be performed by the Deputy Speaker or, if the office of Deputy Speaker is also vacant, by such member of the House of the People as the President may appoint for the purpose.

(2) During the absence of the Speaker from any sitting of the House of the People the Deputy Speaker or, if he is also absent, such person as may be determined by the rules of procedure of the House, or, if no such person is present, such other person as may be determined by the House, shall act as Speaker.

96. The Speaker or the Deputy Speaker not to preside while a resolution for his removal from office is under consideration.—

(1) At any sitting of the House of the People, while any resolution for the removal of the Speaker from his office is under consideration, the Speaker, or while any resolution for the removal of the Deputy Speaker from his office is under consideration, the Deputy Speaker, shall not, though he is

present, preside, and the provisions of clause (2) of article 95 shall apply in relation to every such sitting as they apply in relation to a sitting from which the Speaker, or, as the case may be, the Deputy Speaker, is absent.

(2) The Speaker shall have the right to speak in, and otherwise to take part in the proceedings of, the House of the People while any resolution for his removal from office is under consideration in the House and shall, notwithstanding anything in article 100, be entitled to vote only in the first instance on such resolution or on any other matter during such proceedings but not in the case of an equality of votes.

97. Salaries and allowances of the Chairman and Deputy Chairman and the Speaker and Deputy Speaker.— There shall be paid to the Chairman and the Deputy Chairman of the Council of States, and to the Speaker and the Deputy Speaker of the House of the People, such salaries and allowances as may be respectively fixed by Parliament by law and, until provision in that behalf is so made, such salaries and allowances as are specified in the Second Schedule.

98. Secretariat of Parliament.—

(1) Each House of Parliament shall have a separate secretarial staff:

Provided that nothing in this clause shall be construed as preventing the creation of posts common to both Houses of Parliament.

(2) Parliament may by law regulate the recruitment, and the conditions of service of persons appointed, to the secretarial staff of either House of Parliament.

(3) Until provision is made by Parliament under clause (2), the President may, after consultation with the Speaker of the House of the People or the Chairman of the Council of States, as the case may be, make rules regulating the recruitment, and the conditions of service of persons appointed, to the secretarial staff of the House of the People or the Council of States, and any rules so made shall have effect subject to the provisions of any law made under the said clause.

Conduct of Business

99. Oath or affirmation by members.— Every member of either House of Parliament shall, before taking his seat, make and subscribe before the President, or some person appointed in that behalf by him, an oath or affirmation according to the form set out for the purpose in the Third Schedule.

100. Voting in Houses, power of Houses to act notwithstanding vacancies and quorum.—

(1) Save as otherwise provided in this Constitution, all questions at any sitting of either House or joint sitting of the Houses shall be determined by a majority of votes of the members present and voting, other than the Speaker or person acting as Chairman or Speaker.

The Chairman or Speaker, or person acting as such, shall not vote in the first instance, but shall have and exercise a casting vote in the case of an equality of votes.

(2) Either House of Parliament shall have power to act notwithstanding any vacancy in the membership thereof, and any proceedings in Parliament shall be valid notwithstanding that it is discovered subsequently that some person who was not entitled so to do sat or voted or otherwise took part in the proceedings.

(3) Until Parliament by law otherwise provides, the quorum to constitute a meeting of either House of Parliament shall be one-tenth of the total number of members of the House.

(4) If at any time during a meeting of a House there is no quorum, it shall be the duty of the Chairman or Speaker, or person acting as such, either to adjourn the House or to suspend the meeting until there is a quorum.

Disqualifications of Members

101. Vacation of seats.—

(1) No person shall be a member of both Houses of Parliament and provision shall be made by Parliament by law for the vacation by a person who is chosen a member of both Houses of his seat in one House or the other.

(2) No person shall be a member both of Parliament and of a House of the Legislature of a State, and if a person is chosen a member both of Parliament and of a House of the Legislature of a State, then, at the expiration of such period as may be specified in rules made by the President, that person's seat in Parliament shall become vacant, unless he has previously resigned his seat in the Legislature of the State.

(3) If a member of either House of Parliament—

(a) becomes subject to any of the disqualifications mentioned in clause (1) or clause (2) of article 102, or

(b) resigns his seat by writing under his hand addressed to the Chairman or the Speaker, as the case may be, and his resignation is accepted by the Chairman or the Speaker, as the case may be, his seat shall thereupon become vacant:

Provided that in the case of any resignation referred to in sub-clause *(b)*, if from information received or otherwise and after making such inquiry as he thinks fit, the Chairman or the Speaker, as the case may be, is satisfied that such resignation is not voluntary or genuine, he shall not accept such resignation.

(4) If for a period of sixty days a member of either House of Parliament is without permission of the House absent from all meetings thereof, the House may declare his seat vacant:

Provided that in computing the said period of sixty days no account shall be taken of any period during which the House is prorogued or is adjourned for more than four consecutive days.

102. Disqualifications for membership.—

(1) A person shall be disqualified for being chosen as, and for being, a member of either House of Parliament—

(a) if he holds any office of profit under the Government of India or the Government of any State, other than an office declared by Parliament by law not to disqualify its holder;

(b) if he is of unsound mind and stands so declared by a competent court;

(c) if he is an undischarged insolvent;

(d) if he is not a citizen of India, or has voluntarily acquired

the citizenship of a foreign State, or is under any acknowledgment of allegiance or adherence to a foreign State;

(e) if he is so disqualified by or under any law made by Parliament.

Explanation.—For the purposes of this clause a person shall not be deemed to hold an office of profit under the Government of India or the Government of any State by reason only that he is a Minister either for the Union or for such State.

(2) A person shall be disqualified for being a member of either House of Parliament if he is so disqualified under the Tenth Schedule.

103. Decision on questions as to disqualifications of members.—

(1) If any question arises as to whether a member of either House of Parliament has become subject to any of the disqualifications mentioned in clause (1) of article 102, the question shall be referred for the decision of the President and his decision shall be final.

(2) Before giving any decision on any such question, the President shall obtain the opinion of the Election Commission and shall act according to such opinion.

104. Penalty for sitting and voting before making oath or affirmation under article 99 or when not qualified or when disqualified.—If a person sits or votes as a member of either House of Parliament before he has complied with the requirements of article 99, or when he knows that he is not qualified or that he is disqualified for membership thereof, or that he is prohibited from so doing by the provisions of any law made by Parliament, he shall be liable in respect of each day on which he so sits or votes to a penalty of five hundred rupees to be recovered as a debt due to the Union.

Powers, Privileges and Immunities of Parliament and its Members

105. Powers, privileges, etc., of the Houses of Parliament and of the members and committees thereof.—

(1) Subject to the provisions of this Constitution and to the rules and standing orders regulating the procedure of Parliament, there shall be freedom of speech in Parliament.

(2) No member of Parliament shall be liable to any proceedings in any court in respect of any thing said or any vote given by him in Parliament or any committee thereof, and no person shall be so liable in respect of the publication by or under the authority of either House of Parliament of any report, paper, votes or proceedings.

(3) In other respects, the powers, privileges and immunities of each House of Parliament, and of the members and the committees of each House, shall be such as may from time to time be defined by Parliament by law, and, until so defined, shall be those of that House and of its members and committees immediately before the coming into force of section 15 of the Constitution (Forty-fourth Amendment) Act, 1978.

(4) The provisions of clauses (1), (2) and (3) shall apply in relation to persons who by virtue of this Constitution have the right to speak in, and otherwise to take part in the proceedings of, a House of Parliament or any committee thereof as they apply in relation to members of Parliament.

106. Salaries and allowances of members.— Members of either House of Parliament shall be entitled to receive such salaries and allowances as may from time to time be determined by Parliament by law and, until provision in that respect is so made, allowances at such rates and upon such conditions as were immediately before the commencement of this Constitution applicable in the case of members of the Constituent Assembly of the Dominion of India.

Legislative Procedure

107. Provisions as to introduction and passing of Bills.—

(1) Subject to the provisions of articles 109 and 117 with respect to Money Bills and other financial Bills, a Bill may originate in either House of Parliament.

(2) Subject to the provisions of articles 108 and 109, a Bill

shall not be deemed to have been passed by the Houses of Parliament unless it has been agreed to by both Houses, either without amendment or with such amendments only as are agreed to by both Houses.

(3) A Bill pending in Parliament shall not lapse by reason of the prorogation of the Houses.

(4) A Bill pending in the Council of States which has not been passed by the House of the People shall not lapse on a dissolution of the House of the People.

(5) A Bill which is pending in the House of the People, or which having been passed by the House of the People is pending in the Council of States, shall, subject to the provisions of article 108, lapse on a dissolution of the House of the People.

108. Joint sitting of both Houses in certain cases.—

(1) If after a Bill has been passed by one House and transmitted to the other House—

(*a*) the Bill is rejected by the other House; or

(*b*) the Houses have finally disagreed as to the amendments to be made in the Bill; or

(*c*) more than six months elapse from the date of the reception of the Bill by the other House without the Bill being passed by it, the President may, unless the Bill has elapsed by reason of a dissolution of the House of the People, notify to the Houses by message if they are sitting or by public notification if they are not sitting, his intention to summon them to meet in a joint sitting for the purpose of deliberating and voting on the Bill:

Provided that nothing in this clause shall apply to a Money Bill.

(2) In reckoning any such period of six months as is referred to in clause (1), no account shall be taken of any period during which the House referred to in sub-clause (*c*) of that clause is prorogued or adjourned for more than four consecutive days.

(3) Where the President has under clause (1) notified his intention of summoning the Houses to meet in a joint sitting,

neither House shall proceed further with the Bill, but the President may at any time after the date of his notification summon the Houses to meet in a joint sitting for the purpose specified in the notification and, if he does so, the Houses shall meet accordingly.

(4) If at the joint sitting of the two Houses the Bill, with such amendments, if any, as are agreed to in joint sitting, is passed by a majority of the total number of members of both Houses present and voting, it shall be deemed for the purposes of this Constitution to have been passed by both Houses:

Provided that at a joint sitting—

(*a*) if the Bill, having been passed by one House, has not been passed by the other House with amendments and returned to the House in which it originated, no amendment shall be proposed to the Bill other than such amendments (if any) as are made necessary by the delay in the passage of the Bill;

(*b*) if the Bill has been so passed and returned, only such amendments as aforesaid shall be proposed to the Bill and such other amendments as are relevant to the matters with respect to which the Houses have not agreed;

and the decision of the person presiding as to the amendments which are admissible under this clause shall be final.

(5) A joint sitting may be held under this article and a Bill passed thereat, notwithstanding that a dissolution of the House of the People has intervened since the President notified his intention to summon the Houses to meet therein.

109. Special procedure in respect of Money Bills.—

(1) A Money Bill shall not be introduced in the Council of States.

(2) After a Money Bill has been passed by the House of the People it shall be transmitted to the Council of States for its recommendations and the Council of States shall within a period of fourteen days from the date of its receipt of the Bill return the Bill to the House of the People with its recommendations and the House of the People may thereupon

either accept or reject all or any of the recommendations of the Council of States.

(3) If the House of the People accepts any of the recommendations of the Council of States, the Money Bill shall be deemed to have been passed by both Houses with the amendments recommended by the Council of States and accepted by the House of the People.

(4) If the House of the People does not accept any of the recommendations of the Council of States, the Money Bill shall be deemed to have been passed by both Houses in the form in which it was passed by the House of the People without any of the amendments recommended by the Council of States.

(5) If a Money Bill passed by the House of the People and transmitted to the Council of States for its recommendations is not returned to the House of the People within the said period of fourteen days, it shall be deemed to have been passed by both Houses at the expiration of the said period in the form in which it was passed by the House of the People.

110. Definition of "Money Bills".—

(1) For the purposes of this Chapter, a Bill shall be deemed to be a Money Bill if it contains only provisions dealing with all or any of the following matters, namely:—

(*a*) the imposition, abolition, remission, alteration or regulation of any tax;

(*b*) the regulation of the borrowing of money or the giving of any guarantee by the Government of India, or the amendment of the law with respect to any financial obligations undertaken or to be undertaken by the Government of India;

(*c*) the custody of the Consolidated Fund or the Contingency Fund of India, the payment of moneys into or the withdrawal of moneys from any such Fund;

(*d*) the appropriation of moneys out of the Consolidated Fund of India;

(*e*) the declaring of any expenditure to be expenditure charged on the Consolidated Fund of India or the increasing of the amount of any such expenditure;

((*f*) the receipt of money on account of the Consolidated Fund of India or the public account of India or the custody or issue of such money or the audit of the accounts of the Union or of a State; or

(*g*) any matter incidental to any of the matters specified in sub-clauses (*a*) to (*f*).

(2) A Bill shall not be deemed to be a Money Bill by reason only that it provides for the imposition of fines or other pecuniary penalties, or for the demand or payment of fees for licences or fees for services rendered, or by reason that it provides for the imposition, abolition, remission, alteration or regulation of any tax by any local authority or body for local purposes.

(3) If any question arises whether a Bill is a Money Bill or not, the decision of the Speaker of the House of the People thereon shall be final.

(4) There shall be endorsed on every Money Bill when it is transmitted to the Council of States under article 109, and when it is presented to the President for assent under article 111, the certificate of the Speaker of the House of the People signed by him that it is a Money Bill.

111. Assent to Bills.—When a Bill has been passed by the Houses of Parliament, it shall be presented to the President, and the President shall declare either that he assents to the Bill, or that he withholds assent therefrom:

Provided that the President may, as soon as possible after the presentation to him of a Bill for assent, return the Bill if it is not a Money Bill to the Houses with a message requesting that they will reconsider the Bill or any specified provisions thereof and, in particular, will consider the desirability of introducing any such amendments as he may recommend in his message, and when a Bill is so returned, the Houses shall reconsider the Bill accordingly, and if the Bill is passed again by the Houses with or without amendment and presented to the President for assent, the President shall not withhold assent therefrom.

Procedure in Financial Matters

112. Annual financial statement.—

(1) The President shall in respect of every financial year

cause to be laid before both the Houses of Parliament a statement of the estimated receipts and expenditure of the Government of India for that year, in this Part referred to as the "annual financial statement".

(2) The estimates of expenditure embodied in the annual financial statement shall show separately—

(*a*) the sums required to meet expenditure described by this Constitution as expenditure charged upon the Consolidated Fund of India; and

(*b*) the sums required to meet other expenditure proposed to be made from the Consolidated Fund of India, and shall distinguish expenditure on revenue account from other expenditure.

(3) The following expenditure shall be expenditure charged on the Consolidated Fund of India—

(*a*) the emoluments and allowances of the President and other expenditure relating to his office;

(*b*) the salaries and allowances of the Chairman and the Deputy Chairman of the Council of States and the Speaker and the Deputy Speaker of the House of the People;

(*c*) debt charges for which the Government of India is liable including interest, sinking fund charges and redemption charges, and other expenditure relating to the raising of loans and the service and redemption of debt;

(*d*) (*i*) the salaries, allowances and pensions payable to or in respect of Judges of the Supreme Court;

(*ii*) the pensions payable to or in respect of Judges of the Federal Court;

(*iii*) the pensions payable to or in respect of Judges of any High Court which exercises jurisdiction in relation to any area included in the territory of India or which at any time before the commencement of this Constitution exercised jurisdiction in relation to any area included in a Governor's Province of the Dominion of India;

(*e*) the salary, allowances and pension payable to or in respect of the Comptroller and Auditor-General of India;

(*f*) any sums required to satisfy any judgment, decree or award of any court or arbitral tribunal;

(*g*) any other expenditure declared by this Constitution or by Parliament by law to be so charged.

113. Procedure in Parliament with respect to estimates.—

(1) So much of the estimates as relates to expenditure charged upon the Consolidated Fund of India shall not be submitted to the vote of Parliament, but nothing in this clause shall be construed as preventing the discussion in either House of Parliament of any of those estimates.

(2) So much of the said estimates as relates to other expenditure shall be submitted in the form of demands for grants to the House of the People, and the House of the People shall have power to assent, or to refuse to assent, to any demand, or to assent to any demand subject to a reduction of the amount specified therein.

(3) No demand for a grant shall be made except on the recommendation of the President.

114. Appropriation Bills.—

(1) As soon as may be after the grants under article 113 have been made by the House of the People, there shall be introduced a Bill to provide for the appropriation out of the Consolidated Fund of India of all moneys required to meet—

(*a*) the grants so made by the House of the People; and

(*b*) the expenditure charged on the Consolidated Fund of India but not exceeding in any case the amount shown in the statement previously laid before Parliament.

(2) No amendment shall be proposed to any such Bill in either House of Parliament which will have the effect of varying the amount or altering the destination of any grant so made or of varying the amount of any expenditure charged on the Consolidated Fund of India, and the decision of the person presiding as to whether an amendment is inadmissible under this clause shall be final.

(3) Subject to the provisions of articles 115 and 116, no money shall be withdrawn from the Consolidated Fund of India except under appropriation made by law passed in accordance with the provisions of this article.

115. Supplementary, additional or excess grants.—

(1) The President shall—

(*a*) if the amount authorised by any law made in accordance with the provisions of article 114 to be expended for a particular service for the current financial year is found to be insufficient for the purposes of that year or when a need has arisen during the current financial year for supplementary or additional expenditure upon some new service not contemplated in the annual financial statement for that year, or

(*b*) if any money has been spent on any service during a financial year in excess of the amount granted for that service and for that year, cause to be laid before both the Houses of Parliament another statement showing the estimated amount of that expenditure or cause to be presented to the House of the People a demand for such excess, as the case may be.

(2) The provisions of articles 112, 113 and 114 shall have effect in relation to any such statement and expenditure or demand and also to any law to be made authorising the appropriation of moneys out of the Consolidated Fund of India to meet such expenditure or the grant in respect of such demand as they have effect in relation to the annual financial statement and the expenditure mentioned therein or to a demand for a grant and the law to be made for the authorisation of appropriation of moneys out of the Consolidated Fund of India to meet such expenditure or grant.

116. Votes on account, votes of credit and exceptional grants.—

(1) Notwithstanding anything in the foregoing provisions of this Chapter, the House of the People shall have power—

(*a*) to make any grant in advance in respect of the estimated expenditure for a part of any financial year pending the completion of the procedure prescribed in article 113 for the voting of such grant and the passing of the law in accordance with the provisions of article 114 in relation to that expenditure;

(*b*) to make a grant for meeting an unexpected demand upon the resources of India when on account of the magnitude or the indefinite character of the service the demand cannot be stated with the details ordinarily given in an annual financial statement;

(*c*) to make an exceptional grant which forms no part of the current service of any financial year; and Parliament shall have power to authorise by law the withdrawal of moneys from the Consolidated Fund of India for the purposes for which the said grants are made.

(2) The provisions of articles 113 and 114 shall have effect in relation to the making of any grant under clause (1) and to any law to be made under that clause as they have effect in relation to the making of a grant with regard to any expenditure mentioned in the annual financial statement and the law to be made for the authorisation of appropriation of moneys out of the Consolidated Fund of India to meet such expenditure.

117. Special provisions as to financial Bills.—

(1) A Bill or amendment making provision for any of the matters specified in sub-clauses (*a*) to (*f*) of clause (1) of article 110 shall not be introduced or moved except on the recommendation of the President and a Bill making such provision shall not be introduced in the Council of States: Provided that no recommendation shall be required under this clause for the moving of an amendment making provision for the reduction or abolition of any tax.

(2) A Bill or amendment shall not be deemed to make provision for any of the matters aforesaid by reason only that it provides for the imposition of fines or other pecuniary penalties, or for the demand or payment of fees for licences or fees for services rendered, or by reason that it provides for the imposition, abolition, remission, alteration or regulation of any tax by any local authority or body for local purposes.

(3) A Bill which, if enacted and brought into operation, would involve expenditure from the Consolidated Fund of India

shall not be passed by either House of Parliament unless the President has recommended to that House the consideration of the Bill.

Procedure Generally

118. Rules of procedure.—

(1) Each House of Parliament may make rules for regulating, subject to the provisions of this Constitution, its procedure and the conduct of its business.

(2) Until rules are made under clause (1), the rules of procedure and standing orders in force immediately before the commencement of this Constitution with respect to the Legislature of the Dominion of India shall have effect in relation to Parliament subject to such modifications and adaptations as may be made therein by the Chairman of the Council of States or the Speaker of the House of the People, as the case may be.

(3) The President, after consultation with the Chairman of the Council of States and the Speaker of the House of the People, may make rules as to the procedure with respect to joint sittings of, and communications between, the two Houses.

(4) At a joint sitting of the two Houses the Speaker of the House of the People, or in his absence such person as may be determined by rules of procedure made under clause (3), shall preside.

Regulation by law of procedure in Parliament in relation to financial business.— Parliament may, for the purpose of the timely completion of financial business, regulate by law the procedure of, and the conduct of business in, each House of Parliament in relation to any financial matter or to any Bill for the appropriation of moneys out of the Consolidated Fund of India, and, if and so far as any provision of any law so made is inconsistent with any rule made by a House of Parliament under clause (1) of article 118 or with any rule or standing order having effect in relation to Parliament under clause (2) of that article, such provision shall prevail.

Language to be used in Parliament.—

(1) Notwithstanding anything in Part XVII, but subject to

the provisions of article 348, business in Parliament shall be transacted in Hindi or in English:

Provided that the Chairman of the Council of States or Speaker of the House of the People, or person acting as such, as the case may be, may permit any member who cannot adequately express himself in Hindi or in English to address the House in his mother-tongue.

(2) Unless Parliament by law otherwise provides, this article shall, after the expiration of a period of fifteen years from the commencement of this Constitution, have effect as if the words "or in English" were omitted therefrom.

Restriction on discussion in Parliament.— No discussion shall take place in Parliament with respect to the conduct of any Judge of the Supreme Court or of a High Court in the discharge of his duties except upon a motion for presenting an address to the President praying for the removal of the Judge as hereinafter provided.

Courts not to inquire into proceedings of Parliament.—

(1) The validity of any proceedings in Parliament shall not be called in question on the ground of any alleged irregularity of procedure.

(2) No officer or member of Parliament in whom powers are vested by or under this Constitution for regulating procedure or the conduct of business, or for maintaining order, in Parliament shall be subject to the jurisdiction of any court in respect of the exercise by him of those powers.

LEGISLATIVE POWERS OF THE PRESIDENT

Power of President to promulgate Ordinances during recess of Parliament.—

(1) If at any time, except when both Houses of Parliament are in session, the President is satisfied that circumstances exist which render it necessary for him to take immediate action, he may promulgate such Ordinances as the circumstances appear to him to require.

(2) An Ordinance promulgated under this article shall have

the same force and effect as an Act of Parliament, but every such Ordinance—

(*a*) shall be laid before both Houses of Parliament and shall cease to operate at the expiration of six weeks from the reassembly of Parliament, or, if before the expiration of that period resolutions disapproving it are passed by both Houses, upon the passing of the second of those resolutions; and

(*b*) may be withdrawn at any time by the President.

Explanation.—Where the Houses of Parliament are summoned to reassemble on different dates, the period of six weeks shall be reckoned from the later of those dates for the purposes of this clause.

(3) If and so far as an Ordinance under this article makes any provision which Parliament would not under this Constitution be competent to enact, it shall be void.

The Union Judiciary

Establishment and constitution of Supreme Court.—

(1) There shall be a Supreme Court of India consisting of a Chief Justice of India and, until Parliament by law prescribes a larger number, of not more than seven other Judges.

(2) Every Judge of the Supreme Court shall be appointed by the President by warrant under his hand and seal after consultation with such of the Judges of the Supreme Court and of the High Courts in the States as the President may deem necessary for the purpose and shall hold office until he attains the age of sixty-five years:

Provided that in the case of appointment of a Judge other than the Chief Justice, the Chief Justice of India shall always be consulted:

Provided further that—

(*a*) a Judge may, by writing under his hand addressed to the President, resign his office;

(*b*) a Judge may be removed from his office in the manner provided in clause (4).

(2A) The age of a Judge of the Supreme Court shall be

determined by such authority and in such manner as Parliament may by law provide.

(3) A person shall not be qualified for appointment as a Judge of the Supreme Court unless he is a citizen of India and—

(*a*) has been for at least five years a Judge of a High Court or of two or more such Courts in succession; or

(*b*) has been for at least ten years an advocate of a High Court or of two or more such Courts in succession; or

(*c*) is, in the opinion of the President, a distinguished jurist.

Explanation I.—In this clause "High Court" means a High Court which exercises, or which at any time before the commencement of this Constitution exercised, jurisdiction in any part of the territory of India.

Explanation II.—In computing for the purpose of this clause the period during which a person has been an advocate, any period during which a person has held judicial office not inferior to that of a district judge after he became an advocate shall be included.

(4) A Judge of the Supreme Court shall not be removed from his office except by an order of the President passed after an address by each House of Parliament supported by a majority of the total membership of that House and by a majority of not less than two-thirds of the members of that House present and voting has been presented to the President in the same session for such removal on the ground of proved misbehaviour or incapacity.

(5) Parliament may by law regulate the procedure for the presentation of an address and for the investigation and proof of the misbehaviour or incapacity of a Judge under clause (4).

(6) Every person appointed to be a Judge of the Supreme Court shall, before he enters upon his office, make and subscribe before the President, or some person appointed in that behalf by him, an oath or affirmation according to the form set out for the purpose in the Third Schedule.

(7) No person who has held office as a Judge of the Supreme Court shall plead or act in any court or before any authority within the territory of India.

Salaries, etc., of Judges.—

(1) There shall be paid to the Judges of the Supreme Court such salaries as may be determined by Parliament by law and, until provision in that behalf is so made, such salaries as are specified in the Second Schedule.

(2) Every Judge shall be entitled to such privileges and allowances and to such rights in respect of leave of absence and pension as may from time to time be determined by or under law made by Parliament and, until so determined, to such privileges, allowances and rights as are specified in the Second Schedule:

Provided that neither the privileges nor the allowances of a Judge nor his rights in respect of leave of absence or pension shall be varied to his disadvantage after his appointment.

Appointment of acting Chief Justice.—When the office of Chief Justice of India is vacant or when the Chief Justice is, by reason of absence or otherwise, unable to perform the duties of his office, the duties of the office shall be performed by such one of the other Judges of the Court as the President may appoint for the purpose.

Appointment of *ad hoc* Judges.—

(1) If at any time there should not be a quorum of the Judges of the Supreme Court available to hold or continue any session of the Court, the Chief Justice of India may, with the previous consent of the President and after consultation with the Chief Justice of the High Court concerned, request in writing the attendance at the sittings of the Court, as an *ad hoc* Judge, for such period as may be necessary, of a Judge of a High Court duly qualified for appointment as a Judge of the Supreme Court to be designated by the Chief Justice of India.

(2) It shall be the duty of the Judge who has been so designated, in priority to other duties of his office, to attend the sittings of the Supreme Court at the time and for the period for which his attendance is required, and while so attending he shall have all the jurisdiction, powers and privileges, and shall discharge the duties, of a Judge of the Supreme Court.

Attendance of retired Judges at sittings of the Supreme Court.—Notwithstanding anything in this Chapter, the Chief Justice of India may at any time, with the previous consent of the President, request any person who has held the office of a Judge of the Supreme Court or of the Federal Court or who has held the office of a Judge of a High Court and is duly qualified for appointment as a Judge of the Supreme Court to sit and act as a Judge of the Supreme Court, and every such person so requested shall, while so sitting and acting, be entitled to such allowances as the President may by order determine and have all the jurisdiction, powers and privileges of, but shall not otherwise be deemed to be, a Judge of that Court:

Provided that nothing in this article shall be deemed to require any such person as aforesaid to sit and act as a Judge of that Court unless he consents so to do.

Supreme Court to be a court of record.—The Supreme Court shall be a court of record and shall have all the powers of such a court including the power to punish for contempt of itself.

Seat of Supreme Court.—The Supreme Court shall sit in Delhi or in such other place or places, as the Chief Justice of India may, with the approval of the President, from time to time, appoint.

Original jurisdiction of the Supreme Court.—Subject to the provisions of this Constitution, the Supreme Court shall, to the exclusion of any other court, have original jurisdiction in any dispute—

(*a*) between the Government of India and one or more States; or

(*b*) between the Government of India and any State or States on one side and one or more other States on the other; or

(*c*) between two or more States, if and in so far as the dispute involves any question (whether of law or fact) on which the existence or extent of a legal right depends:

Provided that the said jurisdiction shall not extend to a dispute arising out of any treaty, agreement, covenant, engagement, *sanad* or other similar instrument which, having been entered into or executed before the commencement of this Constitution, continues in operation after such commencement, or which provides that the said jurisdiction shall not extend to such a dispute.

[*Exclusive jurisdiction of the Supreme Court in regard to questions as to constitutional validity of Central laws.*] *Rep. by the Constitution (Forty-third Amendment) Act,* 1977, *s.* 4 *(w.e.f.* 13-4-1978*)*.

Appellate jurisdiction of Supreme Court in appeals from High Courts in certain cases.— (1) An appeal shall lie to the Supreme Court from any judgment, decree or final order of a High Court in the territory of India, whether in a civil, criminal or other proceeding, if the High Court certifies under article 134A that the case involves a substantial question of law as to the interpretation of this Constitution.

(3) Where such a certificate is given, any party in the case may appeal to the Supreme Court on the ground that any such question as aforesaid has been wrongly decided.

Explanation.— For the purposes of this article, the expression "final order" includes an order deciding an issue which, if decided in favour of the appellant, would be sufficient for the final disposal of the case.

Appellate jurisdiction of Supreme Court in appeals from High Courts in regard to civil matters.— (1) An appeal shall lie to the Supreme Court from any judgment, decree or final order in a civil proceeding of a High Court in the territory of India if the High Court certifies under article 134A—

(*a*) that the case involves a substantial question of law of general importance; and

(*b*) that in the opinion of the High Court the said question needs to be decided by the Supreme Court.

(2) Notwithstanding anything in article 132, any party appealing to the Supreme Court under clause (1) may urge as one of the grounds in such appeal that a substantial question of law as to the interpretation of this Constitution has been wrongly decided.

(3) Notwithstanding anything in this article, no appeal shall, unless Parliament by law otherwise provides, lie to the Supreme Court from the judgment, decree or final order of one Judge of a High Court.

Appellate jurisdiction of Supreme Court in regard to criminal matters.—(1) An appeal shall lie to the Supreme Court from any judgment, final order or sentence in a criminal proceeding of a High Court in the territory of India if the High Court—

(*a*) has on appeal reversed an order of acquittal of an accused person and sentenced him to death; or

(*b*) has withdrawn for trial before itself any case from any court subordinate to its authority and has in such trial convicted the accused person and sentenced him to death; or

(*c*) certifies under article 134A that the case is a fit one for appeal to the Supreme Court:

Provided that an appeal under sub-clause (*c*) shall lie subject to such provisions as may be made in that behalf under clause (1) of article 145 and to such conditions as the High Court may establish or require.

(2) Parliament may by law confer on the Supreme Court any further powers to entertain and hear appeals from any judgment, final order or sentence in a criminal proceeding of a High Court in the territory of India subject to such conditions and limitations as may be specified in such law.

Certificate for appeal to the Supreme Court.—Every High Court, passing or making a judgment, decree, final order, or sentence, referred to in clause (1) of article 132 or clause (1) of article 133, or clause (1) of article 134, —

(*a*) may, if it deems fit so to do, on its own motion; and

(*b*) shall, if an oral application is made, by or on behalf of the party aggrieved, immediately after the passing or making of such judgment, decree, final order or sentence, determine, as soon as may be after such passing or making, the question whether a certificate of the nature referred to in clause (1) of article 132, or clause (1) of article 133 or, as the case may be, sub-clause (*c*) of clause (1) of article 134, may be given in respect of that case.

Jurisdiction and powers of the Federal Court under existing law to be exercisable by the Supreme Court.— Until Parliament by law otherwise provides, the Supreme Court shall also have jurisdiction and powers with respect to any matter to which the provisions of article 133 or article 134 do not apply if jurisdiction and powers in relation to that matter were exercisable by the Federal Court immediately before the commencement of this Constitution under any existing law.

Special leave to appeal by the Supreme Court.—(1) Notwithstanding anything in this Chapter, the Supreme Court may, in its discretion, grant special leave to appeal from any judgment, decree, determination, sentence or order in any cause or matter passed or made by any court or tribunal in the territory of India.

(2) Nothing in clause (1) shall apply to any judgment, determination, sentence or order passed or made by any court or tribunal constituted by or under any law relating to the Armed Forces.

Review of judgments or orders by the Supreme Court.— Subject to the provisions of any law made by Parliament or any rules made under article 145, the Supreme Court shall have power to review any judgment pronounced or order made by it.

Enlargement of the jurisdiction of the Supreme Court.— (1) The Supreme Court shall have such further jurisdiction and powers with respect to any of the matters in the Union List as Parliament may by law confer.

(2) The Supreme Court shall have such further jurisdiction and powers with respect to any matter as the Government of India and the Government of any State may by special agreement confer, if Parliament by law provides for the exercise of such jurisdiction and powers by the Supreme Court.

Conferment on the Supreme Court of powers to issue certain writs.— Parliament may by law confer on the Supreme Court power to issue directions, orders or writs, including writs in the nature of *habeas corpus, mandamus,* prohibition, *quo warranto* and *certiorari,* or any of them, for any purposes other than those mentioned in clause (2) of article 32.

Transfer of certain cases.— (1) Where cases involving the same or substantially the same questions of law are pending before the Supreme Court and one or more High Courts or before two or more High Courts and the Supreme Court is satisfied on its own motion or on an application made by the Attorney-General of India or by a party to any such case that such questions are substantial questions of general importance, the Supreme Court may withdraw the case or cases pending before the High Court or the High Courts and dispose of all the cases itself:

Provided that the Supreme Court may after determining the said questions of law return any case so withdrawn together with a copy of its judgment on such questions to the High Court from which the case has been withdrawn, and the High Court shall on receipt thereof, proceed to dispose of the case in conformity with such judgment.

(2) The Supreme Court may, if it deems it expedient so to do for the ends of justice, transfer any case, appeal or other proceedings pending before any High Court to any other High Court.

Ancillary powers of Supreme Court.— Parliament may by law make provision for conferring upon the Supreme Court such supplemental powers not inconsistent with any of the provisions of this Constitution as may appear to be necessary or desirable for the purpose of enabling the Court more effectively to exercise the jurisdiction conferred upon it by or under this Constitution.

Law declared by Supreme Court to be binding on all courts.— The law declared by the Supreme Court shall be binding on all courts within the territory of India.

Enforcement of decrees and orders of Supreme Court and orders as to discovery, etc.— (1) The Supreme Court in the exercise of its jurisdiction may pass such decree or make such order as is necessary for doing complete justice in any cause or matter pending before it, and any decree so passed or order so made shall be enforceable throughout the territory of India in such manner as may be prescribed by or under any law made by Parliament and, until provision in that behalf is so made, in such manner as the President may by order prescribe.

(2) Subject to the provisions of any law made in this behalf by Parliament, the Supreme Court shall, as respects the whole of the territory of India, have all and every power to make any order for the purpose of securing the attendance of any person, the discovery or production of any documents, or the investigation or punishment of any contempt of itself.

Power of President to consult Supreme Court.— (1) If at any time it appears to the President that a question of law or fact has arisen, or is likely to arise, which is of such a nature and of such public importance that it is expedient to obtain the opinion of the Supreme Court upon it, he may refer the question to that Court for consideration and the Court may, after such hearing as it thinks fit, report to the President its opinion thereon.

(2) The President may, notwithstanding anything in the proviso to article 131, refer a dispute of the kind mentioned in the said proviso to the Supreme Court for opinion and the Supreme Court shall, after such hearing as it thinks fit, report to the President its opinion thereon.

Civil and judicial authorities to act in aid of the Supreme Court.—All authorities, civil and judicial, in the territory of India shall act in aid of the Supreme Court.

[Special provisions as to disposal of questions relating to constitutional validity of laws.] Rep. by the Constitution (Forty-third Amendment) Act, 1977, *s.* 5 (*w.e.f.* 13-4-1978).

Rules of Court, etc.— (1) Subject to the provisions of any law made by Parliament, the Supreme Court may from time to time, with the approval of the President, make rules for regulating generally the practice and procedure of the Court including—

(*a*) rules as to the persons practising before the Court;

(*b*) rules as to the procedure for hearing appeals and other matters pertaining to appeals including the time within which appeals to the Court are to be entered;

(*c*) rules as to the proceedings in the Court for the enforcement of any of the rights conferred by Part III;

(*cc*) rules as to the proceedings in the Court under article 139A;

(*d*) rules as to the entertainment of appeals under sub-clause (*c*) of clause (1) of article 134;

(*e*) rules as to the conditions subject to which any judgment pronounced or order made by the Court may be reviewed and the procedure for such review including the time within which applications to the Court for such review are to be entered;

((*f*) rules as to the costs of and incidental to any proceedings in the Court and as to the fees to be charged in respect of proceedings therein;

(*g*) rules as to the granting of bail;

(*h*) rules as to stay of proceedings;

(*i*) rules providing for the summary determination of any appeal which appears to the Court to be frivolous or vexatious or brought for the purpose of delay;

(*j*) rules as to the procedure for inquiries referred to in clause (1) of article 317.

(2) Subject to the provisions of clause (3), rules made under this article may fix the minimum number of Judges who are to sit for any purpose, and may provide for the powers of single Judges and Division Courts.

(3) The minimum number of Judges who are to sit for the purpose of deciding any case involving a substantial question of law as to the interpretation of this Constitution or for the purpose of hearing any reference under article 143 shall be five:

Provided that, where the Court hearing an appeal under any of the provisions of this Chapter other than article 132 consists of less than five Judges and in the course of the hearing of the appeal the Court is satisfied that the appeal involves a substantial question of law as to the interpretation of this Constitution the determination of which is necessary for the disposal of the appeal, such Court shall refer the question for opinion to a Court constituted as required by this clause for the purpose of deciding any case involving such a question and shall on receipt of the opinion dispose of the appeal in conformity with such opinion.

(4) No judgment shall be delivered by the Supreme Court save in open Court, and no report shall be made under article 143 save in accordance with an opinion also delivered in open Court.

(5) No judgment and no such opinion shall be delivered by the Supreme Court save with the concurrence of a majority of the Judges present at the hearing of the case, but nothing in this clause shall be deemed to prevent a Judge who does not concur from delivering a dissenting judgment or opinion.

Officers and servants and the expenses of the Supreme Court.—(1) Appointments of officers and servants of the Supreme Court shall be made by the Chief Justice of India or such other Judge or officer of the Court as he may direct:

Provided that the President may by rule require that in such cases as may be specified in the rule, no person not already attached to the Court shall be appointed to any office connected with the Court, save after consultation with the Union Public Service Commission.

(2) Subject to the provisions of any law made by Parliament, the conditions of service of officers and servants of the Supreme Court shall be such as may be prescribed by rules made by the Chief Justice of India or by some other Judge or officer of the Court authorised by the Chief Justice of India to make rules for the purpose:

Provided that the rules made under this clause shall, so far as they relate to salaries, allowances, leave or pensions, require the approval of the President.

(3) The administrative expenses of the Supreme Court, including all salaries, allowances and pensions payable to or

in respect of the officers and servants of the Court, shall be charged upon the Consolidated Fund of India, and any fees or other moneys taken by the Court shall form part of that Fund.

Interpretation.—In this Chapter and in Chapter V of Part VI, references to any substantial question of law as to the interpretation of this Constitution shall be construed as including references to any substantial question of law as to the interpretation of the Government of India Act, 1935 (including any enactment amending or supplementing that Act), or of any Order in Council or order made thereunder, or of the Indian Independence Act, 1947, or of any order made thereunder.

REFERENCES

- Barber B.R.: *Strong Democracy. Participatory Politics for a New Age*. Berkeley, University of California Press, 1984.
- Chandra, R.: *Judicial System in India*, Lucknow, Print House (India), 1992.
- Gerald, J. : *Handbook of Research Methods in Public Administration*, New York, Marcel Dekker, 1999.
- Thomas, R. : *Elements of Government,* New York, Random House, 1960.

7

The States, The State Legislature and The Union Territories

General

Definition.—In this Part, unless the context otherwise requires, the expression "State" does not include the State of Jammu and Kashmir.

The Governor

Governors of States.—There shall be a Governor for each State:

Provided that nothing in this article shall prevent the appointment of the same person as Governor for two or more States.

Executive power of State.—(1) The executive power of the State shall be vested in the Governor and shall be exercised by him either directly or through officers subordinate to him in accordance with this Constitution.

(2) Nothing in this article shall—

(*a*) be deemed to transfer to the Governor any functions conferred by any existing law on any other authority; or

(*b*) prevent Parliament or the Legislature of the State from conferring by law functions on any authority subordinate to the Governor.

Appointment of Governor.—The Governor of a State shall be appointed by the President by warrant under his hand and seal.

Term of office of Governor.—(1) The Governor shall hold office during the pleasure of the President.

(2) The Governor may, by writing under his hand addressed to the President, resign his office.

(3) Subject to the foregoing provisions of this article, a Governor shall hold office for a term of five years from the date on which he enters upon his office:

Provided that a Governor shall, notwithstanding the expiration of his term, continue to hold office until his successor enters upon his office.

Qualifications for appointment as Governor.—No person shall be eligible for appointment as Governor unless he is a citizen of India and has completed the age of thirty-five years.

Conditions of Governor's office.—(1) The Governor shall not be a member of either House of Parliament or of a House of the Legislature of any State specified in the First Schedule, and if a member of either House of Parliament or of a House of the Legislature of any such State be appointed Governor, he shall be deemed to have vacated his seat in that House on the date on which he enters upon his office as Governor.

(2) The Governor shall not hold any other office of profit.

(3) The Governor shall be entitled without payment of rent to the use of his official residences and shall be also entitled to such emoluments, allowances and privileges as may be determined by Parliament by law and, until provision in that behalf is so made, such emoluments, allowances and privileges as are specified in the Second Schedule.

(3A) Where the same person is appointed as Governor of two or more States, the emoluments and allowances payable to the Governor shall be allocated among the States in such proportion as the President may by order determine.

(4) The emoluments and allowances of the Governor shall not be diminished during his term of office.

Oath or affirmation by the Governor.—Every Governor and every person discharging the functions of the Governor shall, before entering upon his office, make and subscribe in the presence of the Chief Justice of the High Court exercising jurisdiction in relation to the State, or, in his absence, the senior most Judge of that Court available, an oath or affirmation in the following form, that is to say—

"I, A. B., do swear in the name of God that I will solemnly affirm faithfully execute the office of Governor (or discharge the functions of the Governor) of.............*(name of the State)* and will to the best of my ability preserve, protect and defend the Constitution and the law and that I will devote myself to the service and well-being of the people of..........*(name of the State).*"

Discharge of the functions of the Governor in certain contingencies.—The President may make such provision as he thinks fit for the discharge of the functions of the Governor of a State in any contingency not provided for in this Chapter.

Power of Governor to grant pardons, etc., and to suspend, remit or commute sentences in certain cases.—The Governor of a State shall have the power to grant pardons, reprieves, respites or remissions of punishment or to suspend, remit or commute the sentence of any person convicted of any offence against any law relating to a matter to which the executive power of the State extends.

Extent of executive power of State.—Subject to the provisions of this Constitution, the executive power of a State shall extend to the matters with respect to which the Legislature of the State has power to make laws:

Provided that in any matter with respect to which the Legislature of a State and Parliament have power to make laws, the executive power of the State shall be subject to, and limited by, the executive power expressly conferred by this Constitution or by any law made by Parliament upon the Union or authorities thereof.

Council of Ministers

Council of Ministers to aid and advise Governor.—(1) There shall be a Council of Ministers with the Chief Minister at the head to aid and advise the Governor in the exercise of his functions, except in so far as he is by or under this Constitution required to exercise his functions or any of them in his discretion.

(2) If any question arises whether any matter is or is not a matter as respects which the Governor is by or under this Constitution required to act in his discretion, the decision of the Governor in his discretion shall be final, and the validity of anything done by the Governor shall not be called in question on the ground that he ought or ought not to have acted in his discretion.

(3) The question whether any, and if so what, advice was tendered by Ministers to the Governor shall not be inquired into in any court.

Other provisions as to Ministers.—(1) The Chief Minister shall be appointed by the Governor and the other Ministers shall be appointed by the Governor on the advice of the Chief Minister, and the Ministers shall hold office during the pleasure of the Governor:

Provided that in the States of Bihar, Madhya Pradesh and Orissa, there shall be a Minister in charge of tribal welfare who may in addition be in charge of the welfare of the Scheduled Castes and backward classes or any other work.

(1A) The total number of Ministers, including the Chief Minister, in the Council of Ministers in a State shall not exceed fifteen per cent. of the total number of members of the Legislative Assembly of that State:

Provided that the number of Ministers, including the Chief Minister in a State shall not be less than twelve:

Provided further that where the total number of Ministers including the Chief Minister in the Council of Ministers in any State at the commencement of the Constitution (Ninety-first Amendment) Act, 2003 exceeds the said fifteen per cent. or the number specified in the first proviso, as the case may be, then the total number of Ministers in that State shall be brought in conformity with the provisions of this clause within six months from such date* as the President may by public notification appoint. *7.1.2004: *vide* Notification No. S.O. 21(E), dated 7.1.2004.

(1B) A member of the Legislative Assembly of a State or either House of the Legislature of a State having Legislative Council belonging to any political party who is disqualified for being a member of that House under paragraph 2 of the Tenth Schedule shall also be disqualified to be appointed as a Minister under clause (1) for duration of the period commencing from the date of his disqualification till the date on which the term of his office as such member would expire or where he contests any election to the Legislative Assembly of a State or either House of the Legislature of a State having Legislative Council, as the case may be, before the expiry of such period, till the date on which he is declared elected, whichever is earlier.

(2) The Council of Ministers shall be collectively responsible to the Legislative Assembly of the State.

(3) Before a Minister enters upon his office, the Governor shall administer to him the oaths of office and of secrecy according to the forms set out for the purpose in the Third Schedule.

(4) A Minister who for any period of six consecutive months is not a member of the Legislature of the State shall at the expiration of that period cease to be a Minister.

(5) The salaries and allowances of Ministers shall be such as the Legislature of the State may from time to time by law determine and, until the Legislature of the State so determines, shall be as specified in the Second Schedule.

The Advocate-General for the State

Advocate-General for the State.—(1) The Governor of each State shall appoint a person who is qualified to be appointed a Judge of a High Court to be Advocate-General for the State.

(2) It shall be the duty of the Advocate-General to give advice to the Government of the State upon such legal matters, and to perform such other duties of a legal character, as may from time to time be referred or assigned to him by the Governor, and to discharge the functions conferred on him by or under this Constitution or any other law for the time being in force.

(3) The Advocate-General shall hold office during the pleasure of the Governor, and shall receive such remuneration as the Governor may determine.

Conduct of Government Business

Conduct of business of the Government of a State.— (1) All executive action of the Government of a State shall be expressed to be taken in the name of the Governor.

(2) Orders and other instruments made and executed in the name of the Governor shall be authenticated in such manner as may be specified in rules to be made by the Governor, and the validity of an order or instrument which is so authenticated shall not be called in question on the ground that it is not an order or instrument made or executed by the Governor.

(3) The Governor shall make rules for the more convenient transaction of the business of the Government of the State, and for the allocation among Ministers of the said business in so far as it is not business with respect to which the Governor is by or under this Constitution required to act in his discretion.

Duties of Chief Minister as respects the furnishing of information to Governor, etc.—It shall be the duty of the Chief Minister of each State—

(*a*) to communicate to the Governor of the State all decisions of the Council of Ministers relating to the administration of the affairs of the State and proposals for legislation;

(*b*) to furnish such information relating to the administration of the affairs of the State and proposals for legislation as the Governor may call for; and

(*c*) if the Governor so requires, to submit for the consideration of the Council of Ministers any matter on which a decision has been taken by a Minister but which has not been considered by the Council.

THE STATE LEGISLATURE

Constitution of Legislatures in States.—(1) For every State there shall be a Legislature which shall consist of the Governor, and—

(*a*) in the States of Bihar, Maharashtra, Karnataka and Uttar Pradesh, two Houses;

(*b*) in other States, one House.

(2) Where there are two Houses of the Legislature of a State, one shall be known as the Legislative Council and the other as the Legislative Assembly, and where there is only one House, it shall be known as the Legislative Assembly.

Abolition or creation of Legislative Councils in States.—(1) Notwithstanding anything in article 168, Parliament may by law provide for the abolition of the Legislative Council of a State having such a Council or for the creation of such a Council in a State having no such Council, if the Legislative Assembly of the State passes a resolution to that effect by a majority of the total membership of the Assembly and by a majority of not less than two-thirds of the members of the Assembly present and voting.

(2) Any law referred to in clause (1) shall contain such provisions for the amendment of this Constitution as may be necessary to give effect to the provisions of the law and may also contain such supplemental, incidental and consequential provisions as Parliament may deem necessary.

(3) No such law as aforesaid shall be deemed to be an amendment of this Constitution for the purposes of article 368.

Composition of the Legislative Assemblies.—(1) Subject to the provisions of article 333, the Legislative Assembly of each State shall consist of not more than five hundred, and not less than sixty, members chosen by direct election from territorial constituencies in the State.

(2) For the purposes of clause (1), each State shall be divided into territorial constituencies in such manner that the ratio between the population of each constituency and the number of seats allotted to it shall, so far as practicable, be the same throughout the State.

Explanation.—In this clause, the expression "population" means the population as ascertained at the last preceding census of which the relevant figures have been published:

Provided that the reference in this *Explanation* to the last preceding census of which the relevant figures have been published shall, until the relevant figures for the first census taken after the year 2026 have been published, be construed as a reference to the 2001 census.

(3) Upon the completion of each census, the total number of seats in the Legislative Assembly of each State and the division of each State into territorial constituencies shall be readjusted by such authority and in such manner as Parliament may by law determine:

Provided that such readjustment shall not affect representation in the Legislative Assembly until the dissolution of the then existing Assembly:

Provided further that such readjustment shall take effect from such date as the President may, by order, specify and until such readjustment takes effect, any election to the Legislative Assembly may be held on the basis of the territorial constituencies existing before such readjustment:

Provided also that until the relevant figures for the first census taken after the year 2026 have been published, it shall not be necessary to readjust—

(*i*) the total number of seats in the Legislative Assembly of each State as readjusted on the basis of the 1971 census; and

(*ii*) the division of such State into territorial constituencies as may be readjusted on the basis of the 2001 census, under this clause.

Composition of the Legislative Councils.—(1) The total number of members in the Legislative Council of a State having such a Council shall not exceed one third of the total number of members in the Legislative Assembly of that State:

Provided that the total number of members in the Legislative Council of a State shall in no case be less than forty.

(2) Until Parliament by law otherwise provides, the composition of the Legislative Council of a State shall be as provided in clause (3).

(3) Of the total number of members of the Legislative Council of a State—

(*a*) as nearly as may be, one-third shall be elected by electorates consisting of members of municipalities, district boards and such other local authorities in the State as Parliament may by law specify;

(*b*) as nearly as may be, one-twelfth shall be elected by electorates consisting of persons residing in the State who have been for at least three years graduates of any university in the territory of India or have been for at least three years in possession of qualifications prescribed by or under any law made by Parliament as equivalent to that of a graduate of any such university;

(*c*) as nearly as may be, one-twelfth shall be elected by electorates consisting of persons who have been for at least three years engaged in teaching in such educational institutions within the State, not lower in standard than that of a secondary school, as may be prescribed by or under any law made by Parliament;

(*d*) as nearly as may be, one-third shall be elected by the members of the Legislative Assembly of the State from amongst persons who are not members of the Assembly;

(*e*) the remainder shall be nominated by the Governor in accordance with the provisions of clause (5).

(4) The members to be elected under sub-clauses (*a*), (*b*) and (*c*) of clause (3) shall be chosen in such territorial constituencies as may be prescribed by or under any law made by Parliament, and the elections under the said sub-clauses and under sub-clause (*d*) of the said clause shall be held in accordance with the system of proportional representation by means of the single transferable vote.

(5) The members to be nominated by the Governor under sub-clause (*e*) of clause (3) shall consist of persons having special knowledge or practical experience in respect of such matters as the following, namely:—

Literature, science, art, co-operative movement and social service.

Duration of State Legislatures.—(1) Every Legislative Assembly of every State, unless sooner dissolved, shall continue for five years from the date appointed for its first meeting and no longer and the expiration of the said period of five years shall operate as a dissolution of the Assembly:

Provided that the said period may, while a Proclamation of Emergency is in operation, be extended by Parliament by law for a period not exceeding one year at a time and not extending in any case beyond a period of six months after the Proclamation has ceased to operate.

(2) The Legislative Council of a State shall not be subject to dissolution, but as nearly as possible one-third of the members thereof shall retire as soon as may be on the expiration of every second year in accordance with the provisions made in that behalf by Parliament by law.

Qualification for membership of the State Legislature.—A person shall not be qualified to be chosen to fill a seat in the Legislature of a State unless he—

(*a*) is a citizen of India, and makes and subscribes before some person authorised in that behalf by the Election Commission an oath or affirmation according to the form set out for the purpose in the Third Schedule;

(*b*) is, in the case of a seat in the Legislative Assembly, not less than twenty-five years of age and, in the case of a seat in the Legislative Council, not less than thirty years of age; and

(*c*) possesses such other qualifications as may be prescribed in that behalf by or under any law made by Parliament.

Sessions of the State Legislature, prorogation and dissolution.—(1) The Governor shall from time to time summon the House or each House of the Legislature of the State to meet at such time and place as he thinks fit, but six months shall not intervene between its last sitting in one session and the date appointed for its first sitting in the next session.

(2) The Governor may from time to time—

(*a*) prorogue the House or either House;

(*b*) dissolve the Legislative Assembly.

Right of Governor to address and send messages to the House or Houses.—(1) The Governor may address the

Legislative Assembly or, in the case of a State having a Legislative Council, either House of the Legislature of the State, or both Houses assembled together, and may for that purpose require the attendance of members.

(2) The Governor may send messages to the House or Houses of the Legislature of the State, whether with respect to a Bill then pending in the Legislature or otherwise, and a House to which any message is so sent shall with all convenient despatch consider any matter required by the message to be taken into consideration.

Special address by the Governor.—(1) At the commencement of the first session after each general election to the Legislative Assembly and at the commencement of the first session of each year, the Governor shall address the Legislative Assembly or, in the case of a State having a Legislative Council, both Houses assembled together and inform the Legislature of the causes of its summons.

(2) Provision shall be made by the rules regulating the procedure of the House or either House for the allotment of time for discussion of the matters referred to in such address.

Rights of Ministers and Advocate-General as respects the Houses.—Every Minister and the Advocate-General for a State shall have the right to speak in, and otherwise to take part in the proceedings of, the Legislative Assembly of the State or, in the case of a State having a Legislative Council, both Houses, and to speak in, and otherwise to take part in the proceedings of, any committee of the Legislature of which he may be named a member, but shall not, by virtue of this article, be entitled to vote.

Officers of the State Legislature

The Speaker and Deputy Speaker of the Legislative Assembly.—Every Legislative Assembly of a State shall, as soon as may be, choose two members of the Assembly to be respectively Speaker and Deputy Speaker thereof and, so often as the office of Speaker or Deputy Speaker becomes vacant, the Assembly shall choose another member to be Speaker or Deputy Speaker, as the case may be.

Vacation and resignation of, and removal from, the offices of Speaker and Deputy Speaker.—A member holding office as Speaker or Deputy Speaker of an Assembly—

(*a*) shall vacate his office if he ceases to be a member of the Assembly;

(*b*) may at any time by writing under his hand addressed, if such member is the Speaker, to the Deputy Speaker, and if such member is the Deputy Speaker, to the Speaker, resign his office; and

(*c*) may be removed from his office by a resolution of the Assembly passed by a majority of all the then members of the Assembly:

Provided that no resolution for the purpose of clause (*c*) shall be moved unless at least fourteen days' notice has been given of the intention to move the resolution:

Provided further that, whenever the Assembly is dissolved, the Speaker shall not vacate his office until immediately before the first meeting of the Assembly after the dissolution.

Power of the Deputy Speaker or other person to perform the duties of the office of, or to act as, Speaker.—(1) While the office of Speaker is vacant, the duties of the office shall be performed by the Deputy Speaker or, if the office of Deputy Speaker is also vacant, by such member of the Assembly as the Governor may appoint for the purpose.

(2) During the absence of the Speaker from any sitting of the Assembly the Deputy Speaker or, if he is also absent, such person as may be determined by the rules of procedure of the Assembly, or, if no such person is present, such other person as may be determined by the Assembly, shall act as Speaker.

The Speaker or the Deputy Speaker not to preside while a resolution for his removal from office is under consideration.—(1) At any sitting of the Legislative Assembly, while any resolution for the removal of the Speaker from his office is under consideration, the Speaker, or while any resolution for the removal of the Deputy Speaker from his office is under consideration, the Deputy Speaker, shall not, though he is present, preside, and the provisions of clause (2) of article 180 shall apply in relation to every such sitting as they apply in relation to a sitting from which the Speaker or, as the case may be, the Deputy Speaker, is absent.

(2) The Speaker shall have the right to speak in, and otherwise to take part in the proceedings of, the Legislative Assembly while any resolution for his removal from office is under consideration in the Assembly and shall, notwithstanding anything in article 189, be entitled to vote only in the first instance on such resolution or on any other matter during such proceedings but not in the case of an equality of votes.

The Chairman and Deputy Chairman of the Legislative Council.—The Legislative Council of every State having such Council shall, as soon as may be, choose two members of the Council to be respectively Chairman and Deputy Chairman thereof and, so often as the office of Chairman or Deputy Chairman becomes vacant, the Council shall choose another member to be Chairman or Deputy Chairman, as the case may be.

Vacation and resignation of, and removal from, the offices of Chairman and Deputy Chairman.—A member holding office as Chairman or Deputy Chairman of a Legislative Council—

(*a*) shall vacate his office if he ceases to be a member of the Council;

(*b*) may at any time by writing under his hand addressed, if such member is the Chairman, to the Deputy Chairman, and if such member is the Deputy Chairman, to the Chairman, resign his office; and

(*c*) may be removed from his office by a resolution of the Council passed by a majority of all the then members of the Council:

Provided that no resolution for the purpose of clause (*c*) shall be moved unless at least fourteen days' notice has been given of the intention to move the resolution.

Power of the Deputy Chairman or other person to perform the duties of the office of, or to act as, Chairman.—(1) While the office of Chairman is vacant, the duties of the office shall be performed by the Deputy Chairman or, if the office of Deputy Chairman is also vacant, by such member of the Council as the Governor may appoint for the purpose.

(2) During the absence of the Chairman from any sitting of the Council the Deputy Chairman or, if he is also absent, such person as may be determined by the rules of procedure of the Council, or, if no such person is present, such other person as may be determined by the Council, shall act as Chairman.

The Chairman or the Deputy Chairman not to preside while a resolution for his removal from office is under consideration.—(1) At any sitting of the Legislative Council, while any resolution for the removal of the Chairman from his office is under consideration, the Chairman, or while any resolution for the removal of the Deputy Chairman from his office is under consideration, the Deputy Chairman, shall not, though he is present, preside, and the provisions of clause (2) of article 184 shall apply in relation to every such sitting as they apply in relation to a sitting from which the Chairman or, as the case may be, the Deputy Chairman is absent.

(2) The Chairman shall have the right to speak in, and otherwise to take part in the proceedings of, the Legislative Council while any resolution for his removal from office is under consideration in the Council and shall, notwithstanding anything in article 189, be entitled to vote only in the first instance on such resolution or on any other matter during such proceedings but not in the case of an equality of votes.

Salaries and allowances of the Speaker and Deputy Speaker and the Chairman and Deputy Chairman.— There shall be paid to the Speaker and the Deputy Speaker of the Legislative Assembly, and to the Chairman and the Deputy Chairman of the Legislative Council, such salaries and allowances as may be respectively fixed by the Legislature of the State by law and, until provision in that behalf is so made, such salaries and allowances as are specified in the Second Schedule.

Secretariat of State Legislature.—(1) The House or each House of the Legislature of a State shall have a separate secretarial staff:

Provided that nothing in this clause shall, in the case of the Legislature of a State having a Legislative Council, be construed as preventing the creation of posts common to both Houses of such Legislature.

(2) The Legislature of a State may by law regulate the recruitment, and the conditions of service of persons appointed, to the secretarial staff of the House or Houses of the Legislature of the State.

(3) Until provision is made by the Legislature of the State under clause (2), the Governor may, after consultation with the Speaker of the Legislative Assembly or the Chairman of the Legislative Council, as the case may be, make rules regulating the recruitment, and the conditions of service of persons appointed, to the secretarial staff of the Assembly or the Council, and any rules so made shall have effect subject to the provisions of any law made under the said clause.

Conduct of Business

Oath or affirmation by members.—Every member of the Legislative Assembly or the Legislative Council of a State shall, before taking his seat, make and subscribe before the Governor, or some person appointed in that behalf by him, an oath or affirmation according to the form set out for the purpose in the Third Schedule.

Voting in Houses, power of Houses to act notwithstanding vacancies and quorum.—(1) Save as otherwise provided in this Constitution, all questions at any sitting of a House of the Legislature of a State shall be determined by a majority of votes of the members present and voting, other than the Speaker or Chairman, or person acting as such.

The Speaker or Chairman, or person acting as such, shall not vote in the first instance, but shall have and exercise a casting vote in the case of an equality of votes.

(2) A House of the Legislature of a State shall have power to act notwithstanding any vacancy in the membership thereof, and any proceedings in the Legislature of a State shall be valid notwithstanding that it is discovered subsequently that some person who was not entitled so to do sat or voted or otherwise took part in the proceedings.

(3) Until the Legislature of the State by law otherwise provides, the quorum to constitute a meeting of a House of the Legislature of a State shall be ten members or one-tenth of the total number of members of the House, whichever is greater.

(4) If at any time during a meeting of the Legislative Assembly or the Legislative Council of a State there is no quorum, it shall be the duty of the Speaker or Chairman, or person acting as such, either to adjourn the House or to suspend the meeting until there is a quorum.

Disqualifications of Members

Vacation of seats.—(1) No person shall be a member of both Houses of the Legislature of a State and provision shall be made by the Legislature of the State by law for the vacation by a person who is chosen a member of both Houses of his seat in one house or the other.

(2) No person shall be a member of the Legislatures of two or more States specified in the First Schedule and if a person is chosen a member of the Legislatures of two or more such States, then, at the expiration of such period as may be specified in rules made by the President, that person's seat in the Legislatures of all such States shall become vacant, unless he has previously resigned his seat in the Legislatures of all but one of the States.

(3) If a member of a House of the Legislature of a State—

(*a*) becomes subject to any of the disqualifications mentioned in clause (1) or clause (2) of article 191; or

(*b*) resigns his seat by writing under his hand addressed to the speaker or the Chairman, as the case may be, and his resignation is accepted by the Speaker or the Chairman, as the case may be, his seat shall thereupon become vacant:

Provided that in the case of any resignation referred to in sub-clause (*b*), if from information received or otherwise and after making such inquiry as he thinks fit, the Speaker or the Chairman, as the case may be, is satisfied that such resignation is not voluntary or genuine, he shall not accept such resignation.

(4) If for a period of sixty days a member of a House of the Legislature of a State is without permission of the House absent from all meetings thereof, the House may declare his seat vacant:

Provided that in computing the said period of sixty days no account shall be taken of any period during which the House is prorogued or is adjourned for more than four consecutive days.

Disqualifications for membership.—(1) A person shall be disqualified for being chosen as, and for being, a member of the Legislative Assembly or Legislative Council of a State—

(*a*) if he holds any office of profit under the Government of India or the Government of any State specified in the First Schedule, other than an office declared by the Legislature of the State by law not to disqualify its holder;

(*b*) if he is of unsound mind and stands so declared by a competent court;

(*c*) if he is an undischarged insolvent;

(*d*) if he is not a citizen of India, or has voluntarily acquired the citizenship of a foreign State, or is under any acknowledgment of allegiance or adherence to a foreign State;

(*e*) if he is so disqualified by or under any law made by Parliament.

Explanation.—For the purposes of this clause, a person shall not be deemed to hold an office of profit under the Government of India or the Government of any State specified in the First Schedule by reason only that he is a Minister either for the Union or for such State.

(2) A person shall be disqualified for being a member of the Legislative Assembly or Legislative Council of a State if he is so disqualified under the Tenth Schedule.

Decision on questions as to disqualifications of members.—(1) If any question arises as to whether a member of a House of the Legislature of a State has become subject to any of the disqualifications mentioned in clause (1) of article 191, the question shall be referred for the decision of the Governor and his decision shall be final.

(2) Before giving any decision on any such question, the Governor shall obtain the opinion of the Election Commission and shall act according to such opinion.

Penalty for sitting and voting before making oath or affirmation under article 188 or when not qualified or when disqualified.—If a person sits or votes as a member of the Legislative Assembly or the Legislative Council of a State before he has complied with the requirements of article 188, or when he knows that he is not qualified or that he is disqualified for membership thereof, or that he is prohibited from so doing by the provisions of any law made by Parliament or the Legislature of the State, he shall be liable in respect of each day on which he so sits or votes to a penalty of five hundred rupees to be recovered as a debt due to the State.

Powers, Privileges and Immunities of State Legislatures and their Members

Powers, privileges, etc., of the Houses of Legislatures and of the members and committees thereof.—(1) Subject to the provisions of this Constitution and to the rules and standing orders regulating the procedure of the Legislature, there shall be freedom of speech in the Legislature of every State.

(2) No member of the Legislature of a State shall be liable to any proceedings in any court in respect of anything said or any vote given by him in the Legislature or any committee thereof, and no person shall be so liable in respect of the publication by or under the authority of a House of such a Legislature of any report, paper, votes or proceedings.

(3) In other respects, the powers, privileges and immunities of a House of the Legislature of a State, and of the members and the committees of a House of such Legislature, shall be

such as may from time to time be defined by the Legislature by law, and, until so defined, shall be those of that House and of its members and committees immediately before the coming into force of section 26 of the Constitution (Forty-fourth Amendment) Act, 1978.

(4) The provisions of clauses (1), (2) and (3) shall apply in relation to persons who by virtue of this Constitution have the right to speak in, and otherwise to take part in the proceedings of, a House of the Legislature of a State or any committee thereof as they apply in relation to members of that Legislature.

Salaries and allowances of members.—Members of the Legislative Assembly and the Legislative Council of a State shall be entitled to receive such salaries and allowances as may from time to time be determined, by the Legislature of the State by law and, until provision in that respect is so made, salaries and allowances at such rates and upon such conditions as were immediately before the commencement of this Constitution applicable in the case of members of the Legislative Assembly of the corresponding Province.

Legislative Procedure

Provisions as to introduction and passing of Bills.—(1) Subject to the provisions of articles 198 and 207 with respect to Money Bills and other financial Bills, a Bill may originate in either House of the Legislature of a State which has a Legislative Council.

(2) Subject to the provisions of articles 197 and 198, a Bill shall not be deemed to have been passed by the Houses of the Legislature of a State having a Legislative Council unless it has been agreed to by both Houses, either without amendment or with such amendments only as are agreed to by both Houses.

(3) A Bill pending in the Legislature of a State shall not lapse by reason of the prorogation of the House or Houses thereof.

(4) A Bill pending in the Legislative Council of a State which has not been passed by the Legislative Assembly shall not lapse on a dissolution of the Assembly.

(5) A Bill which is pending in the Legislative Assembly of a State, or which having been passed by the Legislative Assembly is pending in the Legislative Council, shall lapse on a dissolution of the Assembly.

Restriction on powers of Legislative Council as to Bills other than Money Bills.—(1) If after a Bill has been passed by the Legislative Assembly of a State having a Legislative Council and transmitted to the Legislative Council—

(*a*) the Bill is rejected by the Council; or

(*b*) more than three months elapse from the date on which the Bill is laid before the Council without the Bill being passed by it; or

(*c*) the Bill is passed by the Council with amendments to which the Legislative Assembly does not agree; the Legislative Assembly may, subject to the rules regulating its procedure, pass the Bill again in the same or in any subsequent session with or without such amendments, if any, as have been made, suggested or agreed to by the Legislative Council and then transmit the Bill as so passed to the Legislative Council.

(2) If after a Bill has been so passed for the second time by the Legislative Assembly and transmitted to the Legislative Council—

(*a*) the Bill is rejected by the Council; or

(*b*) more than one month elapses from the date on which the Bill is laid before the Council without the Bill being passed by it; or

(*c*) the Bill is passed by the Council with amendments to which the Legislative Assembly does not agree;

the Bill shall be deemed to have been passed by the Houses of the Legislature of the State in the form in which it was passed by the Legislative Assembly for the second time with such amendments, if any, as have been made or suggested by the Legislative Council and agreed to by the Legislative Assembly.

(3) Nothing in this article shall apply to a Money Bill.

Special procedure in respect of Money Bills.—(1) A Money Bill shall not be introduced in a Legislative Council.

(2) After a Money Bill has been passed by the Legislative Assembly of a State having a Legislative Council, it shall be transmitted to the Legislative Council for its recommendations, and the Legislative Council shall within a period of fourteen days from the date of its receipt of the Bill return the Bill to the Legislative Assembly with its recommendations, and the Legislative Assembly may thereupon either accept or reject all or any of the recommendations of the Legislative Council.

(3) If the Legislative Assembly accepts any of the recommendations of the Legislative Council, the Money Bill shall be deemed to have been passed by both Houses with the amendments recommended by the Legislative Council and accepted by the Legislative Assembly.

(4) If the Legislative Assembly does not accept any of the recommendations of the Legislative Council, the Money Bill shall be deemed to have been passed by both Houses in the form in which it was passed by the Legislative Assembly without any of the amendments recommended by the Legislative Council.

(5) If a Money Bill passed by the Legislative Assembly and transmitted to the Legislative Council for its recommendations is not returned to the Legislative Assembly within the said period of fourteen days, it shall be deemed to have been passed by both Houses at the expiration of the said period in the form in which it was passed by the Legislative Assembly.

Definition of "Money Bills".—(1) For the purposes of this Chapter, a Bill shall be deemed to be a Money Bill if it contains only provisions dealing with all or any of the following matters, namely:—

(a) the imposition, abolition, remission, alteration or regulation of any tax;

(b) the regulation of the borrowing of money or the giving of any guarantee by the State, or the amendment of the law with respect to any financial obligations undertaken or to be undertaken by the State;

(c) the custody of the Consolidated Fund or the Contingency Fund of the State, the payment of moneys into or the withdrawal of moneys from any such Fund;

(d) the appropriation of moneys out of the Consolidated Fund of the State;

(e) the declaring of any expenditure to be expenditure charged on the Consolidated Fund of the State, or the increasing of the amount of any such expenditure;

(f) the receipt of money on account of the Consolidated Fund of the State or the public account of the State or the custody or issue of such money; or

(g) any matter incidental to any of the matters specified in sub-clauses *(a)* to *(f)*.

(2) A Bill shall not be deemed to be a Money Bill by reason only that it provides for the imposition of fines or other pecuniary penalties, or for the demand or payment of fees for licences or fees for services rendered, or by reason that it provides for the imposition, abolition, remission, alteration or regulation of any tax by any local authority or body for local purposes.

(3) If any question arises whether a Bill introduced in the Legislature of a State which has a Legislative Council is a Money Bill or not, the decision of the Speaker of the Legislative Assembly of such State thereon shall be final.

(4) There shall be endorsed on every Money Bill when it is transmitted to the Legislative Council under article 198, and when it is presented to the Governor for assent under article 200, the certificate of the Speaker of the Legislative Assembly signed by him that it is a Money Bill.

Assent to Bills.—When a Bill has been passed by the Legislative Assembly of a State or, in the case of a State having a Legislative Council, has been passed by both Houses of the Legislature of the State, it shall be presented to the Governor and the Governor shall declare either that he assents to the Bill or that he withholds assent therefrom or that he reserves the Bill for the consideration of the President:

Provided that the Governor may, as soon as possible after

the presentation to him of the Bill for assent, return the Bill if it is not a Money Bill together with a message requesting that the House or Houses will reconsider the Bill or any specified provisions thereof and, in particular, will consider the desirability of introducing any such amendments as he may recommend in his message and, when a Bill is so returned, the House or Houses shall reconsider the Bill accordingly, and if the Bill is passed again by the House or Houses with or without amendment and presented to the Governor for assent, the Governor shall not withhold assent therefrom: Provided further that the Governor shall not assent to, but shall reserve for the consideration of the President, any Bill which in the opinion of the Governor would, if it became law, so derogate from the powers of the High Court as to endanger the position which that Court is by this Constitution designed to fill.

Bills reserved for consideration.—When a Bill is reserved by a Governor for the consideration of the President, the President shall declare either that he assents to the Bill or that he withholds assent therefrom:

Provided that, where the Bill is not a Money Bill, the President may direct the Governor to return the Bill to the House or, as the case may be, the Houses of the Legislature of the State together with such a message as is mentioned in the first proviso to article 200 and, when a Bill is so returned, the House or Houses shall reconsider it accordingly within a period of six months from the date of receipt of such message and, if it is again passed by the House or Houses with or without amendment, it shall be presented again to the President for his consideration.

Procedure in Financial Matters

Annual financial statement.—(1) The Governor shall in respect of every financial year cause to be laid before the House or Houses of the Legislature of the State a statement of the estimated receipts and expenditure of the State for that year, in this Part referred to as the "annual financial statement".

(2) The estimates of expenditure embodied in the annual financial statement shall show separately—

(*a*) the sums required to meet expenditure described by this Constitution as expenditure charged upon the Consolidated Fund of the State; and

(*b*) the sums required to meet other expenditure proposed to be made from the Consolidated Fund of the State; and shall distinguish expenditure on revenue account from other expenditure.

(3) The following expenditure shall be expenditure charged on the Consolidated Fund of each State—

(*a*) the emoluments and allowances of the Governor and other expenditure relating to his office;

(*b*) the salaries and allowances of the Speaker and the Deputy Speaker of the Legislative Assembly and, in the case of a State having a Legislative Council, also of the Chairman and the Deputy Chairman of the Legislative Council;

(*c*) debt charges for which the State is liable including interest, sinking fund charges and redemption charges, and other expenditure relating to the raising of loans and the service and redemption of debt;

(*d*) expenditure in respect of the salaries and allowances of Judges of any High Court;

(*e*) any sums required to satisfy any judgment, decree or award of any court or arbitral tribunal;

(*f*) any other expenditure declared by this Constitution, or by the Legislature of the State by law, to be so charged.

Procedure in Legislature with respect to estimates.— (1) So much of the estimates as relates to expenditure charged upon the Consolidated Fund of a State shall not be submitted to the vote of the Legislative Assembly, but nothing in this clause shall be construed as preventing the discussion in the Legislature of any of those estimates.

(2) So much of the said estimates as relates to other expenditure shall be submitted in the form of demands for grants to the Legislative Assembly, and the Legislative Assembly shall have power to assent, or to refuse to assent, to any demand, or to assent to any demand subject to a reduction of the amount specified therein.

(3) No demand for a grant shall be made except on the recommendation of the Governor.

Appropriation Bills.—(1) As soon as may be after the grants under article 203 have been made by the Assembly, there shall be introduced a Bill to provide for the appropriation out of the Consolidated Fund of the State of all moneys required to meet—

(*a*) the grants so made by the Assembly; and

(*b*) the expenditure charged on the Consolidated Fund of the State but not exceeding in any case the amount shown in the statement previously laid before the House or Houses.

(2) No amendment shall be proposed to any such Bill in the House or either House of the Legislature of the State which will have the effect of varying the amount or altering the destination of any grant so made or of varying the amount of any expenditure charged on the Consolidated Fund of the State, and the decision of the person presiding as to whether an amendment is inadmissible under this clause shall be final.

(3) Subject to the provisions of articles 205 and 206, no money shall be withdrawn from the Consolidated Fund of the State except under appropriation made by law passed in accordance with the provisions of this article.

Supplementary, additional or excess grants.—(1) The Governor shall—

(*a*) if the amount authorised by any law made in accordance with the provisions of article 204 to be expended for a particular service for the current financial year is found to be insufficient for the purposes of that year or when a need has arisen during the current financial year for supplementary or additional expenditure upon some new service not contemplated in the annual financial statement for that year, or

(*b*) if any money has been spent on any service during a financial year in excess of the amount granted for that service and for that year, cause to be laid before the House or the Houses of the Legislature of the State another statement showing the estimated amount of that expenditure or cause to be presented to the Legislative Assembly of the State a demand for such excess, as the case may be.

(2) The provisions of articles 202, 203 and 204 shall have effect in relation to any such statement and expenditure or demand and also to any law to be made authorising the appropriation of moneys out of the Consolidated Fund of the State to meet such expenditure or the grant in respect of such demand as they have effect in relation to the annual financial statement and the expenditure mentioned therein or to a demand for a grant and the law to be made for the authorisation of appropriation of moneys out of the Consolidated Fund of the State to meet such expenditure or grant.

Votes on account, votes of credit and exceptional grants.—(1) Notwithstanding anything in the foregoing provisions of this Chapter, the Legislative Assembly of a State shall have power—

(a) to make any grant in advance in respect of the estimated expenditure for a part of any financial year pending the completion of the procedure prescribed in article 203 for the voting of such grant and the passing of the law in accordance with the provisions of article 204 in relation to that expenditure;

(b) to make a grant for meeting an unexpected demand upon the resources of the State when on account of the magnitude or the indefinite character of the service the demand cannot be stated with the details ordinarily given in an annual financial statement;

(c) to make an exceptional grant which forms no part of the current service of any financial year; and the Legislature of the State shall have power to authorise by law the withdrawal of moneys from the Consolidated Fund of the State for the purposes for which the said grants are made.

(2) The provisions of articles 203 and 204 shall have effect in relation to the making of any grant under clause (1) and to any law to be made under that clause as they have effect in relation to the making of a grant with regard to any expenditure mentioned in the annual financial statement and the law to be made for the authorisation of appropriation of moneys out of the Consolidated Fund of the State to meet such expenditure.

Special provisions as to financial Bills.—(1) A Bill or amendment making provision for any of the matters specified in sub-clauses *(a)* to *(f)* of clause (1) of article 199 shall not be introduced or moved except on the recommendation of the Governor, and a Bill making such provision shall not be introduced in a Legislative Council:

Provided that no recommendation shall be required under this clause for the moving of an amendment making provision for the reduction or abolition of any tax.

(2) A Bill or amendment shall not be deemed to make provision for any of the matters aforesaid by reason only that it provides for the imposition of fines or other pecuniary penalties, or for the demand or payment of fees for licences or fees for services rendered, or by reason that it provides for the imposition, abolition, remission, alteration or regulation of any tax by any local authority or body for local purposes.

(3) A Bill which, if enacted and brought into operation, would involve expenditure from the Consolidated Fund of a State shall not be passed by a House of the Legislature of the State unless the Governor has recommended to that House the consideration of the Bill.

Procedure Generally

Rules of procedure.—(1) A House of the Legislature of a State may make rules for regulating, subject to the provisions of this Constitution, its procedure and the conduct of its business.

(2) Until rules are made under clause (1), the rules of procedure and standing orders in force immediately before the commencement of this Constitution with respect to the Legislature for the corresponding Province shall have effect in relation to the Legislature of the State subject to such modifications and adaptations as may be made therein by the Speaker of the Legislative Assembly, or the Chairman of the Legislative Council, as the case may be.

(3) In a State having a Legislative Council the Governor, after consultation with the Speaker of the Legislative Assembly and the Chairman of the Legislative Council, may make rules

as to the procedure with respect to communications between the two Houses.

Regulation by law of procedure in the Legislature of the State in relation to financial business. —The Legislature of a State may, for the purpose of the timely completion of financial business, regulate by law the procedure of, and the conduct of business in, the House or Houses of the Legislature of the State in relation to any financial matter or to any Bill for the appropriation of moneys out of the Consolidated Fund of the State, and, if and so far as any provision of any law so made is inconsistent with any rule made by the House or either House of the Legislature of the State under clause (1) of article 208 or with any rule or standing order having effect in relation to the Legislature of the State under clause (2) of that article, such provision shall prevail.

Language to be used in the Legislature.—(1) Notwithstanding anything in Part XVII, but subject to the provisions of article 348, business in the Legislature of a State shall be transacted in the official language or languages of the State or in Hindi or in English: Provided that the Speaker of the Legislative Assembly or Chairman of the Legislative Council, or person acting as such, as the case may be, may permit any member who cannot adequately express himself in any of the languages aforesaid to address the House in his mother-tongue.

(2) Unless the Legislature of the State by law otherwise provides, this article shall, after the expiration of a period of fifteen years from the commencement of this Constitution, have effect as if the words "or in English" were omitted therefrom: Provided that in relation to the Legislatures of the States of Himachal Pradesh, Manipur, Meghalaya and Tripura this clause shall have effect as if for the words "fifteen" years occurring therein, the words "twenty-five years" were substituted:

Provided further that in relation to the Legislatures of the States of Arunachal Pradesh, Goa and Mizoram, this clause shall have effect as if for the words "fifteen years" occurring therein, the words "forty years" were substituted.

Restriction on discussion in the Legislature. —No discussion shall take place in the Legislature of a State with respect to the conduct of any Judge of the Supreme Court or of a High Court in the discharge of his duties.

Courts not to inquire into proceedings of the Legislature.—(1) The validity of any proceedings in the Legislature of a State shall not be called in question on the ground of any alleged irregularity of procedure.

(2) No officer or member of the Legislature of a State in whom powers are vested by or under this Constitution for regulating procedure or the conduct of business, or for maintaining order, in the Legislature shall be subject to the jurisdiction of any court in respect of the exercise by him of those powers.

LEGISLATIVE POWER OF THE GOVERNOR

Power of Governor to promulgate Ordinances during recess of Legislature.—(1) If at any time, except when the Legislative Assembly of a State is in session, or where there is a Legislative Council in a State, except when both Houses of the Legislature are in session, the Governor is satisfied that circumstances exist which render it necessary for him to take immediate action, he may promulgate such Ordinances as the circumstances appear to him to require:

Provided that the Governor shall not, without instructions from the President, promulgate any such Ordinance if—

(*a*) a Bill containing the same provisions would under this Constitution have required the previous sanction of the President for the introduction thereof into the Legislature; or

(*b*) he would have deemed it necessary to reserve a Bill containing the same provisions for the consideration of the President; or

(*c*) an Act of the Legislature of the State containing the same provisions would under this Constitution have been invalid unless, having been reserved for the consideration of the President, it had received the assent of the President.

(2) An Ordinance promulgated under this article shall have

the same force and effect as an Act of the Legislature of the State assented to by the Governor, but every such Ordinance—

(*a*) shall be laid before the Legislative Assembly of the State, or where there is a Legislative Council in the State, before both the Houses, and shall cease to operate at the expiration of six weeks from the reassembly of the Legislature, or if before the expiration of that period a resolution disapproving it is passed by the Legislative Assembly and agreed to by the Legislative Council, if any, upon the passing of the resolution or, as the case may be, on the resolution being agreed to by the Council; and

(*b*) may be withdrawn at any time by the Governor.

Explanation.—Where the Houses of the Legislature of a State having a Legislative Council are summoned to reassemble on different dates, the period of six weeks shall be reckoned from the later of those dates for the purposes of this clause.

(3) If and so far as an Ordinance under this article makes any provision which would not be valid if enacted in an Act of the Legislature of the State assented to by the Governor, it shall be void: Provided that, for the purposes of the provisions of this Constitution relating to the effect of an Act of the Legislature of a State which is repugnant to an Act of Parliament or an existing law with respect to a matter enumerated in the Concurrent List, an Ordinance promulgated under this article in pursuance of instructions from the President shall be deemed to be an Act of the Legislature of the State which has been reserved for the consideration of the President and assented to by him.

THE HIGH COURTS IN THE STATES

High Courts for States.—There shall be a High Court for each State.

High Courts to be courts of record.—Every High Court shall be a court of record and shall have all the powers of such a court including the power to punish for contempt of itself.

Constitution of High Courts.—Every High Court shall consist of a Chief Justice and such other Judges as the President may from time to time deem it necessary to appoint.

Appointment and conditions of the office of a Judge of a High Court.—(1) Every Judge of a High Court shall be appointed by the President by warrant under his hand and seal after consultation with the Chief Justice of India, the Governor of the State, and, in the case of appointment of a Judge other than the Chief Justice, the Chief Justice of the High Court, and shall hold office, in the case of an additional or acting Judge, as provided in article 224, and in any other case, until he attains the age of sixty-two years: Provided that—

(*a*) a Judge may, by writing under his hand addressed to the President, resign his office;

(*b*) a Judge may be removed from his office by the President in the manner provided in clause (4) of article 124 for the removal of a Judge of the Supreme Court;

(*c*) the office of a Judge shall be vacated by his being appointed by the President to be a Judge of the Supreme Court or by his being transferred by the President to any other High Court within the territory of India.

(2) A person shall not be qualified for appointment as a Judge of a High Court unless he is a citizen of India and—

(*a*) has for at least ten years held a judicial office in the territory of India; or

(*b*) has for at least ten years been an advocate of a High Court or of two or more such Courts in succession.

Explanation.—For the purposes of this clause—

(*a*) in computing the period during which a person has held judicial office in the territory of India, there shall be included any period, after he has held any judicial office, during which the person has been an advocate of a High Court or has held the office of a member of a tribunal or any post, under the Union or a State, requiring special knowledge of law;

(*aa*) in computing the period during which a person has been an advocate of a High Court, there shall be included any period during which the person has held judicial office or the office of a member of a tribunal or any post, under the Union or a State, requiring special knowledge of law after he became an advocate;

(*b*) in computing the period during which a person has held judicial office in the territory of India or been an advocate of a High Court, there shall be included any period before the commencement of this Constitution during which he has held judicial office in any area which was comprised before the fifteenth day of August, 1947, within India as defined by the Government of India Act, 1935, or has been an advocate of any High Court in any such area, as the case may be.

(3) If any question arises as to the age of a Judge of a High Court, the question shall be decided by the President after consultation with the Chief Justice of India and the decision of the President shall be final.

Application of certain provisions relating to Supreme Court to High Courts.— The provisions of clauses (4) and (5) of article 124 shall apply in relation to a High Court as they apply in relation to the Supreme Court with the substitution of references to the High Court for references to the Supreme Court.

Oath or affirmation by Judges of High Courts.—Every person appointed to be a Judge of a High Court shall, before he enters upon his office, make and subscribe before the Governor of the State, or some person appointed in that behalf by him, an oath or affirmation according to the form set out for the purpose in the Third Schedule.

Restriction on practice after being a permanent Judge.—No person who, after the commencement of this Constitution, has held office as a permanent Judge of a High Court shall plead or act in any court or before any authority in India except the Supreme Court and the other High Courts.

Explanation.—In this article, the expression "High Court" does not include a High Court for a State specified in Part B of the First Schedule as it existed before the commencement of the Constitution (Seventh Amendment) Act, 1956.

Salaries, etc., of Judges.—(1) There shall be paid to the Judges of each High Court such salaries as may be determined by Parliament by law and, until provision in that behalf is so made, such salaries as are specified in the Second Schedule.

(2) Every Judge shall be entitled to such allowances and

to such rights in respect of leave of absence and pension as may from time to time be determined by or under law made by Parliament and, until so determined, to such allowances and rights as are specified in the Second Schedule:

Provided that neither the allowances of a Judge nor his rights in respect of leave of absence or pension shall be varied to his disadvantage after his appointment.

Transfer of a Judge from one High Court to another.—(1) The President may, after consultation with the Chief Justice of India, transfer a Judge from one High Court to any other High Court.

(2) When a Judge has been or is so transferred, he shall, during the period he serves, after the commencement of the Constitution (Fifteenth Amendment) Act, 1963, as a Judge of the other High Court, be entitled to receive in addition to his salary such compensatory allowance as may be determined by Parliament by law and, until so determined, such compensatory allowance as the President may by order fix.

Appointment of acting Chief Justice.—When the office of Chief Justice of a High Court is vacant or when any such Chief Justice is, by reason of absence or otherwise, unable to perform the duties of his office, the duties of the office shall be performed by such one of the other Judges of the Court as the President may appoint for the purpose.

Appointment of additional and acting Judges.—(1) If by reason of any temporary increase in the business of a High Court or by reason of arrears of work therein, it appears to the President that the number of the Judges of that Court should be for the time being increased, the President may appoint duly qualified persons to be additional Judges of the Court for such period not exceeding two years as he may specify.

(2) When any Judge of a High Court other than the Chief Justice is by reason of absence or for any other reason unable to perform the duties of his office or is appointed to act temporarily as Chief Justice, the President may appoint a duly qualified person to act as a Judge of that Court until the permanent Judge has resumed his duties.

(3) No person appointed as an additional or acting Judge of a High Court shall hold office after attaining the age of sixty-two years.

Appointment of retired Judges at sittings of High Courts.—Notwithstanding anything in this Chapter, the Chief Justice of a High Court for any State may at any time, with the previous consent of the President, request any person who has held the office of a Judge of that Court or of any other High Court to sit and act as a Judge of the High Court for that State, and every such person so requested shall, while so sitting and acting, be entitled to such allowances as the President may by order determine and have all the jurisdiction, powers and privileges of, but shall not otherwise be deemed to be, a Judge of that High Court:

Provided that nothing in this article shall be deemed to require any such person as aforesaid to sit and act as a Judge of that High Court unless he consents so to do.

Jurisdiction of existing High Courts.—Subject to the provisions of this Constitution and to the provisions of any law of the appropriate Legislature made by virtue of powers conferred on that Legislature by this Constitution, the jurisdiction of, and the law administered in, any existing High Court, and the respective powers of the Judges thereof in relation to the administration of justice in the Court, including any power to make rules of Court and to regulate the sittings of the Court and of members thereof sitting alone or in Division Courts, shall be the same as immediately before the commencement of this Constitution:

Provided that any restriction to which the exercise of original jurisdiction by any of the High Courts with respect to any matter concerning the revenue or concerning any act ordered or done in the collection thereof was subject immediately before the commencement of this Constitution shall no longer apply to the exercise of such jurisdiction.

Power of High Courts to issue certain writs.—(1) Notwithstanding anything in article 32 every High Court shall have power, throughout the territories in relation to which it exercises jurisdiction, to issue to any person or authority, including in appropriate cases, any Government, within those territories directions, orders or writs, including writs in the nature of *habeas corpus, mandamus,* prohibition, *quo warranto* and *certiorari,* or any of them, for the enforcement of any of the rights conferred by Part III and for any other purpose.

(2) The power conferred by clause (1) to issue directions, orders or writs to any Government, authority or person may also be exercised by any High Court exercising jurisdiction in relation to the territories within which the cause of action, wholly or in part, arises for the exercise of such power, notwithstanding that the seat of such Government or authority or the residence of such person is not within those territories.

(3) Where any party against whom an interim order, whether by way of injunction or stay or in any other manner, is made on, or in any proceedings relating to, a petition under clause (1), without—

(*a*) furnishing to such party copies of such petition and all documents in support of the plea for such interim order; and

(*b*) giving such party an opportunity of being heard, makes an application to the High Court for the vacation of such order and furnishes a copy of such application to the party in whose favour such order has been made or the counsel of such party, the High Court shall dispose of the application within a period of two weeks from the date on which it is received or from the date on which the copy of such application is so furnished, whichever is later, or where the High Court is closed on the last day of that period, before the expiry of the next day afterwards on which the High Court is open; and if the application is not so disposed of, the interim order shall, on the expiry of that period, or, as the case may be, the expiry of the said next day, stand vacated.

(4) The power conferred on a High Court by this article shall not be in derogation of the power conferred on the Supreme Court by clause (2) of article 32.

[*Constitutional validity of Central laws not to be considered in proceedings under article* 226.] *Rep. by the Constitution (Forty-third Amendment) Act,* 1977, *s.* 8 *(w.e.f.* 13-4-1978).

Power of superintendence over all courts by the High Court.—(1) Every High Court shall have superintendence over all courts and tribunals throughout the territories in relation to which it exercises jurisdiction.

(2) Without prejudice to the generality of the foregoing provision, the High Court may—

(*a*) call for returns from such courts;

(*b*) make and issue general rules and prescribe forms for regulating the practice and proceedings of such courts; and

(*c*) prescribe forms in which books, entries and accounts shall be kept by the officers of any such courts.

(3) The High Court may also settle tables of fees to be allowed to the sheriff and all clerks and officers of such courts and to attorneys, advocates and pleaders practising therein:

Provided that any rules made, forms prescribed or tables settled under clause (2) or clause (3) shall not be inconsistent with the provision of any law for the time being in force, and shall require the previous approval of the Governor.

(4) Nothing in this article shall be deemed to confer on a High Court powers of superintendence over any court or tribunal constituted by or under any law relating to the Armed Forces.

Transfer of certain cases to High Court.—If the High Court is satisfied that a case pending in a court subordinate to it involves a substantial question of law as to the interpretation of this Constitution the determination of which is necessary for the disposal of the case, it shall withdraw the case and may—

(*a*) either dispose of the case itself, or

(*b*) determine the said question of law and return the case to the court from which the case has been so withdrawn together with a copy of its judgment on such question, and the said court shall on receipt thereof proceed to dispose of the case in conformity with such judgment.

[Special provisions as to disposal of questions relating to constitutional validity of State laws.] Rep. by the Constitution (Forty-third Amendment) Act, 1977, s. 10 *(w.e.f.* 13-4-1978*).*

Officers and servants and the expenses of High Courts.—(1) Appointments of officers and servants of a High Court shall be made by the Chief Justice of the Court or such other Judge or officer of the Court as he may direct:

Provided that the Governor of the State may by rule require that in such cases as may be specified in the rule no person not already attached to the Court shall be appointed to any office connected with the Court save after consultation with the State Public Service Commission.

(2) Subject to the provisions of any law made by the Legislature of the State, the conditions of service of officers and servants of a High Court shall be such as may be prescribed by rules made by the Chief Justice of the Court or by some other Judge or officer of the Court authorised by the Chief Justice to make rules for the purpose:

Provided that the rules made under this clause shall, so far as they relate to salaries, allowances, leave or pensions, require the approval of the Governor of the State.

(3) The administrative expenses of a High Court, including all salaries, allowances and pensions payable to or in respect of the officers and servants of the Court, shall be charged upon the Consolidated Fund of the State, and any fees or other moneys taken by the Court shall form part of that Fund.

Extension of jurisdiction of High Courts to Union territories.—(1) Parliament may by law extend the jurisdiction of a High Court to, or exclude the jurisdiction of a High Court from, any Union territory.

(2) Where the High Court of a State exercises jurisdiction in relation to a Union territory,—

(*a*) nothing in this Constitution shall be construed as empowering the Legislature of the State to increase, restrict or abolish that jurisdiction; and

(*b*) the reference in article 227 to the Governor shall, in relation to any rules, forms or tables for subordinate courts in that territory, be construed as a reference to the President.

Establishment of a common High Court for two or more States.—(1) Notwithstanding anything contained in the preceding provisions of this Chapter, Parliament may by law establish a common High Court for two or more States or for two or more States and a Union territory.

(2) In relation to any such High Court,—

(*a*) the reference in article 217 to the Governor of the State shall be construed as a reference to the Governors of all the States in relation to which the High Court exercises jurisdiction;

(*b*) the reference in article 227 to the Governor shall, in relation to any rules, forms or tables for subordinate courts, be construed as a reference to the Governor of the State in which the subordinate courts are situate; and

(*c*) the references in articles 219 and 229 to the State shall be construed as a reference to the State in which the High Court has its principal seat:

Provided that if such principal seat is in a Union territory, the references in articles 219 and 229 to the Governor, Public Service Commission, Legislature and Consolidated Fund of the State shall be construed respectively as references to the President, Union Public Service Commission, Parliament and Consolidated Fund of India.

SUBORDINATE COURTS

Appointment of district judges.—(1) Appointments of persons to be, and the posting and promotion of, district judges in any State shall be made by the Governor of the State in consultation with the High Court exercising jurisdiction in relation to such State.

(2) A person not already in the service of the Union or of the State shall only be eligible to be appointed a district judge if he has been for not less than seven years an advocate or a pleader and is recommended by the High Court for appointment.

Validation of appointments of, and judgments, etc., delivered by, certain district judges. —Notwithstanding any judgment, decree or order of any court,—

(*a*) (*i*) no appointment of any person already in the judicial service of a State or of any person who has been for not less than seven years an advocate or a pleader, to be a district judge in that State, and (*ii*) no posting, promotion or transfer of any such person as a district judge, made at any time before the commencement of the Constitution (Twentieth Amendment) Act, 1966, otherwise than in accordance with the provisions of article 233 or article 235 shall be deemed to be illegal or void or ever to have become illegal or void by reason only of the fact that such appointment, posting, promotion or transfer was not made in accordance with the said provisions;

(*b*) no jurisdiction exercised, no judgment, decree, sentence or order passed or made, and no other act or proceedings done or taken, before the commencement of the Constitution (Twentieth Amendment) Act, 1966 by, or before, any person appointed, posted, promoted or transferred as a district judge in any State otherwise than in accordance with the provisions of article 233 or article 235 shall be deemed to be illegal or invalid or ever to have become illegal or invalid by reason only of the fact that such appointment, posting, promotion or transfer was not made in accordance with the said provisions.

Recruitment of persons other than district judges to the judicial service.—Appointments of persons other than district judges to the judicial service of a State shall be made by the Governor of the State in accordance with rules made by him in that behalf after consultation with the State Public Service Commission and with the High Court exercising jurisdiction in relation to such State.

Control over subordinate courts.— The control over district courts and courts subordinate thereto including the posting and promotion of, and the grant of leave to, persons belonging to the judicial service of a State and holding any post inferior to the post of district judge shall be vested in the High Court, but nothing in this article shall be construed as taking away from any such person any right of appeal which he may have under the law regulating the conditions of his service or as authorising the High Court to deal with him otherwise than in accordance with the conditions of his service prescribed under such law.

Interpretation.— In this Chapter—

(*a*) the expression "district judge" includes judge of a city civil court, additional district judge, joint district judge, assistant district judge, chief judge of a small cause court, chief presidency magistrate, additional chief presidency magistrate, sessions judge, additional sessions judge and assistant sessions Judge;

(*b*) the expression "judicial service" means a service consisting exclusively of persons intended to fill the post of district judge and other civil judicial posts inferior to the post of district judge.

Application of the provisions of this Chapter to certain class or classes of magistrates.—The Governor may by public notification direct that the foregoing provisions of this Chapter and any rules made thereunder shall with effect from such date as may be fixed by him in that behalf apply in relation to any class or classes of magistrates in the State as they apply in relation to persons appointed to the judicial service of the State subject to such exceptions and modifications as may be specified in the notification.

PART VII.—[The States in Part B of the First Schedule]. Rep. by the Constitution (Seventh Amendment) Act, 1956, *s.* 29 *and Sch.*

THE UNION TERRITORIES

Administration of Union territories.—(1) Save as otherwise provided by Parliament by law, every Union territory shall be administered by the President acting, to such extent as he thinks fit, through an administrator to be appointed by him with such designation as he may specify.

(2) Notwithstanding anything contained in Part VI, the President my appoint the Governor of a State as the administrator of an adjoining Union territory, and where a Governor is so appointed, he shall exercise his functions as such administrator independently of his Council of Ministers.

Creation of local Legislatures or Council of Ministers or both for certain Union territories.—(1) Parliament may by law create for the Union territory of Pondicherry—

(a) a body, whether elected or partly nominated and partly elected, to function as a Legislature for the Union territory, or

(b) a Council of Ministers, or both with such constitution, powers and functions, in each case, as may be specified in the law.

(2) Any such law as is referred to in clause (1) shall not be deemed to be an amendment of this Constitution for the purposes of article 368 notwithstanding that it contains any provision which amends or has the effect of amending this Constitution.

Special provisions with respect to Delhi.—(1) As from the date of commencement of the Constitution (Sixty-ninth Amendment) Act, 1991, the Union territory of Delhi shall be called the National Capital Territory of Delhi (hereafter in this Part referred to as the National Capital Territory) and the administrator thereof appointed under article 239 shall be designated as the Lieutenant Governor.

(2)*(a)* There shall be a Legislative Assembly for the National Capital Territory and the seats in such Assembly shall be filled by members chosen by direct election from territorial constituencies in the National Capital Territory.

(b) The total number of seats in the Legislative Assembly, the number of seats reserved for Scheduled Castes, the division of the National Capital Territory into territorial constituencies (including the basis for such division) and all other matters relating to the functioning of the Legislative Assembly shall be regulated by law made by Parliament.

(c) The provisions of articles 324 to 327 and 329 shall apply in relation to the National Capital Territory, the Legislative Assembly of the National Capital Territory and the members thereof as they apply, in relation to a State, the Legislative Assembly of a State and the members thereof respectively; and any reference in articles 326 and 329 to "appropriate Legislature" shall be deemed to be a reference to Parliament.

(3) *(a)* Subject to the provisions of this Constitution, the Legislative Assembly shall have power to make laws for the whole or any part of the National Capital Territory with respect to any of the matters enumerated in the State List or in the Concurrent List in so far as any such matter is applicable to

Union territories except matters with respect to Entries 1, 2 and 18 of the State List and Entries 64, 65 and 66 of that List in so far as they relate to the said Entries 1, 2 and 18.

(b) Nothing in sub-clause *(a)* shall derogate from the powers of Parliament under this Constitution to make laws with respect to any matter for a Union territory or any part thereof.

(c) If any provision of a law made by the Legislative Assembly with respect to any matter is repugnant to any provision of a law made by Parliament with respect to that matter, whether passed before or after the law made by the Legislative Assembly, or of an earlier law, other than a law made by the Legislative Assembly, then, in either case, the law made by Parliament, or, as the case may be, such earlier law, shall prevail and the law made by the Legislative Assembly shall, to the extent of the repugnancy, be void:

Provided that if any such law made by the Legislative Assembly has been reserved for the consideration of the President and has received his assent, such law shall prevail in the National Capital Territory:

Provided further that nothing in this sub-clause shall prevent Parliament from enacting at any time any law with respect to the same matter including a law adding to, amending, varying or repealing the law so made by the Legislative Assembly.

(4) There shall be a Council of Ministers consisting of not more than ten per cent. of the total number of members in the Legislative Assembly, with the Chief Minister at the head to aid and advise the Lieutenant Governor in the exercise of his functions in relation to matters with respect to which the Legislative Assembly has power to make laws, except in so far as he is, by or under any law, required to act in his discretion:

Provided that in the case of difference of opinion between the Lieutenant Governor and his Ministers on any matter, the Lieutenant Governor shall refer it to the President for decision and act according to the decision given thereon by the President and pending such decision it shall be competent for the Lieutenant Governor in any case where the matter, in his opinion, is so urgent that it is necessary for him to take immediate action, to take such action or to give such direction in the matter as he deems necessary.

(5) The Chief Minister shall be appointed by the President and other Ministers shall be appointed by the President on the advice of the Chief Minister and the Ministers shall hold office during the pleasure of the President.

(6) The Council of Ministers shall be collectively responsible to the Legislative Assembly.

(7) *(a)* Parliament may, by law, make provisions for giving effect to, or supplementing the provisions contained in the foregoing clauses and for all matters incidental or consequential thereto.

(b) Any such law as is referred to in sub-clause (*a*) shall not be deemed to be an amendment of this Constitution for the purposes of article 368 notwithstanding that it contains any provision which amends or has the effect of amending, this Constitution.

(8) The provisions of article 239B shall, so far as may be, apply in relation to the National Capital Territory, the Lieutenant Governor and the Legislative Assembly, as they apply in relation to the Union territory of Pondicherry, the administrator and its Legislature, respectively; and any reference in that article to "clause (1) of article 239A" shall be deemed to be a reference to this article or article 239AB, as the case may be.

Provision in case of failure of constitutional machinery.—If the President, on receipt of a report from the Lieutenant Governor or otherwise, is satisfied—

(a) that a situation has arisen in which the administration of the National Capital Territory cannot be carried on in accordance with the provisions of article 239AA or of any law made in pursuance of that article; or

(b) that for the proper administration of the National Capital Territory it is necessary or expedient so to do, the President may by order suspend the operation of any provision of article

239AA or of all or any of the provisions of any law made in pursuance of that article for such period and subject to such conditions as may be specified in such law and make such incidental and consequential provisions as may appear to him to be necessary or expedient for administering the National Capital Territory in accordance with the provisions of article 239 and article 239AA.

Power of administrator to promulgate Ordinances during recess of Legislature.—(1) If at any time, except when the Legislature of the Union territory of Pondicherry is in session, the administrator thereof is satisfied that circumstances exist which render it necessary for him to take immediate action, he may promulgate such Ordinances as the circumstances appear to him to require:

Provided that no such Ordinance shall be promulgated by the administrator except after obtaining instructions from the President in that behalf:

Provided further that whenever the said Legislature is dissolved, or its functioning remains suspended on account of any action taken under any such law as is referred to in clause (1) of article 239A, the administrator shall not promulgate any Ordinance during the period of such dissolution or suspension.

(2) An Ordinance promulgated under this article in pursuance of instructions from the President shall be deemed to be an Act of the Legislature of the Union territory which has been duly enacted after complying with the provisions in that behalf contained in any such law as is referred to in clause (1) of article 239A, but every such Ordinance—

(*a*) shall be laid before the Legislature of the Union territory and shall cease to operate at the expiration of six weeks from the reassembly of the Legislature or if, before the expiration of that period, a resolution disapproving it is passed by the Legislature, upon the passing of the resolution; and

(*b*) may be withdrawn at any time by the administrator after obtaining instructions from the President in that behalf.

(3) If and so far as an Ordinance under this article makes any provision which would not be valid if enacted in an Act of

the Legislature of the Union territory made after complying with the provisions in that behalf contained in any such law as is referred to in clause (1) of article 239A, it shall be void.

Power of President to make regulations for certain Union territories.— (1) The President may make regulations for the peace, progress and good government of the Union territory of—

(*a*) the Andaman and Nicobar Islands;

(*b*) Lakshadweep;

(*c*) Dadra and Nagar Haveli;

(*d*) Daman and Diu;

(*e*) Pondicherry:

Provided that when any body is created under article 239A to function as a Legislature for the Union territory of Pondicherry, the President shall not make any regulation for the peace, progress and good government of that Union territory with effect from the date appointed for the first meeting of the Legislature: Provided further that whenever the body functioning as a Legislature for the Union territory of Pondicherry is dissolved, or the functioning of that body as such Legislature remains suspended on account of any action taken under any such law as is referred to in clause (1) of article 239A, the President may, during the period of such dissolution or suspension, make regulations for the peace, progress and good government of that Union territory.

(2) Any regulation so made may repeal or amend any Act made by Parliament or any other law which is for the time being applicable to the Union territory and, when promulgated by the President, shall have the same force and effect as an Act of Parliament which applies to that territory.

High Courts for Union territories—(1) Parliament may by law constitute a High Court for a Union territory or declare any court in any such territory to be a High Court for all or any of the purposes of this Constitution.

(2) The provisions of Chapter V of Part VI shall apply in relation to every High Court referred to in clause (1) as they

apply in relation to a High Court referred to in article 214 subject to such modifications or exceptions as Parliament may by law provide.

(3) Subject to the provisions of this Constitution and to the provisions of any law of the appropriate Legislature made by virtue of powers conferred on that Legislature by or under this Constitution, every High Court exercising jurisdiction immediately before the commencement of the Constitution (Seventh Amendment) Act, 1956, in relation to any Union territory shall continue to exercise such jurisdiction in relation to that territory after such commencement.

(4) Nothing in this article derogates from the power of Parliament to extend or exclude the jurisdiction of a High Court for a State to, or from, any Union territory or part thereof.

[*Coorg.*] *Rep. by the Constitution* (*Seventh Amendment*) *Act,* 1956, *s.* 29 *and Sch.*

THE PANCHAYATS

Definitions.—In this Part, unless the context otherwise requires,—

(*a*) "district" means a district in a State;

(*b*) "Gram Sabha" means a body consisting of persons registered in the electoral rolls relating to a village comprised within the area of Panchayat at the village level;

(*c*) "intermediate level" means a level between the village and district levels specified by the Governor of a State by public notification to be the intermediate level for the purposes of this Part;

(*d*) "Panchayat" means an institution (by whatever name called) of self- government constituted under article 243B, for the rural areas;

(*e*) "Panchayat area" means the territorial area of a Panchayat;

((*f*) "Population" means the population as ascertained at the last preceding census of which the relevant figures have

(*g*) "village" means a village specified by the Governor by public notification to be a village for the purposes of this Part and includes a group of villages so specified.

Gram Sabha.— A Gram Sabha may exercise such powers and perform such functions at the village level as the Legislature of a State may, by law, provide.

Constitution of Panchayats.—(1) There shall be constituted in every State, Panchayats at the village, intermediate and district levels in accordance with the provisions of this Part.

(2) Notwithstanding anything in clause (1), Panchayats at the intermediate level may not be constituted in a State having a population not exceeding twenty lakhs.

Composition of Panchayats.— (1) Subject to the provisions of this Part, the Legislature of a State may, by law, make provisions with respect to the composition of Panchayats:

Provided that the ratio between the population of the territorial area of a Panchayat at any level and the number of seats in such Panchayat to be filled by election shall, so far as practicable, be the same throughout the State.

(2) All the seats in a Panchayat shall be filled by persons chosen by direct election from territorial constituencies in the Panchayat area and, for this purpose, each Panchayat area shall be divided into territorial constituencies in such manner that the ratio between the population of each constituency and the number of seats allotted to it shall, so far as practicable, be the same throughout the panchayat area.

(3) The Legislature of a State may, by law, provide for the representation—

(*a*) of the Chairpersons of the Panchayats at the village level, in the Panchayats at the intermediate level or, in the case of a State not having Panchayats at the intermediate level, in the Panchayats at the district level;

(*b*) of the Chairpersons of the Panchayats at the intermediate level, in the Panchayats at the district level;

(*c*) of the members of the House of the People and the

members of the Legislative Assembly of the State representing constituencies which comprise wholly or partly a Panchayat area at a level other than the village level, in such Panchayat;

(*d*) of the members of the Council of States and the members of the Legislative Council of the State, where they are registered as electors within—

(*i*) a Panchayat area at the intermediate level, in Panchayat at the intermediate level;

(*ii*) a Panchayat area at the district level, in Panchayat at the district level.

(4) The Chairperson of a Panchayat and other members of a Panchayat whether or not chosen by direct election from territorial constituencies in the Panchayat area shall have the right to vote in the meetings of the Panchayats.

(5) The Chairperson of—

(*a*) a panchayat at the village level shall be elected in such manner as the Legislature of a State may, by law, provide; and

(*b*) a Panchayat at the intermediate level or district level shall be elected by, and from amongst, the elected members thereof.

Reservation of seats.—(1) Seats shall be reserved for—

(*a*) the Scheduled Castes; and

(*b*) the Scheduled Tribes,

in every Panchayat and the number of seats so reserved shall bear, as nearly as may be, the same proportion to the total number of seats to be filled by direct election in that Panchayat as the population of the Scheduled Castes in that Panchayat area or of the Scheduled Tribes in that Panchayat area bears to the total population of that area and such seats may be allotted by rotation to different constituencies in a Panchayat.

(2) Not less than one-third of the total number of seats reserved under clause (1) shall be reserved for women belonging to the Scheduled Castes or, as the case may be, the Scheduled Tribes.

(3) Not less than one-third (including the number of seats

reserved for women belonging to the Scheduled Castes and the Scheduled Tribes) of the total number of seats to be filled by direct election in every Panchayat shall be reserved for women and such seats may be allotted by rotation to different constituencies in a Panchayat.

(4) The offices of the Chairpersons in the Panchayats at the village or any other level shall be reserved for the Scheduled Castes, the Scheduled Tribes and women in such manner as the Legislature of a State may, by law, provide:

Provided that the number of offices of Chairpersons reserved for the Scheduled Castes and the Scheduled Tribes in the Panchayats at each level in any State shall bear, as nearly as may be, the same proportion to the total number of such offices in the Panchayats at each level as the population of the Scheduled Castes in the State or of the Scheduled Tribes in the State bears to the total population of the State:

Provided further that not less than one-third of the total number of offices of Chairpersons in the Panchayats at each level shall be reserved for women:

Provided also that the number of offices reserved under this clause shall be allotted by rotation to different Panchayats at each level.

(5) The reservation of seats under clauses (1) and (2) and the reservation of offices of Chairpersons (other than the reservation for women) under clause (4) shall cease to have effect on the expiration of the period specified in article 334.

(6) Nothing in this Part shall prevent the Legislature of a State from making any provision for reservation of seats in any Panchayat or offices of Chairpersons in the Panchayats at any level in favour of backward class of citizens.

Duration of Panchayats, etc.—(1) Every Panchayat, unless sooner dissolved under any law for the time being in force, shall continue for five years from the date appointed for its first meeting and no longer.

(2) No amendment of any law for the time being in force shall have the effect of causing dissolution of a Panchayat at

any level, which is functioning immediately before such amendment, till the expiration of its duration specified in clause (1).

(3) An election to constitute a Panchayat shall be completed—

(*a*) before the expiry of its duration specified in clause (1);

(*b*) before the expiration of a period of six months from the date of its dissolution:

Provided that where the remainder of the period for which the dissolved Panchayat would have continued is less than six months, it shall not be necessary to hold any election under this clause for constituting the Panchayat for such period.

(4) A Panchayat constituted upon the dissolution of a Panchayat before the expiration of its duration shall continue only for the remainder of the period for which the dissolved Panchayat would have continued under clause (1) had it not been so dissolved.

Disqualifications for membership.—(1) A person shall be disqualified for being chosen as, and for being, a member of a Panchayat—

(*a*) if he is so disqualified by or under any law for the time being in force for the purposes of elections to the Legislature of the State concerned:

Provided that no person shall be disqualified on the ground that he is less than twenty-five years of age, if he has attained the age of twenty-one years;

(*b*) if he is so disqualified by or under any law made by the Legislature of the State.

(2) If any question arises as to whether a member of a Panchayat has become subject to any of the disqualifications mentioned in clause (1), the question shall be referred for the decision of such authority and in such manner as the Legislature of a State may, by law, provide.

Powers, authority and responsibilities of Panchayats.—Subject to the provisions of this Constitution, the Legislature of a State may, by law, endow the Panchayats with such powers and authority as may be necessary to enable them to function as institutions of self-government and such law may contain provisions for the devolution of powers and responsibilities upon Panchayats at the appropriate level, subject to such conditions as may be specified therein, with respect to—

(*a*) the preparation of plans for economic development and social justice;

(*b*) the implementation of schemes for economic development and social justice as may be entrusted to them including those in relation to the matters listed in the Eleventh Schedule.

Powers to impose taxes by, and Funds of, the Panchayats.—The Legislature of a State may, by law,—

(*a*) authorise a Panchayat to levy, collect and appropriate such taxes, duties, tolls and fees in accordance with such procedure and subject to such limits;

(*b*) assign to a Panchayat such taxes, duties, tolls and fees levied and collected by the State Government for such purposes and subject to such conditions and limits;

(*c*) provide for making such grants-in-aid to the Panchayats from the Consolidated Fund of the State; and

(*d*) provide for constitution of such Funds for crediting all moneys received, respectively, by or on behalf of the Panchayats and also for the withdrawal of such moneys therefrom, as may be specified in the law.

Constitution of Finance Commission to review financial position.—(1) The Governor of a State shall, as soon as may be within one year from the commencement of the Constitution (Seventy-third Amendment) Act, 1992, and thereafter at the expiration of every fifth year, constitute a Finance Commission to review the financial position of the Panchayats and to make recommendations to the Governor as to—

(*a*) the principles which should govern—

(*i*) the distribution between the State and the Panchayats of the net proceeds of the taxes, duties, tolls and fees leviable by the State, which may be divided between them under this

Part and the allocation between the Panchayats at all levels of their respective shares of such proceeds;

(ii) the determination of the taxes, duties, tolls and fees which may be assigned to, or appropriated by, the Panchayats;

(iii) the grants-in-aid to the Panchayats from the Consolidated Fund of the State;

(b) the measures needed to improve the financial position of the Panchayats;

(*c*) any other matter referred to the Finance Commission by the Governor in the interests of sound finance of the Panchayats.

(2) The Legislature of a State may, by law, provide for the composition of the Commission, the qualifications which shall be requisite for appointment as members thereof and the manner in which they shall be selected.

(3) The Commission shall determine their procedure and shall have such powers in the performance of their functions as the Legislature of the State may, by law, confer on them.

(4) The Governor shall cause every recommendation made by the Commission under this article together with an explanatory memorandum as to the action taken thereon to be laid before the Legislature of the State.

Audit of accounts of Panchayats.—The Legislature of a State may, by law, make provisions with respect to the maintenance of accounts by the Panchayats and the auditing of such accounts.

Elections to the Panchayats.—(1) The superintendence, direction and control of the preparation of electoral rolls for, and the conduct of, all elections to the Panchayats shall be vested in a State Election Commission consisting of a State Election Commissioner to be appointed by the Governor.

(2) Subject to the provisions of any law made by the Legislature of a State, the conditions of service and tenure of office of the State Election Commissioner shall be such as the Governor may by rule determine:

Provided that the State Election Commissioner shall not

be removed from his office except in like manner and on the like grounds as a Judge of a High Court and the conditions of service of the State Election Commissioner shall not be varied to his disadvantage after his appointment.

(3) The Governor of a State shall, when so requested by the State Election Commission, make available to the State Election Commission such staff as may be necessary for the discharge of the functions conferred on the State Election Commission by clause (1).

(4) Subject to the provisions of this Constitution, the Legislature of a State may, by law, make provision with respect to all matters relating to, or in connection with, elections to the Panchayats.

Application to Union territories.—The provisions of this Part shall apply to the Union territories and shall, in their application to a Union territory, have effect as if the references to the Governor of a State were references to the Administrator of the Union territory appointed under article 239 and references to the Legislature or the legislative Assembly of a State were references, in relation to a Union territory having a Legislative Assembly, to that Legislative Assembly: Provided that the President may, by public notification, direct that the provisions of this Part shall apply to any Union territory or part thereof subject to such exceptions and modifications as he may specify in the notification.

Part not to apply to certain areas.—(1) Nothing in this Part shall apply to the Scheduled Areas referred to in clause (1), and the tribal areas referred to in clause (2), of article 244.

(2) Nothing in this Part shall apply to—

(a) the States of Nagaland, Meghalaya and Mizoram;

(b) the hill areas in the State of Manipur for which District Councils exist under any law for the time being in force.

(3) Nothing in this Part—

(a) relating to Panchayats at the district level shall apply to the hill areas of the District of Darjeeling in the State of West Bengal for which Darjeeling Gorkha Hill Council exists under any law for the time being in force;

(b) shall be construed to affect the functions and powers of the Darjeeling Gorkha Hill Council constituted under such law.

(3A) Nothing in article 243D, relating to reservation of seats for the Scheduled Castes, shall apply to the State of Arunachal Pradesh.

(4) Notwithstanding anything in this Constitution, —

(a) the Legislature of a State referred to in sub-clause (*a*) of clause (2) may, by law, extend this part to that State, except the areas, if any, referred to in clause (1), if the Legislative Assembly of that State passes a resolution to that effect by a majority of the total membership of that House and by a majority of not less than two-thirds of the members of that House present and voting;

(b) Parliament may, by law, extend the provisions of this Part to the Scheduled Areas and the tribal areas referred to in clause (1) subject to such exceptions and modifications as may be specified in such law, and no such law shall be deemed to be an amendment of this Constitution for the purposes of article 368.

Continuance of existing laws and Panchayats.— Notwithstanding anything in this Part, any provision of any law relating to Panchayats in force in a State immediately before the commencement of the Constitution (Seventy-third Amendment) Act, 1992, which is inconsistent with the provisions of this Part, shall continue to be in force until amended or repealed by a competent Legislature or other competent authority or until the expiration of one year from such commencement, whichever is earlier:

Provided that all the Panchayats existing immediately before such commencement shall continue till the expiration of their duration, unless sooner dissolved by a resolution passed to that effect by the Legislative Assembly of that State or, in the case of a State having a Legislative Council, by each House of the Legislature of that State.

Bar to interference by courts in electoral matters.— Notwithstanding anything in this Constitution,—

(*a*) the validity of any law relating to the delimitation of constituencies or the allotment of seats to such constituencies, made or purporting to be made under article 243K, shall not be called in question in any court;

(*b*) no election to any Panchayat shall be called in question except by an election petition presented to such authority and in such manner as is provided for by or under any law made by the Legislature of a State.

THE MUNICIPALITIES

Definitions.—In this Part, unless the context otherwise requires,—

(*a*) "Committee" means a Committee constituted under article 243S;

(*b*) "district" means a district in a State;

(*c*) "Metropolitan area" means an area having a population of ten lakhs or more, comprised in one or more districts and consisting of two or more Municipalities or Panchayats or other contiguous areas, specified by the Governor by public notification to be a Metropolitan area for the purposes of this Part;

(*d*) "Municipal area" means the territorial area of a Municipality as is notified by the Governor;

(*e*) "Municipality" means an institution of self-government constituted under article 243Q;

((*f*) "Panchayat" means a Panchayat constituted under article 243B;

(*g*) "population" means the population as ascertained at the last preceding census of which the relevant figures have been published.

Constitution of Municipalities.—(1) There shall be constituted in every State,—

(*a*) a Nagar Panchayat (by whatever name called) for a transitional area, that is to say, an area in transition from a rural area to an urban area;

(*b*) a Municipal Council for a smaller urban area; and

(*c*) a Municipal Corporation for a larger urban area, in accordance with the provisions of this Part.

Provided that a Municipality under this clause may not be constituted in such urban area or part thereof as the Governor may, having regard to the size of the area and the municipal services being provided or proposed to be provided by an industrial establishment in that area and such other factors as he may deem fit, by public notification, specify to be an industrial township.

(2) In this article, "a transitional area", "a smaller urban area" or "a larger urban area" means such area as the Governor may, having regard to the population of the area, the density of the population therein, the revenue generated for local administration, the percentage of employment in non-agricultural activities, the economic importance or such other factors as he may deem fit, specify by public notification for the purposes of this Part.

Composition of Municipalities.—(1) Save as provided in clause (2), all the seats in a Municipality shall be filled by persons chosen by direct election from the territorial constituencies in the Municipal area and for this purpose each Municipal area shall be divided into territorial constituencies to be known as wards.

(2) The Legislature of a State may, by law, provide—

(*a*) for the representation in a Municipality of—

(*i*) persons having special knowledge or experience in Municipal administration;

(*ii*) the members of the House of the People and the members of the Legislative Assembly of the State representing constituencies which comprise wholly or partly the Municipal area;

(*iii*) the members of the Council of States and the members of the Legislative Council of the State registered as electors within the Municipal area;

(*iv*) the Chairpersons of the Committees constituted under clause (5) of article 243S:

Provided that the persons referred to in paragraph (*i*) shall not have the right to vote in the meetings of the Municipality;

(*b*) the manner of election of the Chairperson of a Municipality.

Constitution and composition of Wards Committees, etc.—(1) There shall be constituted Wards Committees, consisting of one or more wards, within the territorial area of a Municipality having a population of three lakhs or more.

(2) The Legislature of a State may, by law, make provision with respect to—

(*a*) the composition and the territorial area of a Wards Committee;

(*b*) the manner in which the seats in a Wards Committee shall be filled.

(3) A member of a Municipality representing a ward within the territorial area of the Wards Committee shall be a member of that Committee.

(4) Where a Wards Committee consists of—

(*a*) one ward, the member representing that ward in the Municipality; or

(*b*) two or more wards, one of the members representing such wards in the Municipality elected by the members of the Wards Committee, shall be the Chairperson of that Committee.

(5) Nothing in this article shall be deemed to prevent the Legislature of a State from making any provision for the constitution of Committees in addition to the Wards Committees.

Reservation of seats.—(1) Seats shall be reserved for the Scheduled Castes and the Scheduled Tribes in every Municipality and the number of seats so reserved shall bear, as nearly as may be, the same proportion to the total number of seats to be filled by direct election in that Municipality as the population of the Scheduled Castes in the Municipal area or of the Scheduled Tribes in the Municipal area bears to the total population of that area and such seats may be allotted by rotation to different constituencies in a Municipality.

(2) Not less than one-third of the total number of seats reserved under clause (1) shall be reserved for women belonging to the Scheduled Castes or, as the case may be, the Scheduled Tribes.

(3) Not less than one-third (including the number of seats reserved for women belonging to the Scheduled Castes and the Scheduled Tribes) of the total number of seats to be filled by direct election in every Municipality shall be reserved for women and such seats may be allotted by rotation to different constituencies in a Municipality.

(4) The offices of Chairpersons in the Municipalities shall be reserved for the Scheduled Castes, the Scheduled Tribes and women in such manner as the Legislature of a State may, by law, provide.

(5) The reservation of seats under clauses (1) and (2) and the reservation of offices of Chairpersons (other than the reservation for women) under clause (4) shall cease to have effect on the expiration of the period specified in article 334.

(6) Nothing in this Part shall prevent the Legislature of a State from making any provision for reservation of seats in any Municipality or offices of Chairpersons in the Municipalities in favour of backward class of citizens.

Duration of Municipalities, etc.—(1) Every Municipality, unless sooner dissolved under any law for the time being in force, shall continue for five years from the date appointed for its first meeting and no longer:

Provided that a Municipality shall be given a reasonable opportunity of being heard before its dissolution.

(2) No amendment of any law for the time being in force shall have the effect of causing dissolution of a Municipality at any level, which is functioning immediately before such amendment, till the expiration of its duration specified in clause (1).

(3) An election to constitute a Municipality shall be completed,—

(*a*) before the expiry of its duration specified in clause (1);

(*b*) before the expiration of a period of six months from the date of its dissolution:

Provided that where the remainder of the period for which the dissolved Municipality would have continued is less than six months, it shall not be necessary to hold any election under this clause for constituting the Municipality for such period.

(4) A Municipality constituted upon the dissolution of a Municipality before the expiration of its duration shall continue only for the remainder of the period for which the dissolved Municipality would have continued under clause (1) had it not been so dissolved.

Disqualifications for membership.—(1) A person shall be disqualified for being chosen as, and for being, a member of a Municipality—

(*a*) if he is so disqualified by or under any law for the time being in force for the purposes of elections to the Legislature of the State concerned:

Provided that no person shall be disqualified on the ground that he is less than twenty-five years of age, if he has attained the age of twenty-one years;

(*b*) if he is so disqualified by or under any law made by the Legislature of the State.

(2) If any question arises as to whether a member of a Municipality has become subject to any of the disqualifications mentioned in clause (1), the question shall be referred for the decision of such authority and in such manner as the Legislature of a State may, by law, provide.

Powers, authority and responsibilities of Municipalities, etc.—Subject to the provisions of this Constitution, the Legislature of a State may, by law, endow—

(*a*) the Municipalities with such powers and authority as may be necessary to enable them to function as institutions of self-government and such law may contain provisions for the devolution of powers and responsibilities upon Municipalities, subject to such conditions as may be specified therein, with respect to—

(*i*) the preparation of plans for economic development and social justice;

(*ii*) the performance of functions and the implementation of schemes as may be entrusted to them including those in relation to the matters listed in the Twelfth Schedule;

(*b*) the Committees with such powers and authority as may be necessary to enable them to carry out the responsibilities conferred upon them including those in relation to the matters listed in the Twelfth Schedule.

Power to impose taxes by, and Funds of, the Municipalities.—The Legislature of a State may, by law,—

(*a*) authorise a Municipality to levy, collect and appropriate such taxes, duties, tolls and fees in accordance with such procedure and subject to such limits;

(*b*) assign to a Municipality such taxes, duties, tolls and fees levied and collected by the State Government for such purposes and subject to such conditions and limits;

(*c*) provide for making such grants-in-aid to the Municipalities from the Consolidated Fund of the State; and

(*d*) provide for constitution of such Funds for crediting all moneys received, respectively, by or on behalf of the Municipalities and also for the withdrawal of such moneys therefrom, as may be specified in the law.

Finance Commission.—(1) The Finance Commission constituted under article 243-I shall also review the financial position of the Municipalities and make recommendations to the Governor as to—

(*a*) the principles which should govern—

(*i*) the distribution between the State and the Municipalities of the net proceeds of the taxes, duties, tolls and fees leviable by the State, which may be divided between them under this Part and the allocation between the Municipalities at all levels of their respective shares of such proceeds;

(*ii*) the determination of the taxes, duties, tolls and fees which may be assigned to, or appropriated by, the Municipalities;

(*iii*) the grants-in-aid to the Municipalities from the Consolidated Fund of the State;

(*b*) the measures needed to improve the financial position of the Municipalities;

(*c*) any other matter referred to the Finance Commission by the Governor in the interests of sound finance of the Municipalities.

(2) The Governor shall cause every recommendation made by the Commission under this article together with an explanatory memorandum as to the action taken thereon to be laid before the Legislature of the State.

Audit of accounts of Municipalities.—The Legislature of a State may, by law, make provisions with respect to the maintenance of accounts by the Municipalities and the auditing of such accounts.

Elections to the Municipalities.—(1) The superintendence, direction and control of the preparation of electoral rolls for, and the conduct of, all elections to the Municipalities shall be vested in the State Election Commission referred to in article 243K.

(2) Subject to the provisions of this Constitution, the Legislature of a State may, by law, make provision with respect to all matters relating to, or in connection with, elections to the Municipalities.

Application to Union territories.—The provisions of this Part shall apply to the Union territories and shall, in their application to a Union territory, have effect as if the references to the Governor of a State were references to the Administrator of the Union territory appointed under article 239 and references to the Legislature or the Legislative Assembly of a State were references in relation to a Union territory having a Legislative Assembly, to that Legislative Assembly:

Provided that the President may, by public notification, direct that the provisions of this Part shall apply to any Union territory or part thereof subject to such exceptions and modifications as he may specify in the notification.

Part not to apply to certain areas.—(1) Nothing in this

Part shall apply to the Scheduled Areas referred to in clause (1), and the tribal areas referred to in clause (2), of article 244.

(2) Nothing in this Part shall be construed to affect the functions and powers of the Darjeeling Gorkha Hill Council constituted under any law for the time being in force for the hill areas of the district of Darjeeling in the State of West Bengal.

(3) Notwithstanding anything in this Constitution, Parliament may, by law, extend the provisions of this Part to the Scheduled Areas and the tribal areas referred to in clause (1) subject to such exceptions and modifications as may be specified in such law, and no such law shall be deemed to be an amendment of this Constitution for the purposes of article 368.

Committee for district planning.—(1) There shall be constituted in every State at the district level a District Planning Committee to consolidate the plans prepared by the Panchayats and the Municipalities in the district and to prepare a draft development plan for the district as a whole.

(2) The Legislature of a State may, by law, make provision with respect to—

(a) the composition of the District Planning Committees;

(b) the manner in which the seats in such Committees shall be filled:

Provided that not less than four-fifths of the total number of members of such Committee shall be elected by, and from amongst, the elected members of the Panchayat at the district level and of the Municipalities in the district in proportion to the ratio between the population of the rural areas and of the urban areas in the district;

(c) the functions relating to district planning which may be assigned to such Committees;

(d) the manner in which the Chairpersons of such Committees shall be chosen.

(3) Every District Planning Committee shall, in preparing the draft development plan,—

(a) have regard to—

(i) matters of common interest between the Panchayats and the Municipalities including spatial planning, sharing of water and other physical and natural resources, the integrated development of infrastructure and environmental conservation;

(ii) the extent and type of available resources whether financial or otherwise;

(b) consult such institutions and organisations as the Governor may, by order, specify.

(4) The Chairperson of every District Planning Committee shall forward the development plan, as recommended by such Committee, to the Government of the State.

Committee for Metropolitan planning.—(1) There shall be constituted in every Metropolitan area a Metropolitan Planning Committee to prepare a draft development plan for the Metropolitan area as a whole.

(2) The Legislature of a State may, by law, make provision with respect to—

(a) the composition of the Metropolitan Planning Committees;

(b) the manner in which the seats in such Committees shall be filled:

Provided that not less than two-thirds of the members of such Committee shall be elected by, and from amongst, the elected members of the Municipalities and Chairpersons of the Panchayats in the Metropolitan area in proportion to the ratio between the population of the Municipalities and of the Panchayats in that area;

(c) the representation in such Committees of the Government of India and the Government of the State and of such organisations and Institutions as may be deemed necessary for carrying out the functions assigned to such Committees;

(d) the functions relating to planning and coordination for the Metropolitan area which may be assigned to such Committees;

(e) the manner in which the Chairpersons of such Committees shall be chosen.

(3) Every Metropolitan Planning Committee shall, in preparing the draft development plan,—

(*a*) have regard to—

(*i*) the plans prepared by the Municipalities and the Panchayats in the Metropolitan area;

(*ii*) matters of common interest between the Municipalities and the Panchayats, including co-ordinated spatial planning of the area, sharing of water and other physical and natural resources, the integrated development of infrastructure and environmental conservation;

(*iii*) the overall objectives and priorities set by the Government of India and the Government of the State;

(*iv*) the extent and nature of investments likely to be made in the Metropolitan area by agencies of the Government of India and of the Government of the State and other available resources whether financial or otherwise;

(*b*) consult such institutions and organisations as the Governor may, by order, specify.

(4) The Chairperson of every Metropolitan Planning Committee shall forward the development plan, as recommended by such Committee, to the Government of the State.

Continuance of existing laws and Municipalities.— Notwithstanding anything in this Part, any provision of any law relating to Municipalities in force in a State immediately before the commencement of the Constitution (Seventy-fourth Amendment) Act, 1992, which is inconsistent with the provisions of this Part, shall continue to be in force until amended or repealed by a competent Legislature or other competent authority or until the expiration of one year from such commencement, whichever is earlier:

Provided that all the Municipalities existing immediately before such commencement shall continue till the expiration of their duration, unless sooner dissolved by a resolution passed to that effect by the Legislative Assembly of that State or, in the case of a State having a Legislative Council, by each House of the Legislature of that State.

Bar to interference by courts in electoral matters.— Notwithstanding anything in this Constitution,—

(*a*) the validity of any law relating to the delimitation of constituencies or the allotment of seats to such constituencies, made or purporting to be made under article 243ZA shall not be called in question in any court;

(*b*) no election to any Municipality shall be called in question except by an election petition presented to such authority and in such manner as is provided for by or under any law made by the Legislature of a State.

REFERENCES

- Morris, W.H.: *The Government and Politics of India*, London, Hutchinson, 1971.
- Keane J.: *Democracy and Civil Liberty*, London, Verso, 1988.
- Goldman, H.: *Co-ordination of Computerization of the Criminal Justice System*, London, Home Office, 1986.
- Manpong, C. M.: *District Administration in Arunachal Pradesh*, New Delhi, Omsons Publications, 1993.

Bibliography

Adam, R.: *Elements of Government,* New York, Random House, 1960.

Austin, Granville: *The Indian Constitution: Cornerstone of a Nation*, Oxford, Clarendon Press, 1966.

Barber B.R.: *Strong Democracy. Participatory Politics for a New Age*. Berkeley, University of California Press, 1984.

Blau, M.: *Bureaucracy in Modern Society,* New York, Random House, 1956.

Brierly, L.: *The Law of Nations,* New York, Oxford University Press, 1955.

Chandra, R.: *Judicial System in India*, Lucknow, Print House (India), 1992.

Derrett, J. : *Religion, Law, and the State in India*, London, Faber, 1968.

Doulton, A.: *Government and Community Information Services*, Oxford, Dragonflair and CDW & Associates, 1994.

Friedrich, J.: *Constitutional Government and Democracy,* Boston, Ginn, 1950.

Goldman, H.: *Co-ordination of Computerization of the Criminal Justice System*, London, Home Office, 1986.

Greer P.: *Transforming Central Government: the Next Steps Initiative*, Buckingham, Open University Press, 1994.

Hans J. : *Politics Among Nations: The Struggle for Power and Peace,* New York, Knopf, 1960.

Hazard, J.N.: *The Soviet System of Government,* Chicago, University of Chicago Press, 1960.

Heimanson, Rudolph: *Dictionary of Political Science and Law*, N.Y.: Oceana Publications, 1967.

Hoggett, P.: *The Politics of Decentralisation*, Basingstoke, MacMillan, 1994.

Howard McIlwain: *Constitutionalism: Ancient and Modern*, N.Y., Cornell University Press, 1958.

Keane J.: *Democracy and Civil Liberty*, London, Verso, 1988.

Keane J.: *Democracy and Civil Liberty*, London, Verso, 1988.

Lenneal, J. : *Urban Administrators: The Politics of Role Elasticity*, Westport, CT, Greenwood Press, 1988.

Lingat, R.: *The Classical Law of India*, Berkeley, University of California Press, 1973.

Manpong, C. M.: *District Administration in Arunachal Pradesh*, New Delhi, Omsons Publications, 1993.

Millward, R: *Public and Private Ownership of British Industry 1820-1990*, Oxford, Clarendon Press, 1994.

Morris, W.H.: *The Government and Politics of India*, London, Hutchinson, 1971.

Peddleton, E.: *Public Administration and the Public Interest*, New York, McGraw-Hill, 1936.

Prahlad, K.: *Governance and Public Administration for Poverty Reduction*, Salvador, Brazil, 1997.

Rosenbloom, H. : *Handbook of Regulation and Administrative Law*, New York, Marcel Dekker, 1994.

Scott, C. : *The Moral Economy of the Peasant*, New Haven, Yale University Press, 1976.

Sullivan, N.: *Bureaucrats and Policy Making*, New York, Holmes & Meier, 1984.

Thomas, R. : *Elements of Government*, New York, Random House, 1960.

Thompson, V.: *Public Administration*, New York, Knopf, 1950.

Victor G. : *Law as a Political Instrument*, New York, Random House, 1955.

Wade, R.: *Public Bureaucracy and the Incentive Problem*, Washington, D.C., World Bank, 1994.

Index

□□□